Shaping Strategic Planning

Frogs, Dragons, Bees, and Turkey Tails

**J. William Pfeiffer,
    Ph.D., J.D.**
Leonard D. Goodstein, Ph.D.
Timothy M. Nolan, Ph.D.

Scott, Foresman and Company
Glenview, Illinois   **London**

In Association with
**University Associates, Inc.
San Diego, California**

Library of Congress Cataloging-in-Publication Data

Pfeiffer, J. William.
    Shaping strategic planning.

    "In association with University Associates, Inc.,
San Diego, California."
    Includes index.
    1. Strategic planning.   I. Goodstein, Leonard David.
II. Nolan, Timothy M.   III. University Associates.
IV. Title
HD30.28.P379   1989   658.4'012   88-37979
ISBN 0-673-38478-0

2   3   4   5   6—KPF—93   92   91   90   89

ISBN 0-673-38478-0

Scott, Foresman professional books are available for bulk sales at quantity discounts.
For information, please contact Marketing Manager, Professional Books Group, Scott,
Foresman and Company, 1900 East Lake Avenue, Glenview, IL 60025.

PREFACE

This book is intended to guide an organization's planning team through the strategic planning process into the successful implementation of the plan. It outlines, step by step, a strategic planning process that has proved to be efficient, logical, and successful. This volume provides the reader with an understanding of what strategic planning really is, how it differs from long-range planning, and how it can be accomplished with any size or type of organization. Faithful adherence to the Applied Strategic Planning Model should enable a planning team to manage its planning process successfully.

The subtitle of this book — *Frogs, Dragons, Bees, and Turkey Tails* — is taken from the first four chapters of the book. Each of those chapters begins with a parable that illustrates an important principle that should be considered by every organization as it embarks on strategic planning. In each parable, we find that things are not always what they seem; and some of our favorite assumptions may have to take a leap, burn up, fly away, or be chopped off before strategies can be optimally planned. Throughout the book we have used examples and metaphors to illustrate the practical side of strategic planning.

The Applied Strategic Planning Model, which is introduced in Chapter 1, represents the synthesis of the authors' experience as consultants and trainers in this arena for the past fifteen years. Although the Applied Strategic Planning Model is in some ways similar to other models, it differs in several important ways. The major differences are found in three of the phases that this model includes: the values audit, strategic business modeling, and integrating functional plans. Also the acid test of this model is the implementation (hence "applied" strategic planning). Not only is implementation the final phase of the model, but implementation considerations are stressed throughout the other phases. Another important ingredient of this model is "environmental scanning," which is an ongoing process that continues from the beginning to the end of the planning period.

A unique aspect of the model is the systematic way in which values clarification is front-end loaded in the process. Although other models of strategic planning may give some attention to the underlying values that drive the planning process, our model gives values clarification a seminal focus and provides specific technology for management that is lacking in other models. Our model requires a greater focus on the psychological components of the planning process, especially during the values audit, in mission formulation, and in the proactive futuring of strategic business modeling.

Our definition of strategic planning—"the process by which the guiding members of an organization envision its future and develop the necessary procedures and operations to achieve that future"—requires a greater emphasis on process consultation than other models typically require. Adhering to the Applied Strategic Planning Model requires more attention to *how* the planning process works and less attention to the plan itself. The model is clearly sequenced, with each phase of the process building on the preceding phase.

The involvement of the planning team (which is composed of key organizational members), the in-depth examination of the social and psychological underpinnings of the organization, the constant environmental surveillance, and the constant focus on the implementation considerations produce a broader and yet more detailed and more immediately applicable plan than do those that result from the use of other models.

This book devotes a complete chapter to each phase of the Applied Strategic Planning Model. Also a chapter is devoted to environmental scanning and implementation considerations. The appendix supplies four instruments that are beneficial during the values audit.

We acknowledge with deep appreciation the work of staff writer Robert Nelson, who worked on an early draft of the book; the expertise and tireless "can-do" spirit of managing editor Mary Kitzmiller, whose efforts enhanced the quality and flavor of this book as well as our enjoyment of the writing process; the dedication of editor Rose Sklare of Editorial Services of New England; and the unique humor of our artist, David Hills.

We are interested in reactions and comments as you read this book. If you have input that will contribute to our continued efforts to help organizations achieve strategic success, please contact us through University Associates, 8517 Production Avenue, San Diego, California 92121; telephone (619)578-5900.

J. William Pfeiffer
Leonard D. Goodstein
Timothy M. Nolan

San Diego, California

CONTENTS

1 SHAPING STRATEGIC SUCCESS: THE MANAGERIAL IMPERATIVE

Let's talk about frogs. Frogs are amphibious creatures. That means they can live on land or in the water. But that's not all. Frogs can adapt to hot arid climates, cold arid climates, hot humid climates, and cold humid climates. From a biological perspective, the frog has survived the ages because of its remarkable adaptability to the environment. But before we say "Hoorah for adaptability," let's take a look at a dimension that surfaced during some experiments with frogs.

In a laboratory, frogs were placed in shallow pans of room-temperature water. They were free to jump out of the pans at any time. Under each pan was a Bunsen burner, which heated the water very gradually. As the temperature rose, degree by degree, the frog adapted to the new temperature. Unfortunately, regardless of how hot the water became, the frog never became uncomfortable enough to jump out of the pan. In fact, it stayed right there until the heat was so intense that the frog died. Now *that's* adaptability!

Some of us, also, are incredibly adaptable. In fact, a major reason for success among human beings is our ability to adapt. When we find ourselves mildly dissatisfied with our jobs, mildly dissatisfied with our significant other, mildly dissatisfied with almost anything, we continue to adapt. For many of us, the more our environment changes, the harder we try to adapt our methods, our services, and our products to the new situation. But, then, alas, far too often we end up boiled frogs!

The secret for the frog would be the ability to realize at some point that it needed to stop adapting and to jump out of the pan — into the unknown — and move in another direction. In strategic planning, a basic question should be, "At what point is adaptability an asset and at what point is it a liability?" But first we must ask another question: "Why is it necessary or even important to do strategic planning?"

If changes did not occur, or if they occurred in a predictable manner, long-range planning would be sufficient. We could just produce more and more of whatever has proved successful. Life

Frogs Are Adaptable Creatures

would be an electronic spreadsheet programmed to reflect consistent and predictable growth in revenues and profit. Since this is not the case, long-range planning alone is inadequate. We must visualize what business we want to be in, how close we are to being there, and what must be done to delete the gap between the two. We must *know* where we want to go. These are the strategic decisions.

ACCELERATED CHANGES

Change is not only certain, but changes are occurring at an accelerating pace. In fact, about half of the technological changes on earth have occurred since 1900. Furthermore, it is predicted that in the last fifteen years of this century we will see as much technological change as in the first eighty-five years. As an illustration, Figure 1-1 lists many familiar items that have come on the scene during the last fifty years. Many people living today can remember

---

Figure 1-1
Some Items Not Available Fifty Years Ago

Air conditioners

Antibiotics

Automatic transmissions

Automatic washers and dryers

Birth-control pills

Commercial jets

Compact discs

Credit cards

Detergents

Disposable diapers

Fast foods

Freeze-dried foods

Health insurance

Latex paint

Magnetic tape

Personal computers

Polio vaccine

Polyester

Refrigerators/freezers

Running shoes

Safety belts

Smoke detectors

Supermarkets

Transparent tape

VCRs

when these things did not exist. Within the next fifteen years another list of "necessities" will emerge—a list so different from anything we have now that we cannot even predict it.

During the last century few people could even imagine life as we live it today. In fact, in 1899 Charles H. Duell thought the U.S. Patent Office had run its course and should be abolished (see Figure 1-2).

Need for Strategic Planning

Technological changes are having a dramatic impact on the social side—the human side—of organizations. Most companies have experienced recent reorganizations in one form or another. Typically in such a reorganization, there is a little change in structure and a little change in roles and not enough clarity on goals. But form follows structure. For example, if you add a thousand pounds to a deer, you no longer have a deer but a rhinoceros. Some organizations add a thousand pounds—perhaps a thousand pounds of bureaucracy—and change the fast, lean deer into a very different creature. There's an adage in the field of consulting that says, "If you just want steady work, look for symptoms in an organization and help cure the symptoms; if you want to do what you are supposed to do, look at the symptoms and help find the problem."

Figure 1-2
1899 Quotation

"Everything that can be invented has already
been invented."
—Charles H. Duell
Director of U.S. Patent Office, 1899

In 1986, approximately 750,000 businesses started up in the United States. This figure is about double the number that started in 1980, and the number keeps increasing. This vast expansion has come in the area of small businesses. People are becoming more and more dissatisfied with working in large businesses, with the traditional way they are treated there. They leave the large organization to work in a small one or to start small businesses of their own.

Given the high degree of flux in today's competitive business climate, strategic planning is especially important. With record numbers of business start-ups, initial stock offerings, mergers, acquisitions, and buy outs, organizations more than ever need a systematic method for managing and coping with change. This method can be found in a revitalized strategic planning process, specifically the Applied Strategic Planning Model (see Figure 1-3).

For managers during this era of rapid technological change the gap lies in the lack of conceptualization. First-line supervisors need a lot of technical competence and human resource skills and just a bit of conceptual skills (see Figure 1-4). Middle management needs about the same amount of human resource skills but less technological knowledge and more conceptual skills. Senior management needs few technical skills but a great deal of conceptual skills. Management training has focused on improving human resource skills, while the need has been for improving conceptual skills.

Some organizations, of course, have been aware of this deficit. When Apple was having problems, did it hire a computer expert as its new CEO? No, it went to PepsiCo and hired John Sculley. Technological knowledge about the product was not important; thinking conceptually about marketing was far more valuable.

Blurred Boundaries

The role of the "boss" and the role of the "subordinate" used to be clear. Now the boundaries are becoming blurred, and the roles are less and less clear. This blurring of traditional boundaries is also occurring between manufacturers and their vendors and between businesses and their customers.

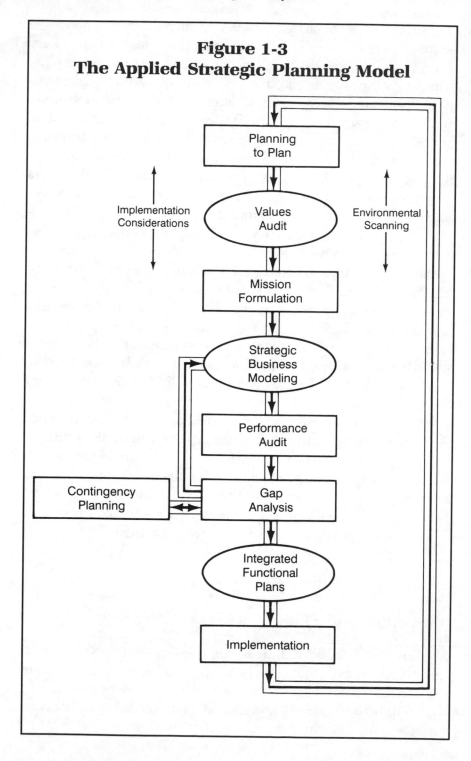

Figure 1-3
The Applied Strategic Planning Model

Planning to Plan

Implementation Considerations

Values Audit

Environmental Scanning

Mission Formulation

Strategic Business Modeling

Performance Audit

Contingency Planning

Gap Analysis

Integrated Functional Plans

Implementation

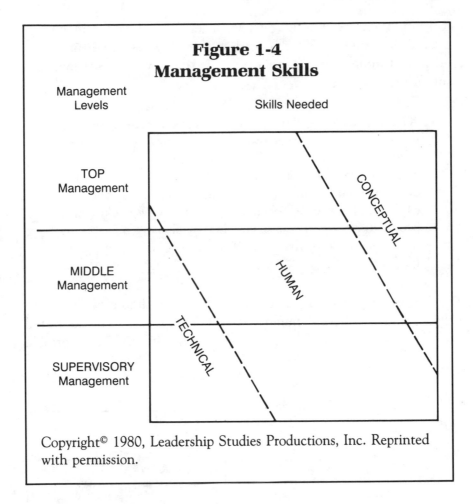

Figure 1-4
Management Skills

We used to think the ideal span of control was five to eight people. By the year 2000, the span will be twenty. How does one person manage twenty people? By devoting all of his or her time to managing rather than to the traditional role of doing. One sociological impact of technological change is that middle-management ranks are being demolished, and organizations are becoming flatter and flatter.

The manager's role is becoming more and more a function of influencing people over whom he or she has no direct control. Lateral relationships — that is, relationships with peers and colleagues — are important parts of the managerial function. According to John Humphrey ("Manager's Manager," *Inc.*, 1987), a manager's overall performance is influenced as much by his or her ability to network through the organization as by the way he or she manages subordinates. He also says:

> "Good managers get their people excited, create a sense of urgency, a sense of empowerment.... They offer people a vision they can believe in. They connect up with their people in a much more personal way, help them deal with the speed of change, empathize with them more—and break the rules when they have to be broken. .... If you're always working with people to reset your course, you don't really have a goal in the traditional sense of the word. What you have is a direction." (p. 55)

Another essential part of managing is the simultaneous loose-tight element, whereby employees—while expected to be dedicated to the central values of the organization—are granted a comfortable

Discontinuous Futures: Don't Try to Adapt

degree of liberty (see Peters & Waterman, 1982). Organizations that encourage this loose-tight element are in sharp contrast to those, on one end of the continuum, that demand strict adherence to every policy and those, on the other end, that allow unrestricted self-expression.

Discontinuous Futures

With technological and sociological changes comes the concept of *discontinuous futures* (see Figure 1-5). Suppose, for example, that your company had been a producer of vacuum tubes for radios. Becoming a manufacturer of transistors would not have been a natural progression, because a vacuum-tube company could not *adapt* to manufacturing transistors. Nor could a transistor company adapt to producing silicon chips. Suppose, further, that your company was the world's most efficient producer of vacuum tubes. It produced the highest-quality tubes, had the lowest production costs, and maintained the most humane working conditions. All of these things would make no difference, because—except for some rare uses—the vacuum tube would no longer be a needed product.

Today we are on the verge of superconductivity. Think of a public utility that controls thousands of miles of high-voltage lines. In twenty to forty years, there will be no more high-voltage transmission lines. Energy may be beamed from a mountaintop or from outer space. Then the power plant will be in the real-estate business, trying to dispose of thousands of miles of property that is only three hundred yards wide.

Figure 1-5
An Example of a Business with
Discontinuous Futures

Vacuum Tubes ——> Transistors ————> Silicon Chips

A drastic change has also occurred in the health-care market. The movement toward outpatient treatment and outpatient surgery is changing the whole picture. One hospital which was unable to fill its rooms with patients quit trying to adapt all its facilities to the sick and turned the top floor into a hotel for those visiting the patients in the hospital. Unlike the frog, the hospital management jumped out of the pan and went in another direction.

What we see in these examples is what we call "discontinuous futures." That is, life in the future is going to be so different that we cannot even predict it, much less adapt to it. More and more, organizations will be faced with an end to the business they have perceived themselves to be in and a need to chart a new future. As the Los Angeles County Public Library embarked on strategic planning, it had to deal with questions such as "Will books *exist* in the year 2000?" and "Will the community library be a continuing viable public service?"

This book will help your organization plan for discontinuous futures. It will help you chart a new course so that your organization—unlike the frog—will see the need to jump out of obsolete situations and into ventures more compatible with the environment. In other words, it will help you to avoid becoming a boiled frog.

THE MANAGERIAL IMPERATIVE

If there ever was a time—and there probably never was—when we had a need for managers who were not leaders, and leaders who were not managers, that day is gone forever. We must have managers who also have a sense of vision, and we must have leaders who have a sense of management. Figure 1-6 illustrates the differences in mixtures of manager and leader. A person low in both skills is an abdicator, leaving decisions to others. Someone who is high in leadership and low in management is merely a dreamer. A person high in management and low in leadership is just an administrator. It takes someone who is high in both management and leadership to be a complete leader, and the future is going to require a blending of both skills.

Figure 1-6
The Management-Leadership Quadrant

Management   Leadership

	Low	High
High	Administrator	Complete Leader
Low	Abdicator	Dreamer

To become a leader in a market sometimes requires entering through the back door or, as some have dubbed it, making a gift of a Trojan horse. For example, the Apple Computer people knew they had to reach beyond the desktop-publishing market to make a niche for their product (see Sculley & Byrne, 1987). Their sales department went after the aerospace corporations and other industries that could use the Macintosh for engineering and designing. Once the systems were in house, the Macintosh began to be used for other computer purposes as well.

Strategic and Tactical Decisions

The difference between strategic decisions and tactical decisions is the what and how. Strategic decisions determine *what* an organization will do; tactical decisions determine *how* something will be done. Most senior executives earned their positions by knowing the how, not the what. Therefore, a real challenge in the strategic planning process lies in the reeducation of managers so they can begin to think in terms of "what," especially when the "whats" are new or perhaps not yet known.

If a manager decides that what the organization is going to do is "go to Maine," then there are numerous ways in which this can be done — by bicycle, for example. Then many tactical questions must be answered: What gear do we pack? Which route do we take?

Where do we stop? Those decisions are much easier if we know we are going to Maine. If we did not know whether we were going to Maine or Georgia or the Baja, the tactical questions would be enormous problems. There is also a dimension that we could label "seasonal." Perhaps we know we are going to Maine, but we do not know *when*. A trip to Maine in June will require answers quite different from those for a trip in December. The same principle is true for the macroeconomic climate.

Strategic planning, then, is "the process by which the guiding members of an organization envision its future and develop the necessary procedures and operations to achieve that future." The operative words in that definition are *guiding members, envision*, and *procedures . . . to achieve that future*. We will meet these terms again in Chapter 5.

Nine Keys to Strategic Success

Sound strategic planning requires outstanding guidance. After becoming virtual coroners of organizations—investigating what went wrong, what caused the heart attack—the authors of this book came up with nine managerial imperatives for shaping strategic success. These "keys" are listed in Figure 1-7.

Figure 1-7
Nine Keys for Shaping Strategic Success

- Base decisions on values.
- Make the mission crystal clear.
- Sound a rallying cry.
- Persevere.
- Empower people—all the people.
- Promote and reward risk taking.
- Encourage innovation.
- Monitor and manage down board.
- Maintain a market focus.

REFERENCES

Managers' Manager John Humphrey. (1987, September). *Inc.*, pp. 49–58.

Peters, T. J., & Waterman, R. H., Jr. (1982). *In search of excellence: Lessons from America's best-run companies.* New York: Harper & Row.

Pfeiffer, J. W., Goodstein, L. D., & Nolan, T. M. (1986). *Applied strategic planning: A how to do it guide.* San Diego, CA: University Associates.

Sculley, J., & Byrne, J. A. (1987). *Odyssey: Pepsi to Apple.* New York: Harper & Row.

SHAPING THE FUTURE OF YOUR ORGANIZATION

In a small, small village in ancient China an old, old man had a magnificent vision. His great vision was for the village to have its own real, live, honest-to-goodness, fire-breathing dragon. The old man said, over and over, "If we had a dragon in our town, our children would behave. If we had a dragon in our town, the government would give us more grants. If we had a dragon in our town, people would come from many miles away to see the dragon, and our economy would soar." And on and on and on. He described his vision to everyone he saw, and he talked about it so frequently that eventually it became the vision of everyone in the village. Now everyone was saying, "If we only had a dragon, all our problems would be solved."

Upon hearing all this, the god of the dragons said, "Hey, these people really want a dragon. And if any group of people in the whole history of mankind ever deserved a dragon, these people deserve one!" So, lo and behold, one morning the old man walks out of his house, and there—standing right in front of him—is a real, full-sized, honest-to-goodness, fire-breathing dragon.

The old man takes one look at the dragon and is so stunned that he falls over with a heart attack and dies. This startles the dragon so much that he roars and spews out flames, and the whole village burns to the ground.

The moral of the story is: There is a helluva big difference between a vision and its implementation.

Many contemporary organizations have dragons. If only we had an infusion of cash! If only we could get rid of Joe (or Mary)!! If we could only get this product on line! If only we had this! If only we had that! With all the emphasis that is given to the potency of a vision, there often is a tremendous gap between an organization's vision and what needs to be done to successfully cope with the organization's real issues.

VALUES-BASED DECISIONS

Rather than hope for the dragon, organizations would be better served by self-examination — self-examination directed toward better understanding of the basis of their operations and what makes them really tick. Organizations make decisions about what to do on a regular basis, and virtually all of these decisions are rooted in the

If Only . . .

values held by the organization. This is a difficult concept for many managers to accept; instead, they insist that the so-called "bottom line" drives all decisions. If we examine some organizational decisions, however, we will see that some underlying values can virtually always be decoded.

For example, a plant of a major computer manufacturer did not have enough units ready to meet its quarterly shipping schedule. It faced the alternatives of not meeting the schedule or sending out equipment that had not been tested adequately. Not shipping would result in a chastisement of the plant manager for failure to meet his goals, but shipping improperly manufactured equipment might impact the organization's strong commitment to high-quality merchandise. The plant manager and his staff reviewed these alternatives for several days before reaching a decision based on their values and their understanding of the overall values of the corporation. Which alternative they selected is not relevant here; what *is* important is that it was rooted in their values, not in a simplistic pursuit of profit.

Consider the dilemma that many large service organizations have faced as a result of a short-term economic recession. Something has to be done to reduce the number of employees on the payroll. Although that decision is based on bottom-line considerations, how it is implemented is clearly a values consideration. Will employees be laid off? If so, on what basis? Last hired, first out? Or will older employees be encouraged to retire early? Another alternative would be to cut down on everyone's hours or to ask employees to volunteer for furloughs. The underlying value on which such decisions are based is the view that is taken of the employees. In an organization in which employees are viewed as disposable commodities, the decision could be quite different from that in an organization that views employees as valuable human resources. The value the organization generally places on employees will determine how they are treated in the organization and how human resource policies are formulated.

Another value that is important in many—or most—business decisions is *risk taking*. Organizations range from being risk-aversive, on one extreme, to risk-seeking on the other, depending primarily on the value that senior managers place on risk. Risk-aversive organizations grow relatively slowly. They generally have personnel policies that protect them from litigation and employee complaints and are relatively low in innovation in both products and marketing. On the other hand, risk-seeking organizations frequently play "bet your company." For risk-seeking managers, much of the thrill of the game is in walking the tight line between reasonable and excessive risking, which has both high payoffs and high downside risks. Risk-aversive managers recognize that their strategy is unlikely to produce rapid change or rapid growth, but neither does it put the entire organization at risk.

Orientation of Decision Making

Organizations can be categorized according to their values. Harrison (1975) suggests an ideology that has four orientations: (a) power, (b) role, (c) task, and (d) self. The *power* orientation places most of the decision-making processes at the top of the organization. Individuals there are expected to yield to leadership, to be loyal followers, and to understand that their leaders will be protective, generous, and indulgent in response to their followership. The *role* orientation is impersonal and has individuals do what is required by the formal system. Concern focuses on rules and regulations and making certain that things are "done right." The *task* orientation is egalitarian, and all people are seen as being able to influence those decisions that concern getting the job done. Individuals are able to use their authority to obtain the resources needed to complete the task. The *self* orientation is represented by those organizations that have as their goal the development of individuals. In such organizations the focus is to help individual members reach their own potential and maximize their own learning.

Deal and Kennedy (1982) identify four cultures (see Figure 2-1): the tough-guy, macho culture; the work-hard/play-hard culture; the bet-your-company culture; and the process culture. Schemes such as Harrison's and that proposed by Deal and Kennedy offer useful ways for an organization to examine its own dominant

---

Figure 2-1
The Deal-and-Kennedy Corporate Cultures

1. The tough-guy, macho culture
2. The work-hard/play-hard culture
3. The bet-your-company culture
4. The process culture

---

values in order to help that organization understand how the values drive the decisions, how human resources are used, how risks are taken, and how people in the organization generally respond to their environment.

Seeking Productive Values

Values of organizations provide a useful anchor in an environment that is constantly in flux. As pointed out in Chapter 1, the rapidity of change in contemporary society creates a sense of uncertainty of direction and lack of clarity about the future. Organizations that clearly recognize the values they espouse and behave congruently with those values will avoid the fate of the Chinese village that had its dream of the dragon come true.

Figure 2-2 compares productive and nonproductive values, on one hand, and also values that overlap between individual managers in an organization and those that do not overlap. Where productive values overlap, there is congruence about the values, and they lead to organizational success.

Organizations work hard to articulate these values, typically in some kind of written statement that is ordinarily widely circulated in the organization. Examples are the "Five Principles of Mars" (see Figure 2-3) and the "Johnson & Johnson Credo" (see Figure 2-4). These statements have evolved over a period of years and represent the explicit values by which managers and employees attempt to run the businesses.

Figure 2-2
Overlap and Productivity Characteristics of Values

OVERLAP   PRODUCTIVE

	Yes	No
Yes	Overlapping Productive Values	Overlapping Nonproductive Values
No	Nonoverlapping Productive Values	Nonoverlapping Nonproductive Values

When nonproductive values overlap, collusion occurs. That is, the dominant values of the organization are nonproductive and do not lead to a functioning organization. Managers, for example, may agree that risk taking is to be avoided at all costs, not recognizing that risk avoidance may be the most risky strategy of all, given the nature of our current environment. When productive values do not overlap, individuals with different values may constantly push to have their positions heard and worked out in the equation of decision making. For example, in our earlier illustration of the computer factory, the quality-control staff argued vehemently that the plant should not ship any equipment that had not been properly "burned in," while the manufacturing group—eager to meet its production schedule—argued that they knew the equipment was satisfactorily manufactured. Such nonoverlapping productive differences produce the kind of dialog that allows an organization to come to a difficult decision where clarity is not readily apparent.

Nonproductive, nonoverlapping values, however, simply produce chaos and conflict. Members of the organization fight, even though winning would have little or no consequence. Their conflict dissipates much of the creative energy of the organization and leaves

> # Figure 2-3
> # The Five Principles of Mars
>
> **1. Quality**
> The consumer is our boss, quality is our work, and value for money is our goal.
> **2. Responsibility**
> As individuals, we demand total responsibility from ourselves; as associates, we support the responsibilities of others.
> **3. Mutuality**
> A mutual benefit is a shared benefit; a shared benefit will endure.
> **4. Efficiency**
> We use resources to the fullest, waste nothing, and do only what we can do best.
> **5. Freedom**
> We need freedom to shape our future; we need profit to remain free.

little room for constructive work. An absurd but lucid example of nonproductive, nonoverlapping values would be if some of the managers believed that a task force should poll employees on the size of the CEO's future office, whereas other managers believed that every employee should be required to sign up with the bowling team.

Behavior Congruent Beliefs

An organization's values need to be congruent with the organization's behaviors, and this presents a problem for many organizations. For example, a driver for an organization that prides itself on customer service accidentally ran over a Wiffle Ball as he backed out of a customer's driveway ("Managers' Manager," 1987). The customer called the manager, who went out of his way to buy a new Wiffle Ball — for $2.67 — and deliver it to the customer. When he turned in the bill, the company refused to reimburse him. Clearly,

Figure 2-4
The Johnson & Johnson Credo

Our Credo

We believe our first responsibility is to the doctors, nurses and patients,
to mothers and all others who use our products and services.
In meeting their needs everything we do must be of high quality.
We must constantly strive to reduce our costs
in order to maintain reasonable prices.
Customers' orders must be serviced promptly and accurately.
Our suppliers and distributors must have an opportunity
to make a fair profit.

We are responsible to our employees,
the men and women who work with us throughout the world.
Everyone must be considered as an individual.
We must respect their dignity and recognize their merit.
They must have a sense of security in their jobs.
Compensation must be fair and adequate,
and working conditions clean, orderly and safe.
Employees must feel free to make suggestions and complaints.
There must be equal opportunity for employment, development
and advancement for those qualified.
We must provide competent management,
and their actions must be just and ethical.

We are responsible to the communities in which we live and work
and to the world community as well.
We must be good citizens — support good works and charities
and bear our fair share of taxes.
We must encourage civic improvements and better health and education.
We must maintain in good order
the property we are privileged to use,
protecting the environment and natural resources.

Our final responsibility is to our stockholders.
Business must make a sound profit.
We must experiment with new ideas.
Research must be carried on, innovative programs developed
and mistakes paid for.
New equipment must be purchased, new facilities provided
and new products launched.
Reserves must be created to provide for adverse times.
When we operate according to these principles,
the stockholders should realize a fair return.

Johnson & Johnson

the values the company articulated about customer service were not carried out into the behaviors that enabled employees to make those modest decisions that provide congruence between behavior and beliefs.

Shaping strategic success requires organizations to recognize and articulate those values that drive its decisions and to disseminate those values throughout the organization. Not only do these values have to be disseminated, but individual members of the organization need to feel empowered to make the decisions that make those values real. Without the congruity, members of the organization feel that the articulated values are fraudulent, and that causes alienation. Under such circumstances, it would be far better not to have such values clearly articulated.

As an example of congruence between behavior and espoused values, look again at Figure 2-3. M & M Mars is one of the largest privately held companies in the world. Throughout the offices of the company—whether in Singapore, or in Waco, Texas, or in the U.S. home office—these five principles are prominently displayed. Adherence to the principles is apparent in the following story, which illuminates the mutuality statement in the "Five Principles of Mars." A buyer who was employed by the Mars company was able to secure cacao beans from a distressed broker at a figure well below the market price. He returned to his company with the self-assurance that he would be lauded for the money he had saved Mars. Much to his surprise, he was disciplined, and the contract was rewritten at a higher price. He was told that his company valued its suppliers too much to take advantage of them during a depressed period, and furthermore, that Mars could some day be the distressed party and would want reciprocal treatment.

Another example of mutuality occurred to one of the authors of this book when he noticed a hole in a two-year-old suit. He took it back to the merchant to ask if it could be rewoven. To his amazement, the merchant located a suit exactly like it, altered it, and presented it in exchange for the old suit.

CLARITY OF MISSION

A second key to shaping strategic success is clarity of mission. That is, individuals need to understand what business the company is in and how its values drive that business. Without such widespread understanding, employees will not develop much commitment or loyalty to the organization and its success. This means that the dominant thrust of the organization needs to be relatively simple, so simple that every employee can understand it and can behave accordingly. One example of clarity of the mission is the motto of Domino's Pizza: "Pizza in thirty minutes." This statement does not suggest that Domino aspires to make the best pizza in the world or that it makes gourmet pizza. It simply says, "If you want a pizza in a hurry, call us." This mission statement also drives Domino employees to meet the challenge of delivering a pizza in thirty minutes. The motto provides high clarity—a clarity that can be understood by every person who works in the organization, from the order taker to the pizza maker to the delivery person, as well as supervisors and managers.

A West Coast motel chain provides a similar lesson on clarity of mission: "Hospitality that brings guests back." It recognizes in this mission statement that the way the guest is treated is the key

A Mission with a Challenge

ingredient in providing repeat business, which is vital in the highly competitive West Coast motel business. This mission statement provides a template for the behavior of the entire staff. Each time an employee of this chain has an encounter with a customer, the question can be asked, "Did I treat this customer in a way that will increase the probability that he or she will use our motels again?"

Challenging the Value of Ambiguity

In contrast to these clear mission statements, many organizations apparently prefer ambiguous statements of mission—probably because such ambiguity does not require individuals to be accountable. It is easy to determine whether or not a pizza has been delivered in thirty minutes, and employees can be held accountable; but statements such as "providing quality" are vague enough to protect employees from accountability. Nevertheless, ambiguous mission statements put the organization at grave risk.

It is often asserted that the organization's mission is too nebulous to define neatly in a few words. However, if the mission cannot be clearly stated, there will be no way to determine when and if it is accomplished. Although not all missions can be as sharply defined as "pizza in thirty minutes," organizations must be able to articulate the goals that they are striving to achieve in a straightforward fashion—one that all employees can understand and to which they can all relate. When managers argue that a clear statement of goals is not possible or even attemptable, one must ask if that is really the case or if perhaps they prefer the ambiguity—and consequent lack of accountability—that results from the failure to address the issue of mission clarity.

Commitment to the Vision

A third key to shaping strategic success is the ability of the organization to sound a clear rallying cry, to make a statement that directly involves and energizes people throughout the organization to achieve the corporate mission. An old apocryphal story illustrates the usefulness of a rallying cry. Three bricklayers were working side by side. In response to the question, "What are you doing?" the first

bricklayer said, "I'm laying bricks." The second one answered, "I'm feeding my family." The third worker, who obviously had a high degree of commitment, responded, "I'm building a cathedral."

The early work of NASA is another illustration of providing a rallying cry. In an interview, a janitor at one of the major NASA installations described his job as "helping to put a man on the moon." Like the cathedral bricklayer, he was involved in and energized by a task that transformed the actual work being done into an achievement that was greater than what the individual alone could achieve. Rallying cries help to bring people to a commitment to the vision. The envisioning process, coupled with strong management that provides constant rallying on the work-unit level, produces the kind of commitment that leads to strategic success.

In another recent example, a computer-software company used a sales goal — breaking the barrier of $100 million dollars — as the rallying cry for the year. "Breaking the $100-million-dollar sales barrier" was seen on banners, shirts, lapel pins, and in other conspicuous places, and it involved every person in the organization. Employees were promised a week-long trip to Hawaii if they helped to break the barrier. The method worked. Sales hit $101 million, up from $50 million the previous year, and the next month, employees started hitting the beaches. Often, organizations are not effective in producing the kind of mission statement that is specific enough to provide the necessary vision, rallying cry, and clarity. Before reading further, look at the mission statement in Figure 2-5.

This mission statement is so vague and so general that one wonders what the product is and, indeed, what the industry is. As you read it, ask yourself if it might not be equally appropriate for your own organization. It may come as a surprise to you to learn that it is the corporate mission statement of General Motors, and that it was developed by the senior executive staff over a period of many months and at a cost of many millions of dollars in staff time and retreat-setting facilities. While there is nothing "wrong" with this mission statement, there is little right about it. It is so general that it has neither the clarity to hold people accountable nor the rallying

---

Figure 2-5
Mission Statement of a Real Organization

The fundamental purpose of [this corporation] is to provide products and services of such quality that our customers will receive superior value, our employees and business partners will share in our success, and our stockholders will receive a sustained, superior return on their investment.

---

cry that is needed for producing the commitment that is vital to an organization's success.

Clarity is a necessary but insufficient precursor to commitment. Both by what they say and, even more important, by what they do managers demonstrate the importance of the mission statement to achieving strategic success. They must articulate the mission on a regular basis, indicate how their day-to-day decision making reflects the importance of the mission, use mission-related criteria in the performance appraisals of their subordinates, and do whatever else they can to clearly communicate their commitment to the mission. Only by such exemplary behavior can they obtain the necessary rank-and-file commitment to the mission. Once that commitment is obtained, however, it has the capacity to energize the entire organization in a new and profoundly different fashion.

REFERENCES

Deal, T. E., & Kennedy, A. A. (1982). *Corporate cultures: The rights and rituals of corporate life*. Reading, MA: Addison-Wesley.

Harrison, R. (1975). Diagnosing organization ideology. In J. E. Jones & J. W. Pfeiffer (Eds.), *The 1975 annual handbook for group facilitators*. San Diego, CA: University Associates.

Managers' Manager John Humphrey. (1987, September). *Inc.*, pp. 49–58.

3 PEOPLE IN CHANGE IN ORGANIZATIONS

This is the way a beehive operates: A worker finds a major source of pollen, flies back to the hive, and performs a dance that shows the other bees the direction of the pollen source. The speed of the dance indicates the distance of the find from the hive. Then the queen bee gives the word, and out of the hive fly the workers directly to the newly found pollen. At least, 85 percent of them do. The other 15 percent don't follow the swarm. They appear not to have comprehended the message and go wandering off in other directions. And what happens to this 15 percent? They look for other sources of pollen, and when they find it the story starts all over again.

15 Percent Seem not to Comprehend

Someone once asked, "Did you know that the mortality rate is higher for the 15 percent?" Being part of that 15 percent in human organizations may mean that the 85 percent try to hammer you into shape. However, for an organization to be effective and survive, it must recognize the value of the behavior of the 15 percent and, in fact, reward that type of behavior. If you look for common denominators in successful organizations, you will see that a strong one is to find a way to get some of the people to do a deviant thing. If a system is too tight for this, if every bee is required to go to a particular source of pollen, there will be no research and development.

SOURCES AND VALUES OF RESISTANCE TO CHANGE

Change is in the eye of the beholder. If the beholder agrees with the change, then it is logical, rational, and well thought out. If not, then it is illogical, irrational, and improperly thought out.

Homeostasis

Try comparing resistance to change with electrical resistance — "a property of a conductor by virtue of which the passage of current is opposed." It is homeostasis, maintaining the status quo. In considering change, we need a balance. We cannot afford to badmouth everyone who is against change. In fact, resistance to change is an important part of stable organizations. If they change too fast, disastrous things can happen. For example, Boise Cascade decided to integrate vertically, and it went all the way from designing seeds to growing trees to building and selling houses. That is about as vertically integrated as an organization can get, and it did not work.

As we go into organizations, we find incredibly rational conversations, but the disagreement is often about what business the organization is in. Whether a group of physicians is in the business of preventive medicine or corrective medicine makes a great deal of difference in the way the doctors behave. What are the values? What will be the rewards?

Changes in the direction of an organization cannot be made if the changes violate employees' values or the traditions that underlie the core culture. Those in favor of change can push, but the value system will not budge. It is like the Pillsbury doughboy; you press on it, and it pops back. Even if a lot of effort is put into the change, if it is contrary to the value system, it springs right back.

In order for an organization to change—according to Lewin (1975)—it must first unfreeze, then change, then refreeze. Many organizations become unfrozen and stay unfrozen ... and they remain unfrozen until at last people become enervated because there has been too much change. They have been in an unfrozen state so long that things become chaotic. Then they begin to reject all change, even logical change. If, however, change comes in increments—unfreeze, change, refreeze; unfreeze, change, refreeze—people are able to get settled before the next change comes.

RISK TAKING

To get people to take more risks, risk taking must be promoted and rewarded. Basically, people have a formula in mind about risk taking. They say, "When there's enough trust in the system, I'm going to take some risks." The trouble is that the formula is 180 degrees off course. The truth is that risk taking results in trust. If people sit around waiting for trust to result in risk taking, they will be waiting a long, long time. Risk taking, when done properly, will create trust.

There is a story about an IBM employee who took a risk that cost his company $500,000. When he was called into the CEO's office, he assumed he would be fired. Instead, he was given a coveted assignment. In essence he replied, "I'm pleased but I'm confused. I cost this company $500,000, and you're giving me one of the real plum jobs in the organization. Why?" We are told that the CEO retorted, "We have just sunk a half-million dollars into your education, and we sure as hell are not going to pour it down the drain!" Most companies, however, do not have that attitude toward risk. They don't say, "What's the positive side? What can we learn from what we've done wrong?"

Harvey (1988) tells a story of Captain Asoh — a pilot of a Japanese commercial airliner — who depended on the power of forgiveness rather than the power of excuses or blame to clear himself of an unforgivable miscalculation. It was said that when Asoh descended too soon and landed on water instead of on land, he set the plane down so gently that many of the ninety-six passengers were not aware of the mistake. Nonetheless, when the National Transportation Safety Board held a preliminary hearing, the press appeared en masse to witness the fiery testimonies and record the numerous accusations. Captain Asoh was the first witness. Harvey tells us the first question was, "Captain Asoh, in your own words can you tell us how you managed to land that DC-8 Stretch Jet 2½ miles out in San Francisco Bay in perfect compass line with the runway?" Although Harvey has not been able to obtain an actual transcript of Captain Asoh's response, rumors say that he merely responded, "As you Americans say, Asoh f____d up!" With those words the hearing was concluded.

Not every system, however, fosters a culture that allows employees to be completely frank and truthful. Mistakes are not tolerated, and the guilty are rewarded for hiding the truth. As Harvey also reminds us, the person who has not made a mistake in the last year is also the person who has been afraid to try anything of significance.

The bees that bat a thousand cannot be flying around looking for new sources of pollen. Somehow the culture has to support the challenges if new lessons are to be learned. Risk taking can be encouraged by modeling, but rewarding can promote it even more. Blanchard (1982) says it in one short phrase, "Catch people doing something right."

EMPOWERMENT

Block (1987) says that politics is the exchange of power, and empowerment is the positive way to be political. *Empowerment* is getting people to believe they are in charge of their destiny, getting them to believe that what they do is going to impact the system. When people feel disempowered, their organization will start on a downward spiral that is difficult to change. People begin to say, "What difference does it make what I do? I don't have control." This can become epidemic in the system. Things that empower people in organizations become key elements in making a vital organization that can respond to change.

A zero-sum activity is an activity in which there are just as many winners as losers. A subzero-sum activity is one in which there are more losers than winners. An organization can provide incentive programs that will produce a net gain that far outweighs the losses. The employees can be empowered to be proactive in their work, and this will produce winning numbers for both the individuals and the organization.

One thing that can be done to empower people is to acknowledge meaningful accomplishments. The term *meaningful* is important, because if an employee is praised for something he or she does not regard as significant, that achievement seems like nonsense. Another way to empower people is to ask for opinions and then really consider those opinions. Some supervisors become trapped into thinking they are practicing participatory management just because they ask for opinions, although they go ahead and do whatever they wanted to do in the first place. Their employees need to know that they are helping to guide destiny.

What is *elegant currency* with regard to empowerment? This, too, is in the eye of the beholder. To one person, "Let's go have a beer after work" is elegant currency for empowerment; to a person who wants to rush home, it can be a pain in the posterior. So the notion of elegant currency is not what is elegant to the person who is trying to empower, but rather to the person who is to be empowered. For some people, a letter of recognition is important and framed and hung. For others, the letter is dropped into a drawer and forgotten.

We can also disempower ourselves. Block mentions five ways (see Figure 3-1). The first is by telling ourselves stories about advancement. For example, we might say, "I'm going to start taking risks as soon as I get tenure," or "If I do that, it will get in the way of my advancement."

Second, all of us need approval, whether it comes from our supervisor, our colleagues, or our significant other. However, if we overdo this quest for approval, we disempower ourselves.

**Elegant Currency for One Person May Be
Trash for Another**

Figure 3-1
Five Ways To Disempower Ourselves

Deception about Advancement	Obsession with Approval	Selling Out for Cash
	Imagined Danger	Control at all Costs

Third, most of us are driven by the desire for hard cash; but if we translate compliant behavior into ways to get hard cash, our action disempowers us.

Fourth, a human wish to remain safe can also be carried too far. We may imagine that we are standing on the brink of the Grand Canyon, when in reality we are on a three-inch curb. We dare not step off the curb for fear of falling into the Grand Canyon. This illusion also disempowers us.

The fifth way we can disempower ourselves is by insisting on keeping control of a situation at all costs. Many senior managers cannot bring themselves to tell their employees, "I don't know." The empowered manager, however, is willing to admit a lack of knowledge and say, "I don't know; we need to figure this out together."

Proactive Futuring

We sometimes talk about how an organization can engage in *proactive futuring*, the act of deciding what you want to happen and then setting out to make it happen. This action is also possible for individuals. It is empowerment at the broadest level. Sculley (Apple's CEO, mentioned in Chapter 1) says, "The best way to predict the future is to invent it" (Sculley & Byrne, 1987, p. 297). You have to imagine what you want and then take charge and make it come true.

You have probably seen the puzzle that has nine dots and instructions to connect the dots with four straight lines without picking up the pen (see Figure 3-2). The secret is to go "outside" the nine dots before changing the direction of your line. We often speak of going "outside the nine dots" as a way of finding creative solutions to problems. If the instructions said, "Connect the nine dots with three lines," a creative person could find the solution by trying a little harder. If the instructions said, "Connect the dots with one straight line," a creative person might realize the line could be any width. One swoop of a wide brush would connect all of them. Or perhaps the person would fold the paper so that one line would connect all of them. The secret of creativity is to push that one step farther, then keep pushing, and keep pushing.

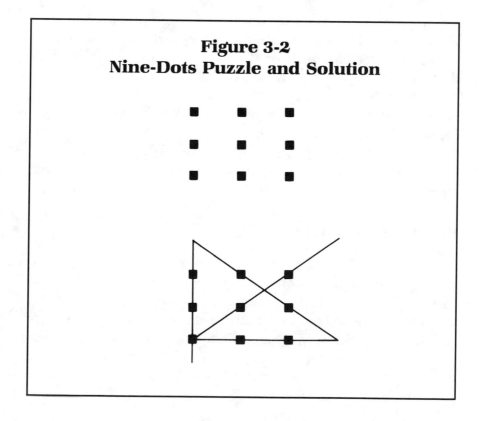

Figure 3-2
Nine-Dots Puzzle and Solution

Perseverance

Change can be made at the knowledge level, at the attitude level, at the individual behavior level, and at the group level. The important variables are (1) the difficulty in making the change and (2) the time it takes to make the change (see Figure 3-3). It can be easy and quick to make changes at the knowledge level. To change attitudes takes longer and is more difficult. Changing individual behavior takes even longer and is increasingly more difficult. And it is extremely difficult and may take a long period of time to change group behavior.

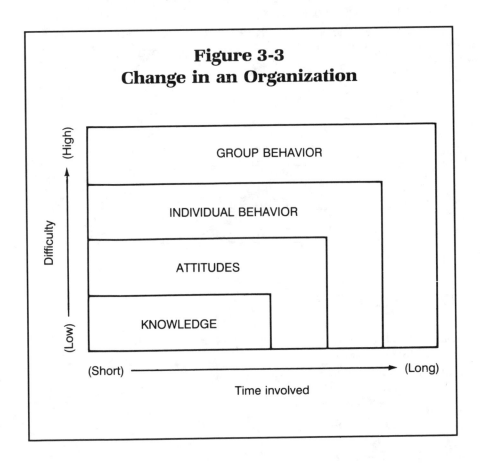

Figure 3-3
Change in an Organization

In many organizations we hear the expression, "We've tried that twice (or three times) and it doesn't work here." That statement brings to mind the "147/805 Rule." This rule is based on two facts: (1) Thomas Edison failed 147 times before he got lucky and (2) the Wright brothers tried 805 times before they achieved sustained flight. Several of our clients have this message posted in their offices: "It is *perseverance* that separates an idea from making it come to life."

An organization's most dynamic strategy of change resides in the alteration of its rewards and sanctions. If you are going to change an organization, you must first change rewards and sanctions. In order to effect the change, you must reward people when they do something right and punish them when they do it wrong. The 15 percent who do not follow the swarm must be assured that they will be rewarded for the occasional big find of new pollen. If you remember the 147/805 Rule, it will take you far. In Pogo's language, "Life is full of unsurmountable opportunities."

147/805 RULE

REFERENCES

Blanchard, K., & Johnson, S. (1982). *The one-minute manager*. New York: William Morrow.

Block, P. (1987). *The empowered manager: Positive political skills at work*. San Francisco: Jossey-Bass.

Harvey, J. B. (1988). *The Abilene paradox and other meditations on management.* San Diego, CA: University Associates.

Lewin, K. (1975). *Field theory in social science.* Westport, CT: Greenwood.

Sculley, J., & Byrne, J. A. (1987). *Odyssey: Pepsi to Apple.* New York: Harper & Row.

FROM VISION TO REALITY

A young man watched his bride carefully prepare a turkey for their first Thanksgiving dinner. With great precision she snipped off the tail of the turkey just before placing the bird in the roasting pan. "Why did you cut off the turkey's tail?" he asked. "Oh," she shrugged, "you *always* cut off the tail before you cook the turkey." "But *why?*" he again asked. "Well, uh," she stammered, "my mother taught me to cut it off. I'll ask her when she arrives."

With an innocent voice, the bride asked her mother, "Why do we cut off the turkey's tail?" The mother exclaimed, "Oh, you should *always* cut off the turkey's tail!" "But *why?*" persisted the daughter. The mother then replied, "I learned it from your grandmother, and she was the best cook in the neighborhood. Many a time I watched her as she was preparing the turkey, so I would know exactly how to do it. Just before cooking it, she always cut off the tail. If you want to know why, call her and ask her."

The bride made a long-distance phone call to wish her grandmother a happy Thanksgiving Day. Then she asked, "Grandmother, why do we cut off the tail of the turkey before cooking it?" The grandmother replied, "I have no idea why *you* cut it off, but I used to cut it off because my roasting pan was so small that a big turkey wouldn't fit unless I cut off the tail."

INNOVATION

Strategic success, for the vast majority of organizations today, pivots directly off their ability to be innovative. There is a difference between creativity and innovation. *Creativity* relates to the generation of ideas, the creating of options, the identification of possibilities. *Innovation*, on the other hand, refers to actual organizational change, improvement, or renewal that comes as a result of the application of ideas. Unfortunately, the literature tends to treat the two as if they were absolutely equivalent. The terms have been used interchangeably. Yet in achieving strategic success, it is far more critical for the organization to make changes, to tune itself, to improve — in other words, to be *innovative*. Some organizations that are highly in need of innovation — that have very low levels of demonstrated successful change — do not, in fact, have a shortage of ideas. A prevalence of ideas and the ability to generate ideas are necessary but not sufficient for achieving strategic success.

Much like the turkey-tail story, organizations frequently function with long periods of tradition, long habit patterns of doing things the way they have previously been done. New ideas do not find an easy home in such organizations. Lewin (1975), in his work

Because We Always Have

on organizational change, developed a model that examined the unfreezing-changing-refreezing kind of sequence (see Figure 4-1) that needs to occur in organizations for proper change to take place. Many organizations, in their process of organizing, have managed to create systems that are relatively impervious to change. According to Lewin, they stay frozen for long periods of time. In a frozen or unready state, an organization can hold off virtually any idea for long periods of time.

Ideas are also an extremely fragile commodity. The major problem in moving from a great idea to organizational innovation is that the person or group who generates the idea frequently believes that the quality of the idea will sell that idea into the organization and that it will, therefore, make a difference. Experience indicates that this is almost never the case. Most ideas die a premature death, because those who are able to do something to turn the idea into innovation simply do not understand the idea, do not identify with it, or are too busy to pay attention to it.

A new idea can be compared with a new baby. Human offspring require years of feeding, clothing, supporting, educating, training, and otherwise nurturing. A newborn colt, on the other hand, is up within minutes after birth and is relatively self-sufficient within days. Many people who generate ideas for change see their ideas—unfortunately—as self-sufficient young horses. Most ideas, however, require the same amount of nurturing as do human offspring. The net result is that many ideas, lacking sufficient support, nurture, guidance, and tuning, are never successfully sold into the organization. As a result, nothing happens.

Figure 4-1
Change Sequence for Organizations

Unfreezing ——> Changing ——> Refreezing

The vast majority of organizations today are clearly finding themselves in the Lewin unfreezing or unfrozen stage of their existence. They have become unfrozen due to rapidly changing business and organizational environments. They are finding their markets changing radically, placing more severe demands on quality of service or quality of product. They are finding competition from sources that were never expected. Profit-making organizations are being challenged by not-for-profit organizations. Manufacturing firms are finding international production capacities that create immeasurable competitive challenges. Even those institutions seemingly solid and free from competition—such as hospitals, schools, and libraries—are finding severe competitive stresses a standard way of life. The net result is that if many organizations were simply to extend their current state of operations out into the future, without innovation of significance, they would at some point—and in many cases a near point—find themselves out of business. What is absolutely clear is that innovation is critical to shaping strategic success.

As those who are charged with leadership functions within organizations examine the risks and the competitive stresses that they are under, many become highly concerned with what all this means. In fact, it has become a significant consulting specialty in Western society to attempt to predict future trends within the economy, within demographics, within those market variables that dictate success or failure of organizations over time. The willingness of tens of thousands of managers and leaders to subscribe to newsletters, to pay consultants, and to otherwise search out some form of "truth" from which they can make decisions about the future illustrates the significance of the problem. Managers should, of course, have the best information available as they guide their organizations into the future. However, no one can fully predict the trends and patterns of even a limited economic sector or marketplace with sufficient accuracy to assure the correct path for management decisions.

There are repeated—and costly—examples of business reversal and failure tied to management decisions made on today's information that gets overturned by shifts in economic and marketplace patterns. One example is Eastern Airlines. In the midst of fuel shortages and high fuel costs, Eastern committed itself to a massive replacement of its fuel-inefficient airplanes with highly fuel-efficient ones. This extensive program, which significantly extended the debt load of Eastern in order to accomplish a long-term goal of being a highly competitive airline, put Eastern at great risk and ultimately caused it to change ownership. This happened because all the data upon which the decision was made shifted. As fuel prices declined and fuel efficiency became less of a significant variable, the extreme expense of massive airplane purchasing was no longer justified. Debt repayment became more difficult, and Eastern became less competitive than some airlines who had chosen to take a less aggressive approach in updating their fleets.

Flexibility

An increasingly important theme for long-term organizational success is that of innovative approaches to developing and maintaining flexibility. In a constantly and sometimes radically changing business environment, flexibility becomes crucial. Given the inability to predict with sufficient accuracy all those events that may cause a given strategy to fail, it becomes important for organizations to develop strategies that allow significant readjustment if key variables change.

Chrysler is an example of a company, which—having successfully brought itself back from near bankruptcy and become a profitable automobile manufacturing operation—went through a series of steps to ensure long-term strategic success by maintaining a flexible stance. Heavy manufacturing companies that do things in traditional ways find flexibility difficult to maintain. The large investment required to develop and maintain manufacturing capacity frequently causes manufacturers to make long-term commitments even when there is no way to assure long-term market needs in a given direction. Chrysler has actively involved itself in the process of attempting to establish sufficient manufacturing capability without making severe long-term investment decisions. It struggled for nearly a year to negotiate the lease of manufacturing capacity—including facilities, employees, and management—from American Motors Corporation. Ultimately Chrysler had to purchase American Motors in order to acquire the facilities—yet Chrysler obtained them at far less expense than would have been required to build new facilities.

A Supplement to the Traditional Library Facility

Strategic plans need to enable organizations to be flexible and to adjust to constantly changing market situations. An example from the not-for-profit sector is the Los Angeles County Public Library. The largest circulating library in the world, this system is currently looking at a significant increase in the population that it will be called upon to serve—possibly a 24-percent increase in the next twelve years. The traditional response in the library world would be a massive building program. The Los Angeles County system, however, has decided that the expense of building, maintaining, heating, and cooling libraries is a major encumbrance on their ability to be flexible. Very few citizens are supportive of ever closing a library facility. Once a library is built and located in a given part of a community, changing that location is not easy. One significant aspect of the strategic plan for the Los Angeles County Public Library is to consider actively a wide variety of service and product delivery systems to supplement the traditional library facility. By providing books in kiosks, in leased space in shopping malls, and through home delivery, a library would have more ability to shift resources as population and library customer needs shift.

As organizations attempt to anticipate those forces that will be important in the future, "paralysis by analysis" becomes a real danger. In the long run, the truly successful organizations will both make use of available information to establish the most likely success scenario and also attempt actively to achieve their optimal level of success.

As mentioned in Chapter 3, John Sculley's notion of inventing the future (see Sculley & Byrne, 1987) is, in our belief, the exact explication of the role of innovation in shaping strategic success. It is the self-belief of those who have empowered themselves to take control of the future of the organization to *invent* their own future. This inventing of the organization's future is the direct, active, creative application of the vision that has been discussed in previous chapters.

Innovation is not limited to Apple computers, manufacturing operations, or any single domain in our economy. In fact, an organization as unlikely as the Milwaukee Sewerage Commission has demonstrated high levels of innovation in tackling its work. In a state that generally has low levels of new business start-ups, the Milwaukee Sewerage Commission has become one of the very few sewage-treatment operations in the Western world that have figured out how to sell the rest of the country their processed sewage! In fact, Milorganite has become a commercial success that has significantly helped offset the charge for sewage treatment to those served by the commission.

Like other organizations that are innovative, the Milwaukee Sewerage Commission does not limit its innovative activity simply to having a product to sell. It has a marketing director and a nine-year plan to link a dramatic reduction in the working force with a retraining program that will prevent workers from losing their jobs. It is claimed that the Milwaukee Sewerage Commission is the only major utility in the United States with a current building project that is both on schedule and under budget. It is currently charted to save the system $300 million in construction costs. This is a good example of the impact that innovation can have on service-oriented or government industries, as well as product-oriented and private enterprises.

Innovation in organizations is dramatically impacted by the organizational environment. One of the more successful programs to encourage internal innovation in a major corporation is that of Kodak. The mission of its Office of Innovation is to significantly increase the internal ideas that are being carried forward to become organizational innovations. An employee who seeks to have an idea become an organizational innovation has a friend in the Office of Innovation. The role of that office is not to carry the idea forward for the employee, but rather to help the employee learn how to carry the idea forward. This stance serves more than one purpose. First, the idea has a better chance of coming to fruition if the person who spawned it stays with it, nurtures it, and helps to carry it forward. Second, the Office of Innovation helps to create idea champions. This approach will greatly enhance the opportunities for innovation in the future.

A classic story among those who concentrate on enhancing innovation in an organization is that of Lipton Soup. Some years ago, Lipton's management decided to compete more effectively with Campbell's Soup. The problem, as the Lipton managers saw it, was that, from the point of opening the package to the point of consumption, Lipton's dry soup took ten minutes to prepare, whereas Campbell's canned soups took only three minutes. Therefore, Lipton's research and development (R&D) people were asked to develop a "three-minute" soup which would enable Lipton to effectively compete with Campbell's. Months passed and still no three-minute soup. Then someone mentioned that they had produced an *instant* soup but were still unable to come up with the specified product. Since the mandate had been a "three-minute" product, the R&D people had rejected the instant soup as a failure. Fortunately for Lipton, someone was able to see the value in the previously rejected instant soup, and this became an innovation that Lipton successfully carried into the marketplace. This story speaks directly to the difficulty experienced when organizations attempt to formalize innovation.

There is great pressure on R&D departments to produce. The R&D function in large organizations is often highly visible. This high visibility and the great amount of pressure results in careful documentation, testing, and retesting of each idea prior to a proposal that the new product or service become an organizational innovation. In fact, in many organizations this cautious procedure has caused the R&D department to be the least likely place to find effective innovation. When R&D does come up with effective innovations, in many cases it is much later than necessary because of the continual testing and retesting. In fact, a new product may come out of R&D far past the optimal period for marketing it. One of the challenges of leaders is to encourage innovation and effective risk taking that will result in an organization that can shape its own strategic success.

MONITORING AND MANAGING DOWN BOARD

In an organization that has successfully charted the desired vision of itself—that has established its strategic directions—implementation of those plans becomes critical. One of the keys to shaping strategic success is effectively monitoring and managing that strategy. Much like a missile, a strategy, once launched, must be carefully guided to its target. This is the monitoring and managing function.

Monitoring is the constant tracking of the strategy as it approaches the target. If this is year one of a five-year plan, are we where we should be? If this is the third quarter of the year, are we where we should be in the third quarter? The monitoring function is critical. It provides feedback on progress frequently enough to allow a redirection of the strategic process if that becomes necessary. Feedback loops must be not only regular but also relatively frequent. Some organizations have only *annual* feedback loops. This is like navigating a ship in the middle of the ocean with only the rising and the setting of the sun to guide you. Gross measures alone are inadequate for managing and shaping strategic success.

Implementation of the strategic plan—managing the strategic directions—is also critical to success. It has been said that a B-quality plan with an A-quality implementation will outperform an A-quality plan with a B-quality implementation. The implementation of a strategic plan is the critical variable that will ultimately determine whether or not that plan will succeed. Managing the plan is facilitated by high-quality information sources, carefully monitored. A second variable is the willingness to adjust, tune, and refocus the plan as necessary in order to react to constantly changing variables in the marketplace. A vast majority of strategic plans break down in this area, for a variety of reasons. Some organizations simply do not have the internal management capacity to guide themselves carefully toward *any* target. Other organizations, although capable of managing themselves successfully, are unwilling to keep a rein on their managers regarding a particular strategy. Often, the careful implementation of a strategy is seen as boring. It is hard work. Implementation may therefore be given a very light pass, resulting in significant failure of the organizational strategy — with the accompanying risk that strategic planning and strategic management will also be seen as a failure.

A significant aspect, both of establishing strategic directions and of managing and monitoring them successfully, is *down-board thinking*. It is analogous to the way world-class chess players think. They must not only decide on their immediate moves, but must also look "down board," consider their opponent's possible responses to their moves, and plan a number of possible moves ahead. Rather than thinking, "What's the best thing I can do right now?" the player must look ahead to see the alternatives available to the opponent and then decide on alternatives to each of the opponent's possible moves . . . for several moves down the board. The modern manager in organizations must become this type of player.

Stories are legion about organizations that made reasonably good decisions for present problems but inadvertently caused themselves great stress by not thinking through the potential implications of their solutions. One example is the DuPont Chemical Corporation. When it needed to reduce its work force, it developed an effective plan to encourage employees to retire early and to take bonuses that enabled them to quit working. Unfortunately, the strategy was *too* effective. The plan was so enticing that many people who were needed for long-term viability took advantage of it. Thus, an extremely well-implemented plan to reduce expenses ate into the very future of the organization.

Another example is People's Express. As a new type of airline, People's was a great success. It identified a market that was in need of service. It selected and motivated a young work force that took an ownership role — both financially and psychologically — in the future success of the company. It became the sweetheart of the business press, apparently destined for even more success. As it sought a way to grow into an even larger business, it made a number of moves that had a short-term payoff but a significant negative impact on the viability of the company. The acquisition of Frontier Airlines created great stresses within People's, which in turn caused the airline to lose customers and necessary profitability. Moves to organize the growing organization better alienated the previously highly motivated work force and caused significant internal human resource problems. The net result of the short-term moves to feed the growth strategy sapped the viability of the airline and made it an easy acquisition target.

Down-board thinking is of particular relevance, both in establishing strategy — looking at what it is that we want to do — and in anticipating what competitors will do in response. It is also significant in the daily management of organizational decisions. Each decision must be made with both a short-term and a long-term view. Each manager of an organization must constantly do a balancing act while asking, "What's the best solution to the problem that I am facing today and *how will that impact our strategic directions?*" or "If we do this to solve today's problem, will it create new problems for tomorrow?" Down-board thinking about how the competition will react to a particular move should become a constant, an automatic response in carefully monitoring and managing the organization's strategic directions.

MARKET-RELEVANT FOCUS

A final key to successfully shaping organizational success is maintaining a constant market-relevant focus. As true as the other eight keys are, they become irrelevant if customers don't want the product, if clients don't want your service, or if potential buyers don't choose to buy. Although this statement may seem unbelievably basic, organization after organization — large, small, private, public — is finding itself out of sync with its customers. In the 1970s most organizations in Western society focused primarily on their own internal needs and only moderately on the needs of customers. The decade of the '80s has created significant strife in external environments. This strife — which has led to the demise of many major corporations and the retrenchment of others that once thought of themselves as invulnerable — has resulted in a shift toward an interest in what the market wants from the organization, what the market is willing to pay for its wants, and how the organization can be effective in satisfying those wants.

The organization that is intent on shaping strategic success will not only learn to react to the demands of the marketplace, but will actively aspire to base its shape on the needs of its customers. Significant shifts in this direction have already occurred among the more successful organizations. Organizations that previously viewed their customers as "clients" or "patients" or "patrons" are now seeing them as customers who have the ability to purchase services elsewhere. This shift toward attending to the customer's wants can dramatically change the way in which business is done, the way organizations carry themselves into the marketplace, and ultimately the way an organization succeeds.

An increasing number of organizations have sought to identify ways of becoming more market-aware. A great deal of attention has been paid to the handful of organizations that have historically been successful in maintaining a marketplace focus. Organizations that have succeeded in the service of customers have thought of themselves in almost an upside-down type of organizational chart. Unlike the hierarchical system in most large organizations, which has the CEO or president at the top of the importance heap, these organizations revere the people who have direct customer contact. In a customer-driven, service-oriented organization, those people who provide the service are the people who ultimately dictate the future success or failure of the organization. In many organizations this is a hard message to sell. It is, nevertheless, a lesson that will be increasingly driven home by the marketplace itself.

Those who adjust their thought patterns, develop marketplace tracking systems, and conceive products and services based on real customer needs will succeed. Those who fail to make such adjustments will not. Customers are increasingly demanding high levels of quality and service. The reality of the marketplace in the '90s will be that almost no organization will be the customer's only choice. As these two factors interact, the customer will shape the market and determine who succeeds and who fails.

Therefore, any successful organization must utilize all nine keys to shaping strategic success: Decisions must be based on values; the mission must be made crystal clear to everyone in the organization; the leadership must sound a rallying cry that excites and involves people. The people must be empowered and encouraged to be innovative and to persevere. They must carry ideas forward tenaciously and successfully overcome hurdles. Productive risk taking must be seen as a desirable investment in establishing strategic success. Strategies must be carefully implemented, with feedback mechanisms well established and tracked. Day-to-day, week-to-week, and month-to-month, the strategic directions must be managed with down-board thinking. But these eight keys alone do not make up the full ring; their use, while creating an organization that is highly effective and strategically focused, is not sufficient for success. Only with the ninth key is the set complete. The ninth key, maintaining a market focus, will determine the success of the organization. Since the ultimate judge of an organization is the customer, the crucial question becomes, "Is the organization desirable in the eyes of the customer?" This makes the ninth key pivotal to strategic success.

REFERENCES

Lewin, K. (1975). *Field theory in social science.* Westport, CT: Greenwood.
Sculley, J., & Byrne, J. A. (1987). *Odyssey: Pepsi to Apple.* New York: Harper & Row.

5 APPLIED STRATEGIC PLANNING

Any organization that is embarking on strategic planning must face a number of important questions. What business is the organization *really* in? How does the organization intend to achieve its long-term objectives? How much commitment to achieving these objectives do mid-level managers have? How much commitment to these objectives do the rank-and-file employees have? How credible is the top-management team? If neither you nor your organization can provide prompt, positive answers to these questions, then your strategic planning process is deficient or nonfunctional.

Most organizations do some kind of long-range or strategic planning; the formal strategic planning process has been available for over thirty years. However, most strategic planning processes are poorly conceptualized and poorly executed, and the resulting strategic plan rarely influences the daily decisions and specific activities of the organization's members. All too often, strategic planning is seen as a top-management exercise that has little or nothing to do with the actual running of the business. In hundreds of organizations, strategic planning is often thought of as a document rather than a process. When completed, these strategic planning documents often are simply filed away until a revision is mandated at some future time.

WHAT IS STRATEGIC PLANNING?

Strategic planning is the process by which the guiding members of an organization envision the organization's future and develop the necessary procedures and operations to achieve that future. The vision of the future provides both a direction and the energy to move in that direction. Our definition of strategic planning focuses on the process of planning, not the plan that is produced. Successful strategic planning is characterized by organizational self-examination, confronting difficult choices, and setting priorities.

This envisioning process, or proactive futuring, is very different from long-range planning. Usually, long-range planning simply extrapolates current business trends in an attempt to anticipate the

Strategic Plans Are for Using

future and prepare accordingly. Proactive futuring, however, involves a belief that the future can be influenced and changed by what we do *now*. Therefore, the model of strategic planning presented in this book helps an organization to understand that the strategic planning process does more than plan for the future; it helps an organization *create* its future.

The need for envisioning is vividly seen in the classic article "Marketing Myopia" by Theodore Levitt (1960). By "marketing myopia" Levitt means a nearsighted view of marketing in terms of the goods or services a company provides. A broader view would include the customer's needs. For example, Levitt contends that the failure of the railroads to see themselves as being in the "transportation business" was the critical reason for their decline. The railroads declined, not because the need for moving people and freight disappeared, but because these needs were filled by other means—by airplanes, automobiles, trucks, and buses. Had the railroads defined their mission as transportation rather than "railroading," they might very well now have truck, airline, and bus divisions and still be a major industry. The only North American railroad that seems to have successfully understood and solved this problem is Canadian Pacific, which has developed into a total transportation company.

A necessary component of effective strategic planning is called "down-board thinking." (See Chapter 4.) The strategic planning team must look down board, consider the implications of its plans, and then base additional plans on those implications. A major benefit of strategic planning is to help an organization see this big picture. Then the organization will be better able to jump out and make the changes that are necessary in the new environment rather than sitting in the pan and trying inappropriately to adapt.

An organization that constantly adapts to smaller changes in its industry may miss the fundamental shifts that can make the business obsolete. In recent years, a company that manufactures personal computers or related products could easily have been caught up in developing faster and more powerful equipment and overlooked the fact that the market had become saturated. The

Buggy-Whip Myopia

reality of the market shift caught many such companies unawares, causing the need for extreme actions such as extensive layoffs and major research-and-development cutbacks.

Strategic planning is, however, more than just an envisioning process. It requires the setting of clear goals and objectives and the attainment of those goals and objectives during specified periods of time in order to reach the planned future state. Targets must be realistic, objective, and attainable. The strategic plan of the Marriott organization to become the market leader in the leisure/hotel industry is a case in point. In addition to large-scale expansion of its existing hotel chain in primary urban centers, such as New York's Times Square, and at major airports, Marriott purchased Host International (a nationwide chain of airport coffee and gift shops and airline catering). It further segmented its hotel business by the addition of Marriott Courtyards, for a somewhat down-scale market at interstate-highway interchanges. It has now begun to enter the time-share condominium market with properties on Hilton Head

Island, South Carolina, and in Tampa, Florida. And in June, 1986, it acquired Saga, the number-one institutional feeder in the United States. Another major thrust has been to expand into retirement homes through its life-care system.

Strategic planning is an iterative process. Strategic planning and strategic management (the day-to-day implementation of the strategic plan) are the most important, never-ending jobs of management, especially top management. The goals and objectives developed within the strategic planning process should provide an organization with its core priorities and a set of guidelines for virtually all day-to-day managerial decisions. Once a strategic planning cycle is completed, the task of management is to ensure its implementation and then to decide on when to begin the next planning cycle. The future, by definition, always faces us; thus, organizations must always be in the simultaneous processes of planning and implementing their plans.

BUSINESS CYCLES

In addition to the planning cycle, there is another important cycle in strategic planning; this is the business cycle. Figures 5-1 and 5-2 demonstrate the relationship between business cycles and an organization's expansion modes. When an organization is new, it will most probably be in a survival mode. As the organization experiences the business cycle rising, it typically starts expanding. While the cycle is still high, even though buying is expensive and good labor scarce, the typical organization accelerates its expansion. As it sees the benefits of expansion, it can easily be trapped into thinking if a little expansion is good, then a lot of expansion is even better. And it continues to expand, even though the business cycle starts to decline (Figure 5-2). In fact, an organization typically will not start contracting until the business cycle has experienced very significant contraction. Then the organization discovers that it has money tied up in machinery and equipment that are lying idle. It also has too many people on the payroll. Because the organization went into expansion at the wrong time and/or stayed in it too long, it reached overexpansion and soon found itself back in the survival mode (Figure 5-1).

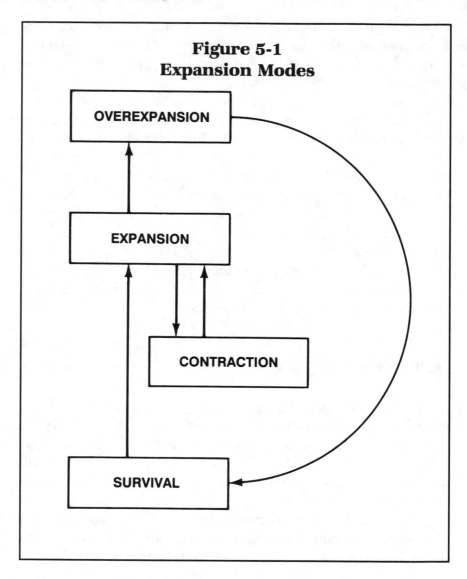

Figure 5-1
Expansion Modes

An important goal in strategic planning is to keep within the expansion/contraction mode and to avoid the overexpansion and survival modes. Let's look at how an organization can do this. If a company begins to expand just as the business cycle begins to rise, it can buy at low prices and will have a good selection of human

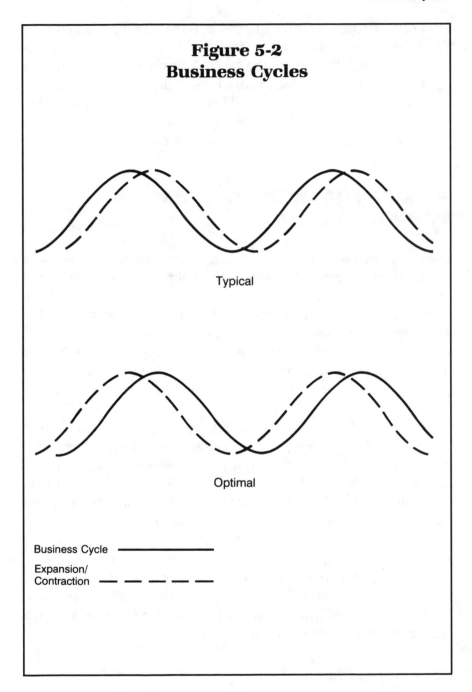

Figure 5-2
Business Cycles

Typical

Optimal

Business Cycle ——————————

Expansion/
Contraction — — — — — —

resources. Then just before the cycle starts to fall, the company should start the contraction process. It should stay in the contraction mode until just *before* the business cycle begins to increase again. Thus, it would continually be moving from expansion to contraction to expansion but would be avoiding the overexpansion and survival modes. Strategic planning enables a business to continue the expansion-contraction-expansion-contraction process.

A NEW STRATEGIC PLANNING MODEL

Based on our research and consulting experience in hundreds of organizations, a new model of strategic planning has been developed (see Figure 5-3). It builds upon several existing models but differs in content, emphasis, and process. The model differs from other strategic planning models in its emphasis on application and implementation. The plan is implemented and applied not only after it is completed, but at nearly every step along the way in the planning process; hence the title "Applied Strategic Planning Model."

The use of this model in strategic planning will provide new direction and new energy to an organization. This planning process — with its clarity and sharpness — harnesses energy that currently may be dissipated in the system, and it reenergizes many who had abandoned hope in the organization. The model was designed for a full range of organizations; it can be applied to large, medium, and small organizations and also to new business start-ups. The model is also as applicable to governmental agencies and not-for-profit organizations as it is to business and industrial organizations. This chapter provides an overview of the specific steps of the model and its overall utility. The succeeding chapters examine each successive step of the model in greater detail.

Planning to Plan

The prework of the strategic planning process involves answering a host of questions and making a number of decisions, all of which are

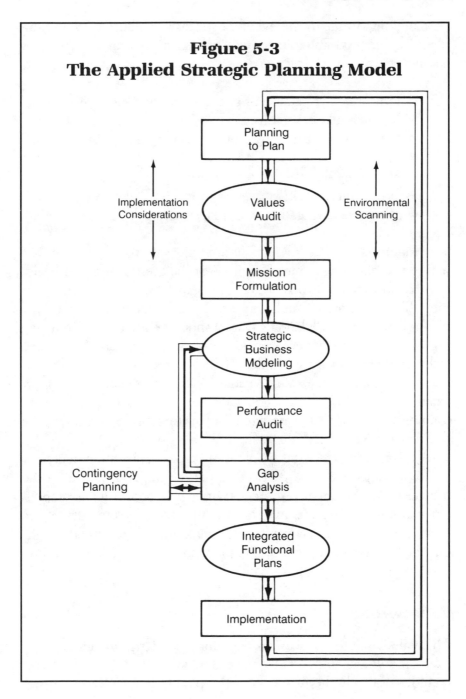

Figure 5-3
The Applied Strategic Planning Model

critically important to the eventual success or failure of the entire planning process. The following questions are typical of those that should be answered:

- How much commitment to the planning process is present?
- Who should be involved?
- How does the organization's fiscal year fit the planning process?
- How long will the strategic planning process take?
- What information is needed in order to plan successfully?
- Who needs to gather and analyze the data?

Planning to plan involves finding answers to these questions before the planning sessions begin. Also before the sessions begin, the expectations that people in the organization have about planning should be clarified, and the people who will be involved with the planning (that is, the "planning team") should be identified. Obtaining organizational commitment from key players in the organization, especially the chief executive officer (CEO) or executive director, is extremely important. Colin Marshall, CEO of British Airways, for example, chose to attend and "kick off" a series of management training programs that were aimed at making British Airways "the world's favorite airline," a capsulization of its strategic plan.

To facilitate the strategic planning process, it is often necessary to use an objective third party. This person can be from inside the organization (a human resources trainer or planner, for example), but it is frequently preferable to bring in someone from outside the organization (that is, a consultant) to maximize objectivity throughout the process. (Chapter 6 will explore the aspects of the planning-to-plan process in greater detail.)

Values Audit

The values audit involves an examination of the values held by every individual and group affected by the strategic plan. This includes not only the members of the planning team, but all other individuals who are major stakeholders in the organization. The values audit includes an examination of the organization's current values, philosophy of operations, assumptions used in operations, and culture.

Early in the planning process, differences in the values of individual members of the planning team need to be identified, clarified, and (where possible) resolved. For example, if individuals' values such as security, risk taking, integrity, and openness are not examined, it is unlikely that the organization's plan can truly reflect the desires and ambitions of the planning team. If these values are not fully examined, there may be little or no agreement about how the organization's future will fit with the expectations of the key members of the management group. For example, a senior-management team that is unconsciously fixed on its perks and retirement benefits is unlikely to adopt any strategy that puts these perks at risk. Once there is clarity and some agreement — or ideally a consensus — on values, the strategic planning process can move ahead.

The values of the organization's other stakeholders also need to be considered. Stakeholders typically include the organization's owner or shareholders (or the funding agency of a not-for-profit or governmental organization), its employees (including all managers), customers, suppliers, unions, and governments. Members of the community who *believe* that they have a stake in the organization, regardless of whether or not such a belief is accurate or reasonable, should not be ignored. The nuclear-power industry, for example, failed to recognize community groups and environmentalists as stakeholders ("What right do they have to dictate to us?"), and currently it has extensive problems, in part because it failed to cultivate a relationship with these external stakeholders.

An organization's values are reflected in the way the organization approaches its work, sometimes referred to as the organization's philosophy of operations. Some organizations have explicit, formal statements of philosophy. An example is the "Five Principles of Mars" (see Chapter 2). This statement by the multinational candy corporation briefly focuses on the importance of the values of quality, responsibility, mutuality, efficiency, and freedom in the operation of the business and in its relations with customers, suppliers, and others.

This type of statement integrates the organization's values into the way the company does business. Organizations that have an explicit philosophy of operations can legitimately expect all employees to abide by the philosophy. True values are supported by rewards and sanctions. At M&M Mars, for example, if any employee violates one of the five principles outlined by the company, the infraction is taken very seriously.

All organizations have philosophies of operation, whether or not those philosophies are stated explicitly. If an organization has an implicit philosophy of operations, then part of the strategic planning process is to make that philosophy explicit. The strategic plan must fit the philosophy, or the philosophy may need to be modified (a task that should only be undertaken with significant organizational support for the change).

The values audit also examines the organization's assumptions about the way things work, the ways in which decisions are made, and the organization's culture. This analysis is one of the most important and—at times—difficult activities of the planning process. It requires an in-depth analysis of the fundamental beliefs that underlie organizational life and organizational decision making. The confrontations that are necessary in the values audit can be long and involved. Without such efforts, however, differences in values, philosophy, and assumptions will continually surface in the planning process and block the group's progress. Once the values are successfully clarified and resolved, the differences are less likely to interfere with the planning process. Then it will be relatively easy to move into the next stage of the planning process. (An in-depth examination of how a values audit can be conducted appears in Chapter 7.)

Mission Formulation

The planning team can next turn its attention to the development of a statement of mission. This step involves identifying and specifically stating what business the organization is in.

The mission statement can be a transformational guide to what management wants the organization to be. For example, when Robert Townsend, as the new CEO at Avis (the car-rental company), asked management to examine its operations, he discovered that a significant portion of the company's business involved the sale of used rental cars. In fact, Avis was one of the world's leading "creators" of used cars. As a result, the company's mission statement was altered to include a statement that the company would seek to provide the best used cars possible. Policies and daily practices (such as vehicle maintenance) soon changed to fall in line with the new goal.

In formulating its mission, an organization needs to answer three primary questions (see Figure 5-4):

1. *What* function does the organization serve?

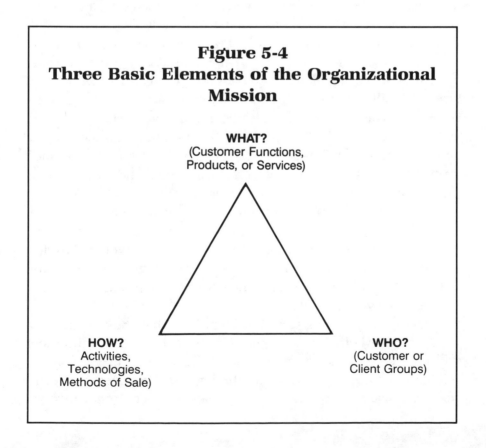

Figure 5-4
Three Basic Elements of the Organizational Mission

WHAT?
(Customer Functions, Products, or Services)

HOW?
Activities, Technologies, Methods of Sale)

WHO?
(Customer or Client Groups)

2. For *whom* does the organization serve this function?
3. *How* does the organization go about filling this function?

Organizations need to answer the "what" question in terms of the needs that the organization meets or attempts to meet for customers or clients. If an organization identifies itself as meeting certain public needs, it will have a clearer and more efficient charter for decisions and operations, making it less likely to experience obsolescence and decline. For example, when a company that manufactured drill bits examined its mission from the standpoint of benefit to the customer, it came to the realization that it was actually in the business of making holes, rather than producing drill bits. The company then began to use the latest laser technology to improve its ability to help customers make holes. If petroleum producers see themselves as being in the business of providing sources of energy to consumers, there are many new options open to them: geothermal, solar- and wind-power generators, and so on. The major issue in mission formulation typically is achieving consensus on how broadly or narrowly the "what" question is answered.

Identifying the "for whom" is the second concern of mission formulation. No organization, no matter how large, can meet all the needs of all its possible clients or customers. The mission-formulation process requires a clear identification of what portion of the total potential customer base an organization considers as its primary market. The process of sorting out the potential customer or client base and identifying which portion should be sought out by the organization is called *market segmentation*. Markets can be segmented in many ways: geographically, ethnically, financially, and so on. For example, needs of Sun Belt consumers are different from those of Frost Belt consumers; kosher foods have devoted consumers, as do soul foods; and Federal Express serves customers who are willing to spend more than the price of ordinary postage to ensure next-day delivery of packages.

Once the planning team has identified what the organization does and for whom, the next step is deciding how the organization will proceed in achieving these targets. The "how" may involve a marketing strategy such as being the low-cost producer, the technological leader, or the high-quality manufacturer. It may involve a distribution system (such as regional warehouses), evening classes that meet in offices or plants, transportation services for clients, or no-appointment medical treatment facilities in shopping centers. It may involve customer service, personalized selling, or any of a variety of organizational processes through which an organization can deliver products or services to a defined consumer group.

Another important ingredient in the mission statement is the organization's distinctive competency, that is, the quality or attribute that sets the organization apart from its competitors. In other words, what is the unique advantage that can be exploited?

Once these elements are identified, they can be woven into the organization's mission statement. This should be a brief statement (one hundred words or less) that identifies the basic business the organization is in. The mission statement should be easily understood by and communicated to all members of the organization.

Developing an effective mission statement can be a time-consuming task, but it must be completed before the planning team moves to the next step. The mission statement provides an enormously valuable management tool to an organization; it clearly charts its future direction and establishes a basis for organizational decision making. (The process of formulating the organization's mission is covered in greater detail in Chapter 8.)

Environmental Scanning

Environmental scanning—perhaps more than any other factor—is responsible for helping the frog see the necessity of jumping out of the pan. Throughout the planning activity, management needs to be aware of things that are happening both inside and outside the organization that might affect the organization. Five environments in particular need to be monitored: the macro environment, the industry environment, the competitive environment, the customer environment, and the organization's internal environment (see Figure 5-5). Naturally, some of these environments overlap one another.

The environmental-scanning process (which includes competitor analysis) should be continual, so that the appropriate information about what is happening or about to happen in the various

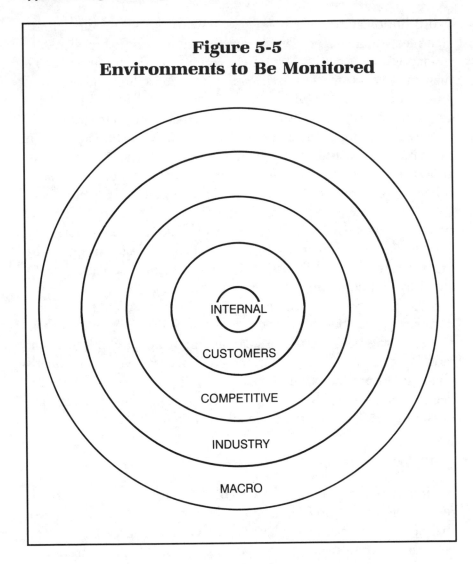

Figure 5-5
Environments to Be Monitored

INTERNAL

CUSTOMERS

COMPETITIVE

INDUSTRY

MACRO

environments is always available to the planning group. Strategic planning provides an opportunity to integrate much of the data the organization has already collected.

The Limited (a highly successful, growth-oriented retail giant) is well known for its unrelenting attention to environmental surveillance. It monitors, primarily through computer-generated information, the internal operations of the organization (for example, sales, inventory, out-of-stock items), and moves quickly to keep its many business elements in alignment. It regularly monitors its customers, and it also monitors the way it is perceived by fashion-conscious, trendy groups of buyers. Equally regularly, it monitors its competitors and the worldwide fashion industry in order to purchase raw materials, choose styles, and establish production schedules. Leslie Waxner, CEO of The Limited, believes that this attention to detail is an important factor in the company's success. (Chapter 9 examines such environmental scanning in more detail.)

Implementation Considerations

Although the implementation of the strategic plan is the final step of the model, there is a continual need to pay attention to the implementation of each step throughout the planning process. As an organization moves through the planning process, it needs to be aware of available resources, the existing culture, and the activities of the competition. Otherwise, the planning process becomes an academic exercise. At each phase of applied strategic planning, certain implementation considerations should be addressed; they should not be postponed until the final implementation phase. (Chapter 9 also discusses implementation considerations.)

Strategic Business Modeling

Strategic business modeling is the process by which the organization specifically defines success in the context of the business(es) it wants to be in, how that success will be measured, and what will be done to achieve it. This definition of success should be consistent with the newly established mission statement.

The strategic business model consists of two parts:

1. The strategic profile, or quantified business objectives, including critical success indicators that are quantitatively specific, such as profitability, market penetration, and liquidity.
2. A narrative description of what business(es) the organization wants to be in at the end of its planning term (for example, in three, five, or ten years).

The strategic-business-modeling phase is another excellent point for determining not to adapt to what is, but to jump out of the pan and engage in proactive futuring. In proactive futuring, the organization takes responsibility for its own future rather than waiting for external forces to dictate the future. Procter & Gamble's disposable diaper is a good example of proactive futuring. The product simply did not exist prior to the P&G marketing program.

Most organizations cite "making a profit" as the organization's primary objective. Yet profit tends—more accurately—to be the result of the successful pursuit of the key business objectives. To overemphasize profit in and of itself is like watching the scoreboard instead of the ball while playing tennis. The objectives and strategies that result from strategic planning should reflect the values and major directions developed in the early stages of the planning process. (Chapter 10 provides a detailed examination of strategic business modeling.)

Performance Audit

The performance audit examines the recent performance of the organization on the same basic performance indices (such as production, quality, service, profit, return on investment, cash flow, and so on) that were identified in the strategic profile. Any data that can help the organization better understand its present capabilities for doing its work should be included in the performance audit. Such data might include life cycles of existing products, employee productivity, inventory turnover, facilities (including capacity and condition), and management capability.

In executing the performance audit, special attention should be paid to obtaining the hard data that indicate the organization's capacity to move in the identified strategic directions. In the summer of 1985, People's Express attempted to expand its market to the business traveler, a market segment to which it had never before appealed. It quickly altered these plans when it learned that its record of 10.38 complaints to the FAA per 100,000 passengers (more than twice that of any other carrier) was a well-known disincentive to business travelers, as was its overloaded reservations system. Then, in an attempt to appeal to the business traveler, People's Express reintroduced first-class service at prices roughly equal to those for coach service on the major airlines.

The need for candor, openness, and nondefensiveness during the performance audit cannot be overstated. Defensiveness in the performance audit leads to finger pointing, avoiding blame, and other trust-destroying behaviors. If such behaviors are allowed to dominate the audit process, they quickly hinder the planning efforts. (The performance audit is discussed in greater detail in Chapter 11.)

Gap Analysis

The gap analysis determines whether or not a gap exists between the strategic business model and the organization's current performance. If a gap does exist, the gap analysis will also determine the degree of the gap. The planning team must then try to be creative in finding strategies to close the gap. If it is impossible to bridge the gap, the planning team must return to the strategic-business-modeling step and rework the business model until the gap between the profile and the organization's capacity to achieve it is reduced to a manageable size. Therefore, the Applied Strategic Planning Model depicts not only arrows running forward from strategic business modeling to performance audit and then to gap analysis, but also an arrow running backward from gap analysis to strategic business modeling (see Figure 5-3).

Examining where the organization is and comparing this picture with where it wants to be may require several iterations before all gaps can be closed. Occasionally the mission statement has to be modified in the process. For example, a small electronics manufacturer had to abandon its growth strategy when its gap analysis revealed that its debt load was too high for the company to obtain the funds necessary to reach the projected growth.

If the gap analysis reveals a substantial disparity between the performance audit and the strategic profile or the strategies identified for achieving the profile, more major changes in the organization may be required. The organization, for example, may be too centralized; it may need to be decentralized to obtain the desired levels of performance. Obviously, either the capability of the organization or the level of expectations of performance needs to be modified in order to close the gaps between the plan and the organization's capacity. (Chapter 12 supplies details about gap analysis.)

Contingency Planning

The strategic planning team needs to identify the major opportunities and threats facing the organization. The team should look for key indicators that suggest these opportunities or threats are apt to become realities. These events or conditions (for example, loss of suppliers, late or reduced funding of key grants, shortage of raw materials, or transportation strikes) are considered because they will necessitate substantial changes *if* they occur.

The planning team should be able to identify the factors that are most likely to affect the organization—such as interest rates, availability of qualified employees, and availability of raw materials—and develop alternative plans based on possible variations in these factors. Contingency planning provides the organization with alternative business-modeling strategies that can be used with a variety of scenarios. For example, producers of building materials are heavily influenced by new housing starts, which in turn are a function of interest rates and general economic conditions. In developing its strategic business model, a producer of building materials may identify several alternative futures, each based on a different volume of housing starts. Housing starts, in turn, are influenced by a variety of governmental actions. For example, if people were no longer allowed tax deductions for mortgage interest paid on their residences, house starts would clearly be threatened. On the other hand, a large governmental program to subsidize residential construction would be an opportunity. Contingency plans should be developed on the basis of both alternatives. (A detailed examination of how to plan for contingencies is provided in Chapter 13.)

Integrating Functional Plans

Next, the planning needs to be moved to the functional units of the organization. New planning teams are then needed for each functional unit (for example, finance, manufacturing, marketing, human resources, and so on). Narratives of functional plans should be developed as a basis for budgeting. For example, in a human resources plan, current and future needs for staffing on the managerial, supervisory, technical, production, and administrative levels should be developed for the time period covered by the plan. Such a plan would take into account employee turnover, staffing requirements, recruitment and training programs, and costs.

Each unit's functional plan must be checked against the organizational values audit and mission statement to determine whether the proposed actions and directions are consistent with what the organization has said it wants to be. Inconsistencies need to be addressed and may reveal a need for further clarification of the values, mission, and strategic business model of the organization, so that all functional plans can be expressed within the same overall objectives and assumptions. Also necessary at this step is a check to determine the level of acceptance of the overall strategic plan by the various functional units.

The planning team then identifies the conflicts among the combined functional plans, and determines how these can be resolved. The integration of the functional plans involves putting together all the pieces in order to ascertain how the overall plan will work and where the potential trouble spots might be. This integration must occur before the normal budgetary cycle. (Chapter 14 provides a detailed analysis of how to integrate functional plans.)

Implementation

At the implementation phase, many strategic plans literally die and are never fully implemented. Careful attention to *doing* what has been planned is critical. The real test of the final implementation of the strategic plan is the degree to which managers and other members of the organization use the strategic plan in their everyday decisions on the job. Ideally, the manager will pause to consider whether or not a proposed solution to a problem is congruent with the organization's strategic plan. (Implementation considerations are discussed in greater length in Chapter 9, and the final implementation process is the subject of Chapter 15.)

SUMMARY

Strategic planning is the process by which the guiding members of an organization envision its future and develop the necessary procedures and operations to achieve that future. This vision of the organization's future state provides a direction in which the organization should move and the energy to begin that move. In today's competitive business environment, strategic planning is more important than ever before. Although many organizations do some kind of long-range or strategic planning, usually these planning processes are poorly conceptualized and more poorly implemented. Furthermore, their strategic plans are rarely used in guiding day-to-day decisions.

Based on research and consulting experience in many organizations, the authors have developed a new model of strategic planning. The Applied Strategic Planning Model differs from existing models in content, emphasis, and process. It contains the following phases: planning to plan, values audit, mission formulation, strategic business modeling, performance audit, gap analysis, contingency planning, integrating functional plans, and implementation. It also provides for environmental scanning and implementation considerations throughout the planning process.

REFERENCE

Levitt, T. (1960, July–August). Marketing myopia. *Harvard Business Review*, pp. 45–56. Reprinted in *Harvard Business Review*, September–October 1975, pp. 26–28, 33–34, 38–39, 44, 173–174, 176–181.

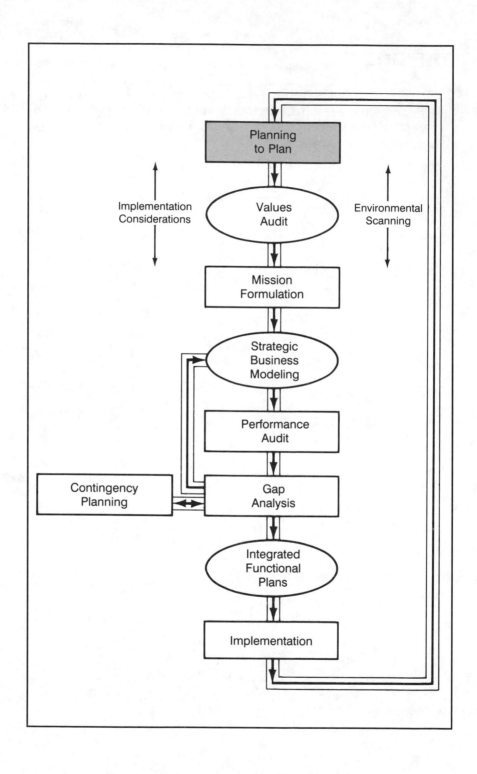

6 PLANNING TO PLAN

"Planning to plan" is the prework activity of the strategic planning process. Individuals who are responsible for making key decisions will determine whether or not the organization is ready to engage in formal strategic planning. If the decision to go ahead is made, this phase will include the careful selection of the planning team and the establishment of methods to feed information back to nonplanning managers and other key staff.

Without planning to plan, it is all too likely that a fire-breathing dragon will crop up in the strategic plan. Perhaps the entire organization will not be engulfed in flames, but a little prework can prevent a lot of heartache and pain.

DETERMINING ORGANIZATIONAL READINESS

In an article entitled "OD Readiness" (Pfeiffer & Jones, 1978), the authors mention an intriguing parallel between the concept of organization development (OD) "readiness" and "reading readiness." If a child is ready to learn to read, it does not make much difference which teaching method is used; the child will learn to read. Conversely, if the child is not ready to learn to read, no strategy will work. Likewise, if an organization has the necessary prerequisites, change is likely to take place regardless of which OD methodology is applied. Conversely, the most sophisticated techniques employed by the most competent and experienced consultants and managers are doomed to failure if the organization itself is unready to undertake a project of planned change.

Inasmuch as applied strategic planning is "a project of planned change," the same overarching principle applies. If an organization is not ready to simultaneously plan *and* apply the planning efforts, it makes little difference to the outcome what set of methodologies is used. Neither does it matter what level of consultation skills are available, because it is highly unlikely that *any* significant outcome will materialize. For example, one of the authors was a consultant for a small electronics-equipment distributor. Although the initial overtures made by that company were for "strategic planning," it quickly became apparent that what was needed was "survival planning." In this case, it would have been futile to devote resources to a five-year plan when everyone's focus should have been on the present quarter's results.

The design group of a major automotive manufacturer had a well-developed strategic plan, driven by the vice president in charge of design. A critical element of the plan was a 25-percent downsizing of personnel. Two years after the "adoption" of the strategic plan, not a single person had been terminated, and there was no implementation plan to begin the process. The inertia that characterized this organization — "resistance to change" — had prevented any significant implementation of the strategic plan. This is another case of overadapting and ending up as boiled frogs.

Readiness for Strategic Planning Is Like Reading Readiness

We have noted that if an organization is ready for change, change will take place regardless of the particular methodology used. An important postscript to that statement is that the particular methodology can make a significant difference in the *translation* of the planning activity. To help managers make day-to-day decisions that will drive the organization in the predetermined direction, the strategic planning method must provide criteria to help the managers make those decisions. Providing these criteria is one of the strong points in the Applied Strategic Planning Model.

DEVELOPING CEO COMMITMENT

Once readiness has been determined, the next major issue is whether or not the chief executive officer (CEO) and other key stakeholders have sufficient commitment to the strategic planning process. (Stakeholders include all those who have or believe they have a stake in the organization.) Resistance to the implementation of a formal planning process must be identified, evaluated, and, where appropriate, dealt with in a decisive manner. In the example of the company that failed to follow through and terminate 25 percent of its personnel, it was necessary to hire a new vice president from outside the company in order to implement the strategic plan. The new vice president was committed to change, was willing to take risks, and had no intention of becoming a boiled frog.

Steiner (1979) defines the CEO as the person or persons with the authority to manage the organization. The CEO can be the president, the president and the executive vice president, or some other individual or combination of individuals. When the term "chief executive officer" does not necessarily refer to just one individual, we will use the term "chief-executive-officer function" (CEOF).

Ultimately, the question that must be posed to the CEOF is threefold:

1. Do you believe that you sufficiently understand the time and energy required for the proposed applied strategic planning process?
2. Are you prepared to make a commitment to ascertain that the cycle is completed in a reasonably thorough manner?
3. Will resources be committed to implementing the plan once it is completed?

Without affirmative responses to these questions, the planning process *must* stop until the CEOF can be convinced. Without such a process of developing CEOF commitment, there is little likelihood of mounting a successful strategic planning process. The CEOF must understand the time and energy that will be required and the importance of committing the necessary resources. Otherwise, the strategic planning activity will commence but will likely have extensive delays and possibly never reach closure. Our previous example is a clear-cut case of the need for the CEO to be committed to the implementation of the plan.

Commitment to the completion and implementation of a strategic plan is often difficult, especially in single-proprietorship organizations. The discipline and rigor required by the planning process often do not fit the energy, vitality, and problem-solving styles of such individuals and organizations. For example, one entre-preneur recently argued, "I make my best deals on airplanes, just by sitting next to a stranger. How are you going to plan for that?"

Nevertheless, it is possible to use a developmental strategy with most executives and help them understand the advantages of developing an applied strategic plan.

In addition to personal commitment, the CEOF must be willing to transfer appropriate levels of responsibility and authority for the planning to the planning team. The CEOF must also

Time Commitment Is Vital

encourage the participation of managers and nonmanagers who, although not a part of the formal planning team, will be responsible for the implementation of planning decisions. Without the commitment of functional managers (and other key staff) the planning process will not be successfully implemented.

It is absolutely necessary for the CEOF to provide overall direction and to assume ultimate responsibility for the creation and execution of the strategic plan. The CEOF must aggressively instill enthusiasm in key staff members while coaching (and, if necessary, cajoling) them through the appropriate use of rewards and sanctions.

Lewin's (1975) force-field analysis (see Figure 6-1) provides a convenient model for examining the forces supporting and opposing the introduction of applied strategic planning and the strength of each force. It may be worthwhile to complete a force-field analysis with the planning team to identify and decide how they can be managed.

THE ROLE OF STAFF PLANNERS

In many settings it is fashionable for senior management to be overcommitted, overextended, and overworked. This frenzied-chic approach to management is often in vogue among entrepreneurially oriented owners/managers, and in such cases there may be an attempt to transfer the responsibility for the planning function to a "staff planner." *This approach categorically does not work!* Although there has been a strong precedent for planning staffs in some large companies (most notably General Electric), there is little (if any) evidence to suggest that planning done by staff will be implemented by line managers.

There are, however, many important administrative functions that can be done by staff planners or by staff assigned to planning-support roles. It is often desirable, particularly in medium-sized companies, to assign a junior manager to be the planning project liaison. Ideally, this role should be offered as a reward, that is, a unique opportunity to learn, firsthand, the essential strategic planning skills needed to become a successful senior manager in today's

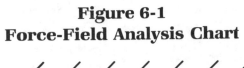

Figure 6-1
Force-Field Analysis Chart

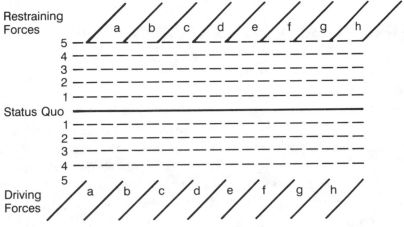

In the above chart, diagram the forces driving toward change and restraining change. First write several key words to identify each of the forces driving toward change (a through h), then repeat the process for forces restraining change. Then rate each force from one to five (five being the strongest) and mark the appropriate dotted line directly above (or underneath) the force. Now draw a vertical arrow for each mark to the status quo line. For example, if you rated the restraining force for item "a" as 3, draw an arrow in column "a" from line 3 down to the status quo line.

increasingly complex business environment. One of our clients assigned a senior human resource manager to this function. He worked closely with us as we guided the planning team through the strategic planning process. His expert detail work between sessions saved at least two days of planning time—and resulted in a stronger, better organized plan.

This planning-coordination role can provide important support as the focal point for data collection and analysis, decision recording and dissemination, and management of clerical and logistic support to ensure that formal planning sessions are optimally effective.

IDENTIFYING THE PLANNING TEAM

Once the full commitment of the CEOF is secured, the next concern is to identify the most effective planning team. Being selected for the planning team should be billed as an opportunity to participate in the shaping of the organization's future. Otherwise, strategic planning may be viewed as just an endless string of meetings that detract from other work assignments without producing any positive impact on day-to-day decisions.

Five to twelve members make a good size for a planning team. (A significant amount of research indicates that groups of five are typically the most effective in problem solving. In a group larger than twelve, the air time per person is so limited that it is difficult for every member to make appropriate contributions. Furthermore, our experience indicates that groups larger than twelve are difficult to "read" in terms of group process.) All other things being equal, the authors prefer to work with a group of seven to nine, the optimal balance between the need to represent stakeholder factions and the need to allow for productive dialogue.

During the planning-to-plan phase the planning team should gain a thorough understanding of what *environmental scanning* entails and how it should operate in the organization. (See Chapter 9.)

Figure 6-2 illustrates the degree to which planning-team members appropriately change their foci from the company to their own functions as strategic planning progresses. When they first join the planning team, their commitment is primarily focused on the organization. As the planning process continues and members begin to see what strategic planning means for their own functional areas, the focus begins to change. Each member becomes more and more concerned with the implications for his or her own department or division. As the planning team develops the strategic plan, the focus

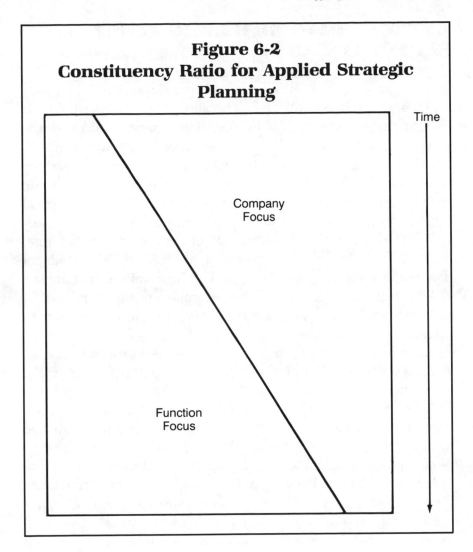

**Figure 6-2
Constituency Ratio for Applied Strategic
Planning**

Time

Company
Focus

Function
Focus

of the plan moves from the global to the narrow. During this process, it is important both to identify the relevant areas that need to be involved and to develop a commitment to taking the necessary steps in each of those areas.

ESTABLISHING REALISTIC TIME EXPECTATIONS

Another key issue that must be faced is the realization of how long the planning process will take. The answer, almost inevitably, is "longer than anticipated." The size of the organization and the complexity of products and/or services offered have some impact on the time needed to complete the planning cycle. Nevertheless, the three most significant factors that influence the time needed to do the necessary work are (1) self-awareness, (2) interpersonal conflict-managementskills, and (3) the degree to which the key stakeholders have a harmonious view of the organization's future. Another factor in determining the time needed is the availability of data required for the performance audit. Organizations that are less skillful in the management of interpersonal data simply take more time and more consultant energy to accomplish the same tasks than do more interpersonally skilled groups of managers.

Realistically, an organization should expect to spend between ten and twenty full days of meetings to complete the planning cycle. Assuming no significant change in the planning team (or key stakeholders) and performance within the targeted ranges, successive alterations can shorten the planning time. One medium-sized manufacturing firm we worked with scheduled twelve days for planning and added an additional two days because of the need to spend more time in building systems to support the performance audit. Another client reduced planning time to nine days by assigning extensive between-session work to internal staff consultants. Later, management acknowledged that it would have liked more time to pursue some aspects of the process to a greater depth.

In an ideal model, the first full process can be completed in six to nine months. In such circumstances, the planning team would meet fairly regularly, perhaps every six weeks, for two or three days at a time. Ideally, the team would work effectively toward values consensus, develop a mission statement that is rapidly and enthusiastically endorsed by the organization, and then create a strategic business model expeditiously. The resulting action plans then would be developed, tested, integrated, and promptly implemented. But it is more likely that significant stumbling blocks will arise at various points in the sequence, blocks that must be addressed and resolved before the team can move on. For example, in the six weeks between planning-team meetings, various members of the organization may be researching, compiling, and cataloging data that are necessary for the team to consider in the next stage of the process. If such data are readily available, the planning team may be able to meet sooner than scheduled. If, however, gathering and processing the required data severely burden the resources of the organization, the planning team may decide to postpone its next meeting for a week or two.

The strategic plan must be at the core of the organization's budget process for the following year. For that reason, the strategic planning schedule should be established so that the results of the planning process can lead directly into the budget considerations for the coming year. In the first year of the strategic planning effort, this may require as much as twelve months' lead time; as the process is repeated and becomes refined, nine, or even six months may suffice. As the strategic planning process is repeated each year, the gathering and processing of information will become easier, and the relationship between the planning process and budgeting considerations will become more obvious, more automatic, and more harmonious.

It is important to note that membership on the applied strategic planning team is for a single year and that the planning team needs to be reconstituted each year. In particular, people who detract from the process should be replaced by people who have the potential to contribute more constructively to the process. Different participants may also be required in order to reflect new directions that the organization is taking.

Location of Planning Sessions

Another significant issue is *where* the strategic planning sessions should be conducted. To be effective, the site used must be away from the interruptions of the daily work routine. We have experienced successful planning sessions in hotel or motel meeting rooms, retreat-type conference facilities, condominium and private clubhouses, vacation homes, and personal residences. The key is to assist the planning-team members in isolating themselves from daily work routines that can inhibit the kind of envisioning and confrontation that is essential to the strategic planning process.

We have also been successful in using the regular conference room in the organization's own facility for weekend sessions. This practice depends partly on the organizational culture. Another factor to consider is the possibility that too much formal weekend work will detract from the day-to-day functioning of the operation.

Educating the Planning Team and Others

Much of the resistance to any change effort comes from misunderstanding or, at least, not understanding. Therefore it is very important to devote significant energy at the end of the planning-to-plan phase to inform the planning-team members of how they were selected and what is expected of them. We recommend that other key members of the organization be given a separate orientation for the purpose of educating them in the process of applied strategic planning.

Another significant step is to inform *all* members of the organization about what is taking place. They should receive either (1) a brief orientation from the CEO or (2) a letter explaining the strategic planning process from the CEO. Either method should stress the CEO's commitment to the process, and it should identify the planning team, its goals, and the projected time frame. "Don't let them guess about what you're up to when you're able to tell them" is a solid axiom for any CEO. Human beings need to have answers. In the absence of data they create data — assumptions fill gaps that facts should have occupied. These assumptions may lead to lots of misallocated resources.

Keeping all members of the organization well informed about the progress of the planning team is also essential. The total organization needs to know about its involvement in the strategic planning process and what benefits can be anticipated from the process. It also needs to know the estimated costs in time, disruption, and so on — not just the monetary costs. Each significant achievement (the new mission statement, the results of the performance audit, and so on) needs to be shared. The mechanism (a meeting or memorandum) that will be used to inform the employees and the frequency of it (for example, quarterly or after each planning session) should be established and communicated as part of the orientation meeting or memorandum. Provisions must also be made for returning feedback from employees to the members of the planning team. This feedback loop is an essential element of the implementation considerations (an ongoing process) as well as the implementation phase (the last step in the Applied Strategic Planning Model).

COST OF DOING FORMAL PLANNING

The two major direct costs associated with applied strategic planning are (1) the meeting time of the planning team and (2) the out-of-meeting time on the part of the planning team and others who must generate the data for the planning meetings.

If an organization makes extensive use of an outside consultant, which we strongly recommend because it adds objectivity and enhances the productivity of the planning team, the consultant should set some realistic expectations with the client regarding the overall costs.

IDENTIFICATION OF OTHER NEEDS

Our experience indicates that the applied strategic planning process will *inevitably* identify needs for the type of activities used in organization development (for example, climate survey/feedback, department team building, conflict resolution on an interpersonal and departmental level, customer service programs, market research, sales training, and market studies). Because such activities have a high potential of distracting the planning team and the CEO from the salient issues, we advocate *not* pursuing these activities during the strategic planning activity. It is difficult enough to complete the strategic planning cycle reasonably close to the target time within expense allocations.

Where possible, these emergent needs should be incorporated into the human resource development plan and be dealt with as yet another competitor for the limited resources of money, time, and energy in the phase of integrating functional plans. If the need cannot be deferred to the next cycle of the planning process, we recommend that appropriate individuals be hired to do the work. This somewhat purist point of view will enable the strategic planning team to keep a focus on its task.

In one organization, the members of the planning group had developed more clients than they could handle. To help with the overload, they sought an M.B.A. with extensive experience in financial-portfolio management; this person would also need a nine-month training program. These requirements kept them from easy access to qualified people. A human resource development plan, triggered by early signs of client overload, would have prevented them from becoming boiled frogs.

SUMMARY

"Planning to plan" involves the prework of the strategic planning process. This phase will determine whether or not the organization is ready to engage in formal strategic planning. A major element of the planning-to-plan phase is the degree of commitment by the CEO or CEOF. In the absence of sufficient commitment, the planning process must be halted—at least until the necessary commitment is developed.

When CEOF commitment is secured and the organization is deemed ready, the planning team will be selected. The optimal size of the planning team is between five and twelve members.

Another important issue that must be faced during the planning-to-plan phase is time commitment. The planning team should expect to spend between ten and twenty full days in meetings to complete the planning cycle. To be effective, the meeting site should be away from the interruptions of the daily work routine. Hotel/motel meeting rooms, retreat-type conference facilities, condominium or private clubhouses, and personal residences have been successful sites for strategic planning meetings.

Members of the planning team should be told how they were selected and what they are expected to do. Other key members of the organization should be kept informed about the process and progress. In fact, every person in the organization should be given information about the process of strategic planning, so that no one will have to wonder or make false assumptions about what is going on.

REFERENCES

Lewin, K. (1975). *Field theory in social science*. Westport, CT: Greenwood.

Pfeiffer, J. W., & Jones, J. E. (1978). OD readiness. In J. W. Pfeiffer & J. E. Jones (Eds.), *The 1978 annual handbook for group facilitators*. San Diego, CA: University Associates.

Steiner, G. A. (1979). *Strategic planning: What every manager should know*. New York: Free Press.

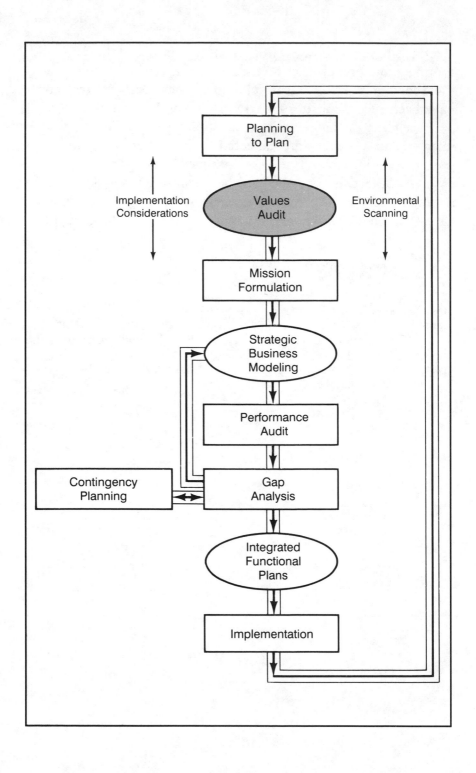

THE VALUES AUDIT

7

One unique aspect of our strategic planning model is the emphasis placed on the values audit. Many others who write about and practice strategic planning suggest that the underlying values of the organization need to be considered in the planning process and that understanding the organizational culture is essential to a successful planning activity. Nevertheless, they typically provide little advice and few suggestions about how to tackle this critically important aspect of strategic planning. Chapter 7 is intended to remedy this problem.

The organization's values and its strategic plan must be congruent. Strategic plans that do not take values into account will be in trouble and will probably fail. For example, consider the acquisition of Fireman's Fund Insurance Company by the American Express Corporation. Although a variety of financial and marketplace considerations affected this acquisition, we feel that the differences in the values of the two organizations — which were largely unexamined — led to many of the problems in making the acquisition work. At the time of the acquisition, Fireman's Fund was an old-line, San Francisco based company that prided itself on its long tradition of service, its commitment to policyholders, and its record of paying off all claims from the turn-of-the-century San Francisco earthquake and fire. American Express, on the other hand, was a comprehensive financial-service organization with a hard-nosed profit orientation. Fireman's Fund was committed to strong humanistic values in dealing with its employees and had very comprehensive HRD programs, whereas American Express was much more traditional in employee relations and had little in the way of HRD programs. The clash of these two cultures was inevitable, and the CEO of American Express found it necessary to devote much time to the direct management of Fireman's Fund, a move that required him to spend the bulk of his time in the Fireman's Fund headquarters. It is clear from the array of newspaper and magazine reports (as well as reports from personal observers) that—although the acquisition of Fireman's Fund made sense in terms of marketing strategy—the failure to check out the differences in values between the two organizations and to make appropriate plans to manage those differences was an important reason for the difficulties that were encountered.

After several years, it was announced in the summer of 1985 that the American Express Company was divesting itself of Fireman's Fund because it was "incompatible with its investment strategy." To continue with the situation would only have produced boiled frogs. The president of American Express announced his resignation "to seek career opportunities elsewhere."

ELEMENTS OF VALUES AUDIT

There are four elements to the values audit in strategic planning:

1. The values audit itself
2. The examination of the organization's operating philosophy
3. An analysis of the organization's culture
4. A stakeholder analysis

Each of these steps is built on the prior step; and each can be both threatening to members of the planning team and, as a consequence, time consuming.

**Values Audit: Include *All* Members
of the Team**

Our view of organizations as social systems leads us to give heavy emphasis to the values audit as an early and critical phase of strategic planning. Many organizations have given little attention to the values underlying the behavior of their members, particularly their leaders, or to the organizational values that have driven organizational decisions. An excellent example is an organization's values about conflict management — how conflict should be handled between the organization and its competitors, between and among organizational units, or between individual members of the organization. These values are always present and are important determinants of behavior; yet rarely are they consciously expressed, and even more rarely are they discussed in an open fashion to determine whether various specific values are warranted. Risk taking is one such value. Two managers who differ strongly on how much risk is acceptable in a new venture will typically argue about whether or not the risks are real and cogent rather than whether or not risk taking is "fun" or "enjoyable."

Figure 7-1 presents guidelines that one organization issued to all employees to help them manage conflict within the organization. Additional material was also distributed to the employees at a workshop on how to manage conflict.

Figure 7-1
Guidelines for Managing Conflict

1. Do not ignore a "pinch." Work on the issue before it becomes a "crunch." However, if needed, a cooling-off period may be established, with an agreed-on time to deal with the issue later.
2. Talk directly to the other person involved and try to solve the issue yourself.
3. It is O.K. to ask one of the organization's consultants for suggestions on how to approach the other person or in defining the issue. Be sure to check back with the consultant for feedback or perspectives on the result.
4. If the solution you work out involves a potential change of work procedure, you *must* get the approval of your manager.
5. If someone approaches you with an issue, be willing to work on it. You may also wish to seek a consultant's help in clarifying your point of view.
6. If someone begins to complain to you about another person who is not present, help that person take a more positive approach to handling the conflict. Do not collude in "triangling."
7. If, after you have tried to work on the issue on your own, there has been no change and the conflict still exists, you may ask for help from one of the consultants on next steps.

Allowing such issues to surface in an organization, especially for the first time, often reveals differences between espoused values and actual values, as well as differences in the values of the several segments of the organization and in the values held by members of the planning team. Without some resolution of these differences — at least at the level of agreeing to disagree and considering how these disagreements need to be built into later decisions — little effective planning can occur.

Consider, for example, an organization whose members cannot agree on how to manage risk taking in an unstable environment.

There may be some key players in the planning group who genuinely prefer to be cautious, given the instability of the environment, whereas other key players may feel that a cautious approach involves the greatest risk. Some of them may feel that the 15 percent of the bees who do not fly with the swarm should be rewarded for their initiative, creativity, and risk-taking efforts, whereas others believe that all workers should concentrate on the current source of pollen or continue to cut off the turkey's tail simply because that is the way it has always been done.

In a real estate development group, the question of how many units to include in a new housing development provides a clear-cut example of this issue. One manager strongly believed that the market would "turn around" in the next six months and that having a good housing stock available would give the group an advantage over its competitors. His counterpart insisted that there was no guarantee that the market would indeed improve and that having an excess inventory that required continued financing would pose an unnecessary risk. Unless such differences are managed at this basic level of values clarification, each later decision that involves risk taking (and how few organizational decisions do not involve risk taking!) will become another battle in the war between these two values positions. Attempting to do strategic planning in a group that has not examined its values also increases the probability of boiled frog(s).

In the above example, the question initially posed was how to determine whether or not the demand for housing would increase over the course of the project—a question that never could be answered to both managers' satisfaction. The question that needed to be resolved was the underlying conflict over the value of risk taking. Once that could be posed and debated, some resolution, or at least compromise, could be attempted.

Because very few groups have the skills to continue to confront such emotionally loaded and difficult-to-resolve issues as values differences and values clarification, attempts to resolve these matters frequently deteriorate into personal arguments and power struggles; or the group may retreat into unrelated and more readily resolvable areas. The frequency and severity of such problems prompt us to insist on a consultant from outside the organization for most groups. The consultant must be able to recognize and bring to the surface legitimate differences among group members, provide a safe environment to test these differences, ensure that all points of view are expressed, and promote enough resolution of the differences to allow the group to move on.

One consequence of the failure to allow differences to surface is a situation that has been termed the "Abilene paradox" (Harvey, 1988). The term comes from a story of a family who drove some one hundred miles to Abilene in a nonair-conditioned car for dinner on a hot summer night. (And when they arrived in Abilene, they literally felt like boiled frogs!) Although nobody wanted to make the trip, each person—thinking all the others wanted to go—was unwilling to express disagreement. Organizations that put a high value on managing agreement, rather than on surfacing and legitimizing disagreement, may often find themselves on a trip to Abilene.[1]

Values Defined

Our work with organizations has convinced us that values lie at the heart of almost all organizational decisions. When managers say that the XYZ department always can be counted on to fulfill its promises or that the ABC organization would never sell unsafe products because it is a highly ethical firm, they are explaining those organizations' behaviors in terms of their value bases.

In this context, we are using Rokeach's (1973) definitions that "a *value* is an enduring belief that a specific mode of conduct or end-state of existence is personally or socially preferable to an opposite or converse mode of conduct or end-state of existence. A *value system* is an enduring organization of beliefs concerning preferable modes of conduct or end-states of existence along a continuum of relative importance."

---

[1]An excellent videocassette based on Harvey's article is also available: The Abilene paradox [Videocassette]. (1985). Del Mar, CA: McGraw-Hill Training Systems. This videocassette may be ordered from McGraw-Hill CRM Films, 674 Via de la Valle, Solana Beach, CA 92075; telephone (619) 453-5000.

Such an "enduring organization of beliefs" determines what both individuals and organizations consider to be appropriate and inappropriate behavior. Such belief systems or values determine *norms* (that is, the standards for action) in organizations. For example, the norm of following the chain of command in an organization is based on the value system that the more senior members of the organization have the experience, expertise, and authority to make appropriate decisions and, even more importantly, that those attributes are the most important factors to consider in making decisions. Thus, organizations with such an underlying value system are unlikely to hold innovation and change as important values unless they come from age and experience. It is often much easier for an organization to identify its norms and not the underlying values that lead to and support the norms. The norms are the observable behavior (for example, politeness: "I don't mean to differ with you, but . . . .") whereas the values are the underlying assumptions that create the norms ("Disagreements among managers lead to unhealthy conflict and hurt feelings").

The Values Audit

Since values exist on both the individual and organizational levels, as well as within various segments of the organization, there needs to be clarity regarding the level at which the assessment is occurring. We recommend that the first values audit take place at the individual level. It is particularly important for the key decision makers in an organization to be clear about their personal values and to recognize any differences in values that exist among them. If these key organizational decision makers are not the only members of the planning team, then the values of the other members also need to be assessed. Next the underlying organizational values, particularly those values that drive organizational decisions — especially the determination of the organization's future direction — should be assessed. Then differences in values that exist among the major segments of the organization should be assessed. The same value-auditing procedures used to measure the values of the organization as a whole are equally useful for the component parts.

There are several techniques for assessing values on the individual level. The one-on-one interview, conducted by a consultant, is a frequently used procedure for tapping personal values on the individual level. Typical questions are, "What are some of your personal beliefs about how this business should be run?" "What are some of the mottos or slogans, such as 'a penny saved is a penny earned,' that guide your actions?" "What are some of your beliefs about other people? Do you tend to be initially trusting or guarded in dealing with others?"

Some consultants use a list of personal values and surface individual values by asking each planning-team member to rank order the list (e.g., Oliver, 1985). A discussion among the group members about both the meaning of the overall pattern of the results and the differences among the group members is a first step in individual values identification and clarification. This type of activity also provides an opportunity for individuals to explain their values and to share them with others before tackling the difficult task of strategic planning.

Still another approach would be to ask each member of the planning team to write out his or her imaginary diary for a typical work day five or ten years in the future, beginning with waking up and ending with going back to bed. Such an activity causes a number of issues to surface—including values around work style, growth of the organization, and commitment—and it helps the team to understand the relationship between personal goals and organizational strategic planning. For example, in a small management group, young managers with heavy family responsibilities may resist projects that will take evening and weekend time whereas more senior managers who have their family-rearing responsibilities largely behind them may be more supportive of such projects.

There are also several approaches for assessing organizational values. A group interview would be a straightforward, relatively direct process for identifying organizational values. The type of questions suggested above for individual interviews are equally useful, with slight modification, for assessing organizational values. Because the data are developed for group involvement and the entire process is public, there is no need for the consultant or facilitator to analyze the data; however, there is still a need for a neutral third person to monitor this process.

Another technique for identifying organizational values is to ask the participants to compare their organization's characteristics with the eight characteristics of the "excellent" organizations identified by Peters and Waterman (1982) in their best-selling book, *In Search of Excellence*. This activity is useful in surfacing organizational values and norms, as well as providing a set of criteria against which organizational values can be compared. The organizational values of IBM are an interesting example. IBM values its customers highly, which leads to a strong marketing and customer-service orientation rather than a technological one. Digital Equipment Corporation, on the other hand, is strongly driven by technological values, that is, on developing "cutting-edge" data-processing equipment. Both organizations have carved out strong market niches for themselves, while appealing to different market segments.

Organizations work hard to protect their own internal values. The employment-interview process typically involves trying to identify individuals who have both the necessary skills and the "right" values. Candidates who are rejected as "not fitting into our organization" are those whose values — too little commitment to career, too ambitious, too flamboyant, and so on — do not fit those of the organization. Occasionally, a deviant does slip by this screening process; but they often find that the organizational culture that is value-driven is not compatible and leave of their own accord.

Operating Philosophy

An organization's values typically are organized and codified into a philosophy of operations. Some organizations have explicit, formal statements of philosophy, such as the "Five Principles of Mars" (see Figure 2-2) or the "Johnson & Johnson Credo" (see Figure 2-3). These statements have evolved over the years and represent the explicit values by which managers and employees attempt to run the businesses.

Both M&M Mars, the candy manufacturer that is probably the world's largest privately held corporation, and Johnson & Johnson, a major health-care products manufacturer, regularly update their explicit philosophy statements, have regular seminars with employees to ensure dissemination of these values, and actually hold managers accountable for operating in accord with these philosophies. For example, given the first sentence of the Johnson & Johnson Credo, that "our first responsibility is to the doctors, nurses, and patients, to mothers and all others who use our products," it is not surprising that the managers of McNeil Consumer Products Company, a wholly owned subsidiary of Johnson & Johnson, decided to recall all of the retail stock of Tylenol (31 million bottles) when several people died after taking capsules into which cyanide had been inserted to taint the medication. Although it was clear that the tampering had taken place after the product reached the retail level (and it was ultimately determined that only 75 capsules in eight bottles had been tampered with), commitment to the end users required this action. Persons knowledgeable about the event state unequivocally that the only issue confronting management was *when* the recall could take place, not *if* a recall was in order. This is a clear example of how a values-driven organization made a decision by applying those explicit values.

Later, after a similar episode, the McNeil company decided to withdraw Tylenol capsules from the market and to supply caplets instead. This decision also reflected adherence to the Johnson & Johnson Credo.

In such values-driven organizations all members of the organization are expected to know and understand the operating philosophy and to use it in their day-to-day work. Furthermore, serious sanctions are invoked against any member who violates the philosophy. In these organizations there is usually a great deal of folklore about the philosophy, and many stories are related—both about the people who were rewarded for acting according to the philosophy and about people who were punished for not acting in accordance with it.

Even those organizations that do not have explicit, written philosophies of operations have implicit philosophies. Members of this type of organization can be asked about its philosophy of

operations in action: how work is done, how conflict is managed, how much customer service is provided, how soon bills are paid, and so on.

Another aspect of an organization's philosophy of operations that is worth discussing in this process is how marginal employees are managed. By "marginal employees" we mean those employees whose performance is never poor enough to warrant discharge but never good enough to make them solid performers. The philosophy of operations about such employees is usually implicit and rarely addressed directly by management. Bringing this issue to the surface is frequently highly cathartic for a planning team and frequently results in an organization's discussing the issue directly—often for the first time.

One important part of the strategic planning process is to create an explicit philosophy of operations, because this philosophy becomes the vehicle for disseminating the organization's values both internally and externally. Also, the strategic plan needs to be built on the organization's philosophy of operations, or that philosophy needs to be changed to conform to the strategic plan. The advertising agency of a small pharmaceutical house proposed an advertising campaign that would increase market share by questioning the reliability of a competitor's products. While the potential positive impact of the campaign was clearly seen, the proposal was rejected as incongruent with the values of "fighting fair" in the competitive arena—a value embedded in the company's philosophy of operations.

There is no simple and direct way for an organization to produce an explicit philosophy of operations if it does not have one. It is often useful for the strategic planning team to attempt to develop a statement of philosophy as part of its work, using examples such as those from Johnson & Johnson and from Mars. It is useful for a member of the strategic planning team (or the consultant) to keep a record of the various organizational assumptions that are encountered during the earlier phases and, at appropriate times in the planning process, to raise them as issues to be examined for truth or falsehood and for agreement or disagreement. Organizations typically make untested assumptions about their

competition, their marketplace, compensation schedules for both exempt and nonexempt workers, the role of the government, the problems of unionization, and so on. Although raising such issues for a reasoned analysis is a difficult, anxiety-arousing task, it is an important part of the strategic planning process and should be performed by the consultant. The following false assumptions (see Zimmerman, 1985) in organizations are frequently accepted by:

1. Top managers share common understandings of the organization's strategy.
2. If something is longer range, it is strategic; if shorter range, it is operational. (Strategy is, in fact, measured in terms of impact on direction.)
3. If the business units' strategies are clear, the organization's strategy is clear.
4. If an organization has a long-range plan, it knows where it is going. (This is an operational trap.)
5. The top team in the organization has the experience and ability to think strategically.

Members of the strategic planning team should examine these false assumptions carefully to determine whether or not they have been accepting the assumptions as truth.

Figure 7-2 provides an instrument that is helpful in determining and discussing the values of the planning team. The following instruments (included in the Appendix) can also be helpful in producing a more open atmosphere for examining organizational assumptions and for causing some of these assumptions and their underlying values to surface: "Organizational Blasphemies: Clarifying Values" (McNulty, 1983), "Organizational Diagnosis Questionnaire" (Preziosi, 1980), and "Organizational Norms Opinionnaire" (Alexander, 1978).

Organizational Culture

It is important for managers to scan the environment for changes, especially in the social and political realms. As we noted earlier, organizational members' individual values, the values of the organization *per se*, the organization's philosophy of operations, and its

---

Figure 7-2
Personal Values Activity

Please rank from 1 to 10
  1 = Most important to you personally
10 = Least important to you personally

1. Getting along with colleagues ☐
2. Professional reputation ☐
3. Achievement of business goals ☐
4. Excitement ☐
5. Leisure time for family or fun ☐
6. Material wealth ☐
7. Respect of peers ☐
8. Contribution to society ☐
9. Pleasing others ☐
10. Accomplishing personal goals ☐

---

assumptions all come together to produce the organization's culture, or "the way we do things around here" (Deal & Kennedy, 1982). An organization's culture ties the people in the organization together and gives meaning and purpose to their day-to-day work lives.

It is becoming more and more obvious that those organizations that have "strong positive cultures," that is, organizations that have a clear system of informal rules that spell out how organizational members should regularly behave and that enable members to feel good about their jobs and their employers, are consistently high-performing systems (Deal & Kennedy, 1982; Peters & Waterman, 1982). As Levering, Moskowitz, and Katz (1984) point out in their analysis of the one hundred best American companies to work for, these are companies whose cultures provide a working life for people that is really worth living and one to which they can look forward on a regular basis. Hewlett-Packard, Citicorp, Dayton Hudson, Herman Miller, and Johnson & Johnson were all among the companies included in the Levering et al. list.

In identifying and understanding an organization's culture, we need to investigate three elements, in addition to the organization's values, that are the heart of the culture: the organization's heroes, its rites and rituals, and its cultural network.

An organization with a strong culture always has a hero or two whose exploits help clarify and personalize organizational values. An organization's heroes are those people who personify the organization's values and about whom stories are told. These are the organizational members who serve as clear role models for others and epitomize the uniqueness of the organization. Learning about an organization's heroes is an integral part of learning about its culture.

It is no surprise that founders of organizations frequently have this role. J. W. Marriott, Sr., the now-deceased chairman of the board of the Marriott Corporation, was a hero in his organization for his faithful reading of customer comment cards in order to make real the Marriott slogan, "We do it right." Forrest Mars, former CEO of Mars, is legendary for his preoccupation with the quality of product and his extravagant temper when he found that his expectations about quality were violated for any reason.

High-performing organizations have a variety of rites and rituals as part of their strong culture, and these need to be identified as part of the strategic planning process. Rites and rituals are the ceremonies and other programmed routines that help define the organization's expectations (and the underlying values) for employees. An organization that regularly rewards career employees for longevity with recognition dinners and five-year pins that are proudly worn is rather different from one that pays no attention to length of service and lavishly rewards its top salespeople and other top performers; and these are both different from organizations that have rites and rituals for both. Such symbolic acts tell much about the organization and need to be carefully observed.

An organization that valued longevity was experiencing a 20-percent compounded growth in staff, resulting in a doubling every four years. Many of its new employees would "accidentally" wash their ID badges in the washing machine with their clothing in order to avoid being seen as a "new hire."

A strong culture requires a cultural network of informal communications to tend and spread the culture. This may consist of "storytellers," who keep the culture alive by telling tales about the organization's heroes (and villains); "priests," who worry about any intrusion of foreign values into the organizational culture; or "whisperers," who transmit cultural information into otherwise inaccessible places. These people are important actors in maintaining and extending the organizational culture and are invaluable informants to the strategic planning process. They also play a critical role in facilitating the acceptance of the strategic planning process and the assimilation of the strategic plan into the ongoing working life of the organization.

Although there is no single system for categorizing an organization's culture, there are several that are useful to the strategic planning process. Deal and Kennedy (1982) identify four generic organizational cultures, namely:

1. *The tough-guy, macho culture.* In this individualistic culture, high risks are taken but the environment provides quick feedback on whether the actions were right or wrong. The entertainment industry, especially motion picture production, is a prime example of this culture, as is advertising.
2. *The work-hard/play-hard culture.* Fun and action are the rule in this culture. Employees take few risks, and even those few provide quick feedback. To succeed, employees must maintain a high level of relatively low-risk activities. Sales-driven organizations, especially retail-sales organizations specializing in door-to-door selling, are outstanding examples of this culture.

3. *The bet-your-company culture.* This culture calls for big-stake decisions with years passing before the environment provides clear feedback on whether or not the decision was correct. This is a high-risk, slow-feedback culture. Many high-tech organizations, especially in aerospace, are prime examples of the bet-your-company culture.

4. *The process culture.* Little or no feedback is provided in this culture, and employees find it difficult to measure what they do. Instead, they concentrate on *how* their work is done. Most highly regulated organizations, including most governmental agencies, are common examples of the process culture.

Although none of these categories may fit an organization exactly, they can help bring that culture into focus as part of the strategic planning process. A successful strategic plan must be built

The Process Culture

on and integrated into the culture of the organization. Otherwise the plan will never become operational. Neglecting the importance of organizational culture was the flaw in the previously mentioned acquisition of Fireman's Fund by American Express. After a year, it was clear that the merger was unsuccessful due to "organizational incompatibility"—two cultures in conflict. The members of the strategic planning team must examine the culture of their organization, understand it, and find ways to integrate that understanding into their vision of the organization's future.

The Stakeholder Analysis

The final step of the values audit is the stakeholder analysis. The stakeholder analysis enables the planning team to identify the various constituencies that need to be considered in the planning process. By "stakeholders," we mean those individuals, groups, and organizations who will be impacted or who are likely to be interested in the organization's strategic plan and the planning process. Included are all who believe, rightly or wrongly, that they have a stake in the organization's future and not merely those who the planning team believes have a reasonable or legitimate right to such a stake. The Grocery Workers Union attempted to block the leveraged buy-out of Safeway Stores because they had not been involved in either the decision making or the negotiations. In many European countries, it is typical for representatives of community councils to be formally represented on corporate boards in the communities in which they operate to bring community concerns to light.

First, each stakeholder needs to be identified. Then the planning team needs to determine how the stakeholders are likely to respond to the plan, the planning process, and the implementation of the plan. The planning team should also take into account the various stakeholder resources, statuses, freedoms of action, relationships, and activities that may be impacted by shifts or changes in the organization's strategic direction.

In his discussion of stakeholder analysis, Ackoff (1981) points out that business organizations engage in six direct exchange processes with stakeholders:

1. An exchange of money for work with *employees*, including managers
2. An exchange of money for goods and services with *suppliers*
3. An exchange of goods and services for money with *consumers*
4. An exchange of money paid later for money received now with *investors* and *lenders*
5. An exchange of money paid now for money received later with *debtors*
6. An exchange of money for goods, services, and regulation with *government* (e.g., police and fire protection, antitrust regulation, water, and sewage)

Ackoff's conceptualization is presented graphically in Figure 7-3. Ackoff insists that the appropriate objective of a business organization is not to serve any one of its stakeholder groups to the exclusion of any other; rather, it should serve all the stakeholders by increasing their ability to pursue their own objectives more efficiently and effectively. In other words, Ackoff argues that the overriding purpose of an organization ought to be to serve the interests of *all* its stakeholders, not just its investors (the group whose interests are typically served by an organization).

The purpose of presenting Ackoff's position is to identify two important issues in the strategic planning process: who the organization's stakeholders are; and how (if at all) the organization intends to meet the interests of these stakeholders. Identification of the stakeholders permits the planning team to consider the impact of various future states on each of them.

A rather straightforward way to approach stakeholder analysis is to have the members of the planning team, first independently and then as a group, identify the various stakeholders and then attempt to understand the nature of the current exchange process

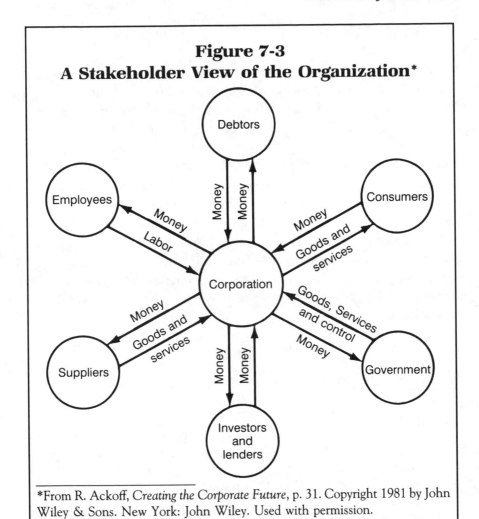

**Figure 7-3
A Stakeholder View of the Organization***

*From R. Ackoff, *Creating the Corporate Future*, p. 31. Copyright 1981 by John Wiley & Sons. New York: John Wiley. Used with permission.

with each of these stakeholders. The construction of a diagram similar to that shown in Figure 7-3 has proven to be a useful way of recording these data.

SUMMARY

The values audit is both a very important and a very difficult aspect of the planning process. The values audit involves an in-depth analysis of the most fundamental values and assumptions that underlie organizational life and organizational decision making. Working on such emotionally charged issues is uncommon in most organizations and such confrontations can be long, tiring, and painful. This process can be very positively impacted by the use of a skilled facilitator. A major goal of the values audit is to reach a working understanding of the values represented. Otherwise, the differences in values, beliefs, philosophies of operations, and assumptions will continually interfere with the more practical planning that also must be done. Once a values audit is successfully completed, it is relatively simple to move into the next stages of the planning process.

REFERENCES

Ackoff, R. (1981). *Creating the corporate future.* New York: John Wiley.

Alexander, M. (1978). Organizational norms opinionnaire. In J. W. Pfeiffer & J. E. Jones (Eds.), *The 1978 annual handbook for group facilitators.* San Diego, CA: University Associates.

Deal, T., & Kennedy, A. (1982). *Corporate cultures: The rites and rituals of corporate life.* Reading, MA: Addison-Wesley.

Harrison, R. (1975). Diagnosing organization ideology. In J. E. Jones & J. W. Pfeiffer (Eds.), *The 1975 annual handbook for group facilitators.* San Diego, CA: University Associates.

Harvey, J. B. (1988). The Abilene paradox and other meditations on management. San Diego, CA University Associates.

Levering, R., Moskowitz, M., & Katz, M. (1984). *The one hundred best companies to work for in America.* Reading, MA: Addison-Wesley.

McNulty, T. (1983). Organizational blasphemies: Clarifying values. In L. D. Goodstein & J. W. Pfeiffer (Eds.), *The 1983 annual for facilitators, trainers, and consultants.* San Diego, CA: University Associates.

Oliver, J. E. (1985). The personal value statement (PVS): An experiential learning instrument. In L. D. Goodstein & J. W. Pfeiffer (Eds.), *The*

1985 annual: Developing human resources. San Diego, CA: University Associates.

Peters, T. J., & Waterman, R. H. (1982). *In search of excellence: Lessons from America's best-run companies.* New York: Harper & Row.

Preziosi, R. C. (1980). Organizational diagnosis questionnaire (ODQ). In J. W. Pfeiffer & J. E. Jones (Eds.), *The 1980 annual handbook for group facilitators.* San Diego, CA: University Associates.

Rokeach, M. (1973). *The nature of human values.* New York: Free Press.

Zimmerman, J. (1985). The frontiers of strategic thinking: An interview with John W. Zimmerman. *Kepner-Tregoe Journal 14* (4), 13–16.

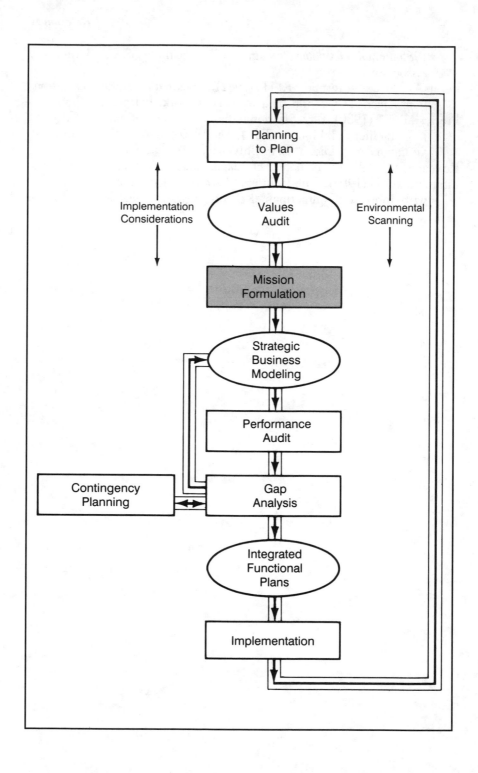

8 MISSION FORMULATION

The mission-formulation phase provides an excellent opportunity for the planning team to consider whether or not it is headed in the direction of the boiled frog. It can pause and examine not only where the organization is, but also what direction it might or should take. Has the organization been trying to hard to adapt its current products or services? Has it been attempting to overadapt to its present customers and clients? Is it using outdated methods to supply its customers and clients? The mission statement will not only *reflect* the posture of the organization, but it can actually *determine* it.

One of the most important aspects of the strategic planning process is the development of the mission statement. Often this is also one of the most difficult aspects. The mission statement is a brief, clear statement of the objectives of the organization. Ideally, it contains no more than one hundred words. The mission statement provides the context for formulating specific program strategies that the organization will engage in; it sets the arena in which the organization will compete; it determines how resources will be allocated by the organization; and it guides the general pattern of growth and the direction the organization will follow for the future.

If members of the planning team understand that the mission statement sets the arena in which the organization will compete, they will more readily understand why some environmental scanning is important prior to the formulation of the mission statement. For example, the social, technological, and political aspects of the macro environment should be considered by the planning team before the mission statement is formulated (see Chapter 9).

Figure 8-1 and 8-2 are two examples of effective mission statements.

A less effective mission statement is presented in Figure 8-3. It is not immediately apparent from its mission statement that the Gamma Corporation is an actual organization that is currently in the business of lawn and carpet care. Its mission statement is so broad that virtually any set of goods and services that met any

The Mission Statement Should Be Brief

Figure 8-1
An Example of a Mission Statement

The Alpha Corporation is a low-cost manufacturer and marketer of consumable food-service items for home and industrial use. We intend to maintain our position as a market leader by meeting customer needs and providing a high level of service and quality while maintaining a level of earnings sufficiently high to satisfy our investors.

Figure 8-2
An Example of a Mission Statement

The Beta Company's principal goal is to develop, manufacture, and market man-made fibers and related products for industrial and textile markets in an innovative manner so as to ensure long-term profitability. Our intent is to utilize worldwide and internally developed technology to enhance our leadership position in the quality of goods and services for our customers.

---

residential or commercial consumer needs could be included. Such a mission statement is hardly likely to influence day-to-day management decisions, and the distinctive competence of the organization is simply not clear. If the planning team defines the business in terms of the customer needs that are met, it can avoid formulating a mission statement that is too limiting. It is sometimes helpful to summarize the mission statement with a slogan (see Figure 8-4 for examples of slogans).

**Figure 8-3
An Example of an Ineffective Mission
Statement**

The Gamma Corporation is a marketing-centered, professional service company that concentrates its efforts on providing services to satisfy the wants and needs of residential and commercial consumers at a value to the consumer superior to the competition.

**Figure 8-4
Examples of Value-Based Slogans**

Sears, Roebuck: "Quality at a Good Price"
Rouse Company: "Create the Best Environment for People"
Dana Corporation: "Productivity Through People"
Price Waterhouse & Company:
                         "Strive for Technical Perfection"

Slogans that have changed:
Dupont: "Better Things for Better Living ~~Through~~

                                        ~~Chemistry~~"
American Telephone & Telegraph: "~~Universal Service~~"

FORMULATING THE MISSION STATEMENT

The purpose of the mission statement is to provide a guiding star by which to steer the organization. The development of a mission statement follows the completion of the values audit. The mission statement must be congruent both with the values and beliefs that were clarified during the values audit and also with the organization's culture. A mission statement that is not congruent with the organization's core values, its culture, and its philosophy of operations will not provide the necessary guiding star. Even worse, any attempt to develop a mission statement without congruence with existing organizational values will likely meet with considerable resistance and fail.

The new mission statement of British Airways, "The World's Favorite Airline," would be difficult to achieve with the traditional bureaucratic and militaristic values of the old British Airways. A massive downsizing leading to earlier retirement of many tradition-oriented, bureaucratic employees, coupled with a prolonged effort at culture change, has been necessary to effect even the beginnings of real change.

A mission statement addresses the organization's fundamental reason for existing and specifies the functional role that the organization is going to adopt in its marketplace. A mission statement should clearly indicate the scope and direction of the organization's activities and, to the extent that it is feasible, provide a template for decision making by employees at all levels.

In formulating its mission statement, an organization must answer three primary questions (see Figures 8-5 and 5-4).

Figure 8-5
Mission Statement Questions

1. *What* function does this organization perform?
2. For *whom* does the organization perform this function?
3. *How* does this organization go about performing this function?

What?

The first question — "what?" — involves defining the needs that the organization is attempting to fill. Chapter 5 pointed out that it is critically important to avoid "marketing myopia" (Levitt, 1960) in answering the "what" question. It is also important not to accept superficial analyses of what business the organization is in. The classic story of Avis (see Chapter 5) nicely illustrates this point.

"Marketing myopia" causes an organization to define the "what" in terms of goods or services provided rather than in terms of *needs to be served.* Thinking about what needs that the organization is attempting to fill for customers or clients helps the organization to identify and monitor those needs. As the needs change, a need-conscious organization is more likely to develop new goods and services in order to meet the emerging needs of its customers and is less likely to become a boiled frog.

A detergent manufacturer that sees itself in the business of helping people clean garments, for example, is likely to view a new ultrasonic cleaning process as an opportunity — and as part of its ongoing mission — whereas a similar organization that sees its mission as making soap products may fail when its narrow line of merchandise loses popularity.

Nevertheless, simply defining the "what" in terms of customer needs is no guarantee of success. It *can* lead to success — as occurred when the oil companies redefined their mission as being in the energy business rather than the oil business and acquired energy companies such as coal mines. On the other hand, when the business is defined *too* broadly, it can lead to failure. This occurred when some oil companies defined themselves as being in the "natural resources" business — and Gulf, for example, acquired Bunker Hill Mining and Smelting operations. Gulf failed to understand this "new" business and was too arrogant to learn how to succeed in it. While a broad definition allows the organization to consider a wider range of options, each of these options needs to be carefully evaluated, and tough decisions will still need to be made. A mission statement is no substitute for good management and intelligent decision making.

Successful organizations spend a great deal of time and energy identifying need-reducing goods and services that meet current and future needs of their markets, and they include these in formulating their mission statements. A typical major issue in mission formulation is achieving consensus on how broadly or narrowly to answer the "what" question. The fact that values regarding risk taking, conflict avoidance, and growth-versus-profit quickly surface during mission formulation is one of the important reasons for completing the values audit prior to the mission statement.

Who?

The second aspect of mission formulation is identifying the "who," that is, which part of the market the organization is attempting to serve. No organization, regardless of size, is large enough to meet the needs of all possible customers or clients. Few, if any, organizations are large enough to attempt to serve everybody; and, in any event, "everybody" does not have the same needs. Mission formulation requires a clear identification of what portion or segment of the total potential customer base the organization is targeting. The process of sorting out a market's actual and potential segments — and where the organization will compete — is called market segmentation.

There are many ways in which a market can be segmented: by geography, age, wealth, ethnicity, and a variety of other factors. An organization can segment its market by single or multiple factors; for example, products can be developed for middle-class homemakers throughout the United States, or middle-class homemakers only in the Northeast, and so on. Until recently, for example, Coors Brewery saw itself as having a regional market. Its unpasteurized beer did not travel well over long distances and this family-owned business was satisfied with its regional market niche. As the marketing strategy of national breweries began to impinge on their once-secure regional marketing niche, Coors believed that it had to "go national" in order to survive.

In 1986 UAL, Inc. (best known for its United Airlines unit) decided to purchase Hilton International, which would complement the Westin Hotels that UAL already owned. UAL also purchased Hertz Corporation. This is another example of a company that defined its mission broadly, by making its target upscaling travelers' services, rather than narrowly by simply providing airline service. This strategy, however, was rejected by a group of shareholders who preferred short-term profitability to long-term strategic growth. These shareholders insisted that UAL divest itself of these operations, and the hotel and car-rental businesses were subsequently sold.

Clarity about its chosen market segment(s) enables an organization to be more sensitive to the needs of that segment and to focus its resources on its prime target. There clearly are different needs and different resources in various market segments. Organizations may elect to serve only one small segment of the market; consider, for example, the difference between a small boutique and a large department store. A small boutique offers personalized, exclusive quality products and services at a high margin to offset its small volume. A large department store provides less personalized, more mass-produced goods and services with a lower margin but at higher volume. There are customers and profits in both segments, provided there is clarity about the mission and skill in its execution.

The changes experienced by Montgomery Ward illustrate what can happen when the market segmentation is too broad. Montgomery Ward's new name ("Focus") and the new "Focus" campaign are clearly attempts to focus in on a specific market segment.

How?

The third question addressed by the mission statement should be concerned with *how* the organization will carry its products or services into the marketplace. For example, what technologies will be used by the organization in meeting the needs identified in its market? The "how" could involve a marketing strategy, such as becoming the low-cost producer, providing innovative products, or providing the most reliable products. It may involve a distribution strategy, such as providing no-appointment dental or medical services in shopping malls, adding regional warehouses, or offering electronic shopping through computers. It may involve direct-mail marketing, door-to-door selling, telemarketing, or any of a variety of processes through which the organization can develop, produce, market, and deliver products and/or services to a defined group of consumers or clients. What is best for your company is determined by experience, testing, intuition, and related factors.

Another important aspect of "how" involves the consideration of acquisitions and mergers. If, for example, growth or movement into new lines of business becomes a significant part of the strategic plan, then such growth or movement can often be most readily obtained through acquisition or merger and should be included as part of the "how" portion of the mission statement. The growth of Continental Airlines with its important subsidiary of New York Air will be greatly enhanced by its acquisition of Eastern, People's Express, and Frontier. In addition to the complementary route systems, the Eastern reservations systems — with its holiday packaging capability — is an important aspect of the merger, because Continental did not have a well-developed reservation system of its own.

In determining what, who, and how, the planning team must make sure that it is not attempting to overadapt. It must look beyond what is and focus on what is possible and what it wants the organization to be. In other words, the organization must not continue to sit in the same old pan if this, indeed, would yield boiled frogs.

Driving Forces

Another important factor that must be considered as part of mission formulation is the identification and prioritization of the organization's *driving forces*. The initial phase of mission formulation is defining the desired "future state." This defining disregards the constraints of the "present state," which needs to be examined later in the process. The driving force analysis is one way to examine these constraints later, after the articulation of the future state. Tregoe and Zimmerman (1980) identify the following nine basic categories of driving forces:[1]

---

[1]We have identified some additional driving forces in client systems; for example, the personal desires of the owner or entrepreneur.

1. **Products or Services Offered.** The organization is committed primarily to providing a product or service, such as retail banking, corn-sugar refining, or automotive manufacturing, and limits its strategy to increasing the quantity and quality of that product or service.
2. **Market Needs.** Market-driven companies continually survey potential customers to discover unfilled needs for goods and services. Once these are identified, the organization develops products or services to fill those needs.
3. **Technology.** Organizations that are technology driven continually try to develop products and services that are based on the latest scientific breakthroughs.
4. **Production Capability.** Capacity-driven organizations have a primary commitment to keeping their existing production capacity utilized, for example, to have hospital beds filled or to keep the continuous-process plant from shutting down.
5. **Method of Sale.** The method of sale, such as door-to-door selling, direct mail, or premiums and bonus programs, directs the strategy of these organizations.
6. **Method of Distribution.** Some organizations are driven by their current method of distribution, which may be regional warehouses, manufacturer's representatives, pipelines, etc.
7. **Natural Resources.** Certain types of organizations are strategically driven by their dependency on natural resources, such as coal, timber, petroleum, land, or metals.
8. **Size and Growth.** Organizations that are driven by set goals regarding size and growth constantly strive for continuing, significant growth above current performance.
9. **Profit/Return on Investment.** Many organizations set high priorities on profit margins or return on investments and make strategic decisions in order to achieve these goals.

Although all nine of these categories need to be considered in mission formulation, Tregoe and Zimmerman believe that an organization must clarify which of the nine factors is its primary driving force. When decisions require choosing from these nine forces, the decision makers in the organization must clearly and mutually understand which one is the primary force. For example, decisions may need to be made on whether resources should be allocated to research and development or to the development of a sales force to achieve growth or whether they should be retained as profits. If there is clarity on the organization's single driving force, these decisions can be made more easily.

In contrast to the conclusions of Tregoe and Zimmerman, we have found it more useful for the strategic planning team to prioritize the driving forces from one to nine in terms of their perceived importance, rather than identify only the primary force. If the organization has other driving forces, they should be added before the list is prioritized. The importance of gaining consensus on these priorities should be apparent. Most major strategic decisions that organizations make involve the allocation of resources according to a set of priorities. If resources are inadequate or if the choices are incompatible, the rank of the nine strategic areas can determine how resources will be allocated or which direction will be chosen. Ranking the driving forces (with the most important driving force in first place) enables the planning team to make otherwise difficult decisions rather easily.

Distinctive Competency

The final ingredient of the mission statement requires the identification of the distinctive competency or competencies of the organization: What quality or attribute of the organization sets it aside from its competitors? What is its unique advantage? An organization's distinctiveness may be a function of the products or services offered or a function of being a low-cost producer or providing superior service. For example, it may be the only educational institution to provide management education after work and on weekends in its geographical market. Another example is Perrier water, which proudly states "All the Perrier in the world comes from this Ice Age Spring." The mystique of the sparkling water in the distinctive green bottle owes much of its success to this distinctiveness campaign.

Identifying its distinctive competencies is a process by which the organization can focus its energies and resources to move in a particular direction. It also helps provide a rallying point for both managers and rank-and-file employees. American Airlines and its employees are extremely proud of being regularly voted "No. 1" by the members of the Airline Passengers Association. Maintaining this ranking has become a source of pride throughout the organization, one of which rank-and-file employees are willing to extend themselves. (Distinctive competency is further discussed in Chapter 11 in relation to the performance audit.)

Some organizations are unable to identify *any* clearly distinctive competency. There is simply nothing of significance that differentiates the organization from others that provide similar products or services. (This situation is dealt with during the performance audit.) During the mission-formulation process care should be taken not to assume the presence of a distinctive competency.

Once the question of what, who, and how are answered and the organization's driving force and distinctive competencies are identified, these elements can be integrated into the organization's mission statement. The mission statement should be brief, typically a hundred words or less, and clearly identify the organization's basic business. The mission statement answers the questions of what the organization does, for whom, and how; and it identifies the organization's major driving force. By answering these questions for both internal and external use, the organization can chart its course of action and provide a guide for making routine day-by-day decisions. The mission statement should be easily understood and communicated to all members of the organization.

If the planning team is large, a subgroup of the team may actually write the mission statement and present it to the total group for discussion and approval. When the planning team leaves the mission-formulation phase, it should have a working model of the mission statement, although it may later need to be revised. However, as soon as possible after an acceptable mission statement is formulated, it should be communicated to the organization.

MISSION FORMULATION IN ORGANIZATIONAL SEGMENTS

Once an overall mission statement has been developed for an organization, mission statements that are more specific and concrete should be developed for significant units or segments of the organization. Those parts of the organization that are large enough and autonomous enough to function relatively independently (that is, the strategic business units) will ordinarily profit by developing their own unit mission statements. Thus in a large organization, units with highly differentiated functions—such as the marketing group or the service department—would each need a mission statement, as would each of the separate plants, regional offices, clinics, schools, and so on, of the organization.

The finance group of one organization with which we are familiar has the mission of providing "completely accurate financial analyses for business unit managers within eight working days after the close of the reporting period." This ambitious goal serves as a model for other service units in the company to be clear and proactive in their efforts. The journal publishing arm of another organization has as its mission "the on-time publication of all major journals with zero defects."

The first step in developing a unit mission statement is to ask the planning team of the unit to review the overall mission statement of the organization and consider how the functioning of their

The Unit Mission Statement Must Reflect the Overall Mission Statement

unit fits into the overall organizational mission. In large organizations it may also be necessary to do a unit values audit before writing a unit mission statement. This is especially true if there are different values, beliefs, and philosophies of operation among the various organizational segments or between the top levels of organizational management and other levels of management.

Once a consensus on values and philosophy of operations is achieved in the unit, the unit planning staff (or the management of the unit) should develop the unit's mission statement, observing the same requirements that governed the preparation of the overall organizational mission statement. The unit mission statement should identify what the unit does, for whom, and how it does what it does, as well as identify its driving force and distinctive competence. And, again, the formulators of the unit mission statement should avoid the boiled-frog syndrome.

When the unit planning staff agrees on the unit mission statement, that statement should be forwarded to the organization's top-level strategic planning team and/or top management for endorsement and approval. It is the responsibility of senior management to make certain that each unit mission statement is based on and reflects the overall organizational mission statement. A similar review and sign-off process from other organizational segments, such as marketing and sales or manufacturing and quality control, may also be important. Such an exchange and dialogue over unit mission statements can clarify the roles and expectations of the various segments of an organization.

In implementing the unit mission statements, it is imperative to inform all personnel of that unit promptly about the unit's mission statement. This can best be accomplished through meeting with them to discuss the mission statement. An actual example of a unit mission statement is presented in Figure 8-6 (Kanter & Buck, 1985, p. 7).

Kanter and Buck also provide an in-depth analysis of the development of this particular unit mission statement, its function as part of an overall unit change strategy, and the way this unit mission statement is intended to fit into the overall corporate mission. The positive effect of using an external consultant to facilitate the mission formulation process is particularly noteworthy in this case.

Figure 8-6
Example of a Unit Mission Statement

The Defense Systems Employee Relations Department provides leadership for progressive human resources planning, policy design, systems, and services which are aimed at fostering productivity, innovation, and a climate of success in the work place. We contribute to business strategy development while being mindful of the self-esteem and well-being of employees and the division's responsibility to the greater community.

TEN CRITERIA FOR EVALUATING MISSION STATEMENTS

For a mission statement to be effective, it should meet the following ten conditions:

1. The mission statement is clear and understandable to all personnel, including rank-and-file employees.
2. The mission statement is brief enough for most people to remember.
3. The mission statement clearly specifies what business the organization is in. This includes a clear statement about:
   a. *What* customer or client needs the organization is attempting to fill (not what products or services are offered);
   b. *Who* the organization's primary customers or clients are; and
   c. *How* the organization plans to go about its business, that is, what its primary technologies are.
4. The mission statement should have a primary focus on a single strategic thrust.
5. The mission statement should reflect the distinctive competence of the organization.

6. The mission statement should be broad enough to allow flexibility in implementation but not so broad as to permit a lack of focus.

7. The mission statement should serve as a template and be the means by which managers and others in the organization can make decisions.

8. The mission statement must reflect the values, beliefs, and philosophy of operations of the organization and reflect the organizational culture.

9. The mission statement should reflect attainable goals.

10. The mission statement should be worded so as to serve as an energy source and rallying point for the organization.

A DIFFICULT BUT CRUCIAL STEP

The process of formulating the mission statement of the organization is critical. It is an extremely difficult and time-consuming task. In fact, the choice of a single word may arouse intense controversy among the planning team. After all, there *is* a major difference between stating that the organization will be "the" leading producer or simply "a" leading producer of a product line. The subsequent plans could be quite different, depending on which word was selected.

The development of a consensus on such issues is what mission formulation is all about, and it is a long, tough process. Despite our insistence on the brevity of the mission statement (or perhaps because of it), the process of writing and editing the mission statement and achieving the consensus necessary for its adoption is rarely accomplished in a single session. It is a process that usually extends over several sessions and seems to require some reflective time between sessions. In spite of this difficulty, developing a truly functional mission statement is well worth the time and effort, because the organization will then have an enormously useful management tool that has significant long-term positive consequences.

A functional mission statement can make a difference in being a more effective, profitable organization and being less effective or unprofitable. A small financial investment company, for example, struggled with the issues of direction, size, organization, and future prospects until a strong consensual agreement was reached on the following statement: "Frontier Financial Service is in the business of providing high-quality, personalized portfolio management to individuals with significant liquid assets." Starting with clients having $500,000 in "significant liquid assets" in 1976, today prospective clients must have a minimum of $4 million. The company has refused to take on several small pension funds as not fitting into its strategy and has achieved an outstanding reputation for the quality of its personalized investment counsel.

SUMMARY

A mission statement provides the context for the formulation of specific program strategies that an organization will engage in. It sets the arena in which the organization will compete, and it determines the future pattern of growth and direction. It also determines how resources will be allocated. The mission statement is, therefore, one of the most important aspects of the strategic planning process. The development of a mission statement is also one of the most difficult aspects of planning. Especially difficult and important is limiting the mission statement to one hundred words or less.

The formulation of the mission statement follows the values audit and should answer the following questions: What function does the organization perform? For whom does the organization perform this function? How does the organization go about performing this function? As the planning team develops the mission statement, it should identify and prioritize the organization's driving forces. It should also identify the organization's distinctive competencies.

REFERENCES

Kanter, R. M., & Buck, J. D. (1985). Reorganizing part of Honeywell: From strategy to structure. *Organizational Dynamics, 13*(3), 4–25.

Levitt, T. (1960, July–August). Marketing myopia. *Harvard Business Review*, pp. 45–56. Reprinted in *Harvard Business Review*,September–October, 1975, pp. 26–28, 33–34, 38–39, 44, 173–174, 176–181.

Tregoe, B. B., & Zimmerman, J. W. (1980). *Top management strategy: What it is and how to make it work.* New York: Simon and Schuster.

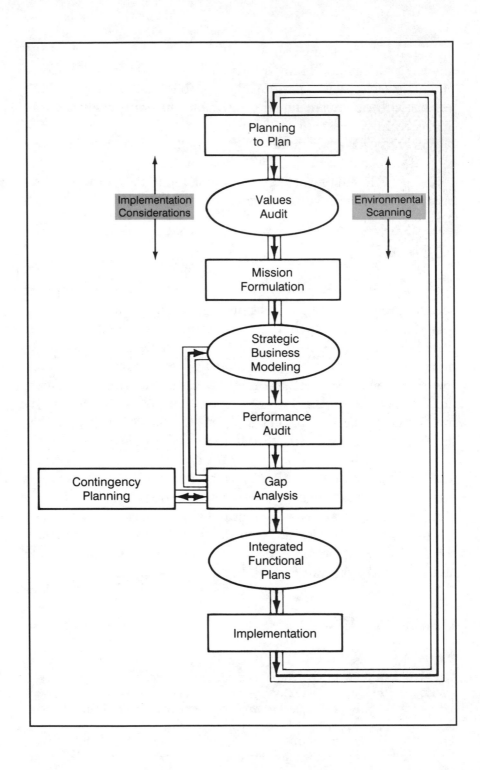

9 ENVIRONMENTAL SCANNING AND IMPLEMENTATION CONSIDERATIONS

Two very important activities that must occur throughout the strategic planning process are addressed in this chapter. The first involves *environmental scanning*, or monitoring the environment that impacts the organization. The second involves *implementation considerations*, that is, an ongoing review at each phase of strategic planning to determine which elements need immediate implementation.

ENVIRONMENTAL SCANNING

Just as some of the worker bees have to continually scan the environment for new sources of pollen in order to successfully maintain the beehive, so must organizations be diligent in scanning the environment if they are to survive. All organizations have a vital need to track what is occurring or about to occur in their environments. While change has been one of the few constants in our world, the rate of change is accelerating; and organizations that do not anticipate and attempt to manage this increasingly rapid rate of change face precarious futures. Only by constantly and carefully monitoring an organization's environments can the organization track and understand these changes. Environmental scanning — perhaps more than any other factor — helps to prevent boiled frogs.

Strategic planning requires that an organization take time to seriously examine how it can systematically monitor the environments that impact its future and how it can process the information obtained. Because the Applied Strategic Planning Model assumes that environmental scanning is an ongoing, continual process in organizations, there is no single point in the planning sequence at which environmental scanning begins or ends. Thus, our model shows environmental scanning as part of the enveloping fabric of the planning process (see Figure 5-3). The information gleaned from the organization's ongoing scanning process should continually provide information to the planning team and to the entire organization about

**Environment Scanning:
An Important Step**

what is happening and what is likely to happen that might affect the organization's planning process and its overall future.

Two essential aspects of environmental scanning need to be confronted in the planning process. The first concerns the types of information that need to be obtained and the ways this information — facts, hypotheses, intuitions, guesses, and the like — should be used. The second aspect concerns the effectiveness of the organization's system for gathering, storing, processing, and disseminating environmental intelligence. In most cases, an organization's data are fragmented and incomplete, and its scanning system — especially its competitor analysis — is woefully inadequate. For example, one large manufacturer of high-style fabrics for the women's apparel industry — a notoriously unstable environment — tracked competitors' fabrics only through their advertisements in fashion magazines. In that industry such an information source clearly provides data too late for a competitor to make appropriate countermoves.

One of the side benefits of the Applied Strategic Planning Model is that it helps the organization confront and evaluate its environmental scanning system and, where necessary, develop a more effective system. In our example of a fabric manufacturer, a more effective system would involve monitoring the opening shows of various fashion designers, interviewing reporters and other trade sources, examining sample books provided by competitors for end-users, and integrating these data points carefully and systematically.

The specific kinds and forms of information that are needed by a specific organization will, of course, depend on the organization and the environmental context in which it is situated. However, this information should identify emerging opportunities and threats and also the organization's strengths and weaknesses for meeting these opportunities and threats. We often refer to these four factors (strengths, weaknesses, opportunities, and threats) with the acronym SWOT.

In general, the following five environments (also see Figure 9-1) should be scanned on a regular basis:

1. The macro environment

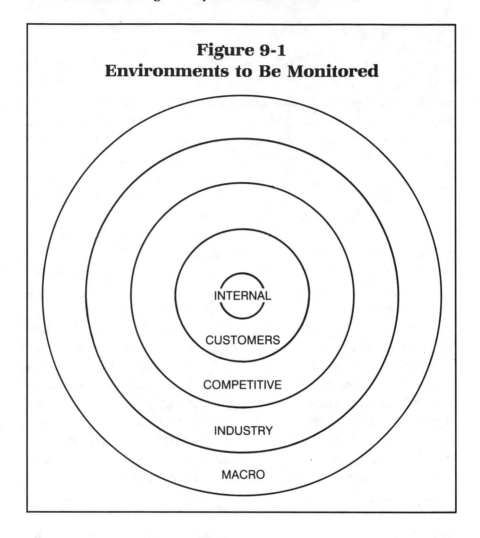

Figure 9-1
Environments to Be Monitored

INTERNAL

CUSTOMERS

COMPETITIVE

INDUSTRY

MACRO

2. The industry environment
3. The competitive environment
4. The customer environment
5. The internal organizational environment

Various aspects of these environments are discussed as appropriate throughout this book. Environmental scanning will identify a variety of factors, both internal and external to the organization, to be considered as part of the strategic planning process. In fact, one of the side benefits of applied strategic planning is that an organization obtains a much better understanding of how environmental scanning should be done and how well it is being done. As mentioned in Chapter 6, during the planning-to-plan phase, the planning team should gain a thorough understanding of what the process entails and how it should operate in the organization.

The following lists indicate what should be monitored in each of the five environments:

1. *Macro-enironmental surveillance* should include the following:
   - Social factors, such as demographic changes
   - Technological factors, such as the large-scale use of microcomputers
   - Economic factors, such as the prime interest rate and the consumer price index
   - Political factors, such as increases or decreases in governmental regulation

Scanning The Macro Environment

2. Among the factors to be monitored as part of the *industry environment* are the following:

- Structure of the industry
- How the industry is financed
- Changes in the degree of governmental regulation
- Changes in typical products offered by the industry
- Changes in typical industry marketing strategies and techniques

3. Surveillance of the *competitive environment* includes consideration of the following:

- Competitor profiles
- Market-segmentation patterns
- Research and development trends
- Emergence of new competitors

4. Scanning the *customer environment* includes the following:

- Tracking customer complaints and compliments
- Monitoring return rates and warranty costs
- Listening to customer needs and concerns

5. Finally, the following factors should be considered as part of the *internal organizational environment:*

- The appropriateness of the organization's structure
- The lessons to be learned from the organization's history
- The organization's climate and culture
- The organization's distinctive competencies
- Shifts in organizational leadership

Tracking these five areas and understanding how changes in any one of these environments may impact the organization over time constitute the essence of environmental scanning.

Effective Environmental Surveillance

Most organizations are exposed to tremendous amounts of environmental information. They have multiple subscriptions to trade journals, association newsletters, and business and financial publications of many sorts. Frequently organizations also send several representatives to trade shows and conventions. Despite all this information, the data are often incompletely surveyed, organized, analyzed, and stored and—as a result—are unavailable for either management decisions or strategic planning. In other words, the surveillance of the environment is, in most cases, undirected, haphazard, and nonfunctional. Like the frog, the organization is surrounded by evidence but fails to use it for its own survival. And so the random collection of data that is never systematically reviewed and integrated is likely to provide little useful environmental data, especially about competitors.

To give some order to this often chaotic state, Aaker (1983) has recommended that organizations utilize a strategic information scanning system (SISS). The SISS is a simple, formal, five-stepsystem for identifying organizational information needs, assigning members of the organization to specific scanning tasks to obtain that information, and feeding the information into the strategic planning and management processes. The five steps are as follows:

1. Identify the organization's information needs, especially for the next round of strategic planning.
2. Generate a list of information sources that provide core inputs (for example, trade shows, publications, trade associations, technical meetings, and customers).
3. Identify those who will participate in the environmental scanning process (they do not have to be members of the planning team).
4. Assign scanning tasks to several members of the organization.
5. Build a system to store and disseminate the information.

The SISS should be as simple and as manageable as possible. All the important areas (such as identifying actual or potential changes in strategy by competitors) should be covered, but the surveillance tasks should be kept manageable. Information needs can be rated on their importance to and impact on the organization. For example, if it is highly probable that a serious threat will occur soon, then information in this area is much more important than data about less likely threats in the more distant future.

An extensive list of information sources should be developed and then the sources that are routinely and regularly accessible should be determined. Those that have been ignored or overlooked should also be identified. This procedure will help an organization to develop a rational core set of information sources.

People from various parts of the organization should be tapped as a source of information from vendors, customers, advertisers, and the like. Many people outside the planning team have easy access to valuable information and will be happy to report their findings.

Figure 9-2 illustrates how the SISS could be conducted and monitored. Various information sources are shown along the horizontal axis, and several information needs are displayed along the vertical axis. The names identify specific people who are assigned to monitor each of the sources in order to meet the information needs. When several people are assigned to the same source, each person monitors that source for a particular information need based on his or her background and interest. For example, a prime technical journal might be monitored by one person for marketing information, by another for new applications, and by still another for competitor information.

The information can be stored in any convenient form, from a simple set of manila folders to a complex computer-data-base system. However, the storage method should be congruent with the work styles and traditional means of information storage and retrieval in the organization. Time and care must be devoted to the development of the storage system so that it can adequately serve the needs of the planning process.

As mentioned in Chapter 8, if members of the planning team understand that the mission statement sets the arena in which the organization will compete, they will more readily understand why a

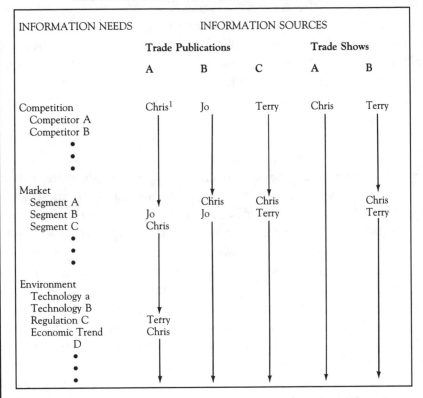

Figure 9-2
Information Needs and Sources

INFORMATION NEEDS	INFORMATION SOURCES				
	Trade Publications			Trade Shows	
	A	B	C	A	B
Competition	Chris[1]	Jo	Terry	Chris	Terry
Competitor A					
Competitor B					
•					
•					
Market		Chris	Chris		Chris
Segment A					
Segment B	Jo	Jo	Terry		Terry
Segment C	Chris				
•					
•					
Environment					
Technology a					
Technology B					
Regulation C	Terry				
Economic Trend	Chris				
D					
•					
•					
•					

[1]Name indicates person responsible.

Based on the strategic information scanning system described in "Using a Strategic Information Scanning System" by D.A. Aaker, 1983. In *California Management Review*, 25, pp. 80–81.

certain amount of environmental scanning is necessary prior to the formulation of the mission statement.

The Macro Environment

The macro environment is involved with large social, technological, economic, and political changes in our society. During the past decade few organizations—if any—have not been affected by the introduction of the microcomputer, the changes in fuel costs, the changes in interest rates, and such broad societal changes as the rise of consumerism, the changing attitudes of employees toward work, and the taxpayer rebellion. These changes in the macro environment clearly affect most or all organizations, but in different ways and to differing degrees. Organizations that monitor broad social changes and integrate the potential impact of such changes into their planning process obviously have a competitive edge over organizations that do not. As mentioned in Chapter 8, the social, technological, and political aspects of the macro environment should be considered by the planning team before the mission statement is formulated.

For an extended period of time, U.S. automobile manufacturers did not fully appreciate the long-range impact of the increase in gasoline prices on consumer behavior. Starting with the fuel crisis of the 1970s, most purchasers of automobiles expected new cars to get higher average miles per gallon regardless of where the car was manufactured. Thus the U.S. automobile manufacturers faced a significant loss of market share to the smaller, more fuel-efficient cars made in Japan, Germany, France, Italy, and more recently, Korea and Yugoslavia. This trend, of course, was enormously augmented by the parallel rise of consumerism, which led to heightened discontent with the perceived low quality of American cars.

Social Aspects.   Social aspects are those broad social changes that occur over time and that directly affect the way organizations operate or should operate. An article in the *New York Times* (1983) that was based on U.S. Census Bureau projections of the "graying" of the U.S. population over the next hundred years made such a point. Consider the vast number of youth-oriented businesses that will require refocusing over time if they are to survive. One clear example is the American film makers who currently focus on adolescent horror films, mindless escape adventures, and the like— scarcely standard fare for a graying audience. Another trend to anticipate is the growing pattern of illiteracy, which became obvious as we helped the Los Angeles County Library System with its strategic plan. These are only two of the many social trends that need to be considered in the strategic planning process.

Technological Aspects.   As mentioned in Chapter 1, many technological changes that have revolutionized our lives have come into existence since about 1930. The influence of such technological changes on the macro environment is as pervasive as that of social changes. Among the clear technological trends that need to be considered are the increasingly widespread use of the microcomputer, the development of robotics, office automation, and electronic information transmission (for example, electronic banking). Although the degree to which any specific organization will be affected by such technology will vary, rarely will an organization be unaffected.

An example of this impact was seen in a financial-service organization to which the authors were consultants. The entire secretarial force was centralized in a secretarial pool, and each manager was given a computer terminal to replace the missing secretary. The managers drafted their correspondence on their terminals and received final copies from the secretarial pool. Although the cost savings will be substantial because the number of secretaries was reduced, the loss of the personal relationship between the remaining secretaries and their former supervisors has been disconcerting to both groups and has resulted in unhappiness. This technological change caused office relationships to become more impersonal and less efficient than they were previously.

Economic Aspects.   Organizations need to become aware of macroeconomic trends and to monitor them carefully. Most people are aware of the impact of economic changes over the past decade. The initial OPEC oil embargo, the subsequent skyrocketing cost of petroleum products followed by a glut from overproduction, the recession of the 1970s, interest rates that soared to 20 percent and then fell to a third of that high, and the shifting values of the U.S. dollar in foreign exchange are only a few of the economic changes that have had both personal and organizational consequences for our entire society. Any organization that became aware of any of these economic trends early and tracked them in its planning process was at a substantial advantage in the marketplace.

Political Aspects.   A number of political trends have also affected broad segments of our society. The most important of these include governmental deregulation, changes in the tax laws, the lobbying of special-interest groups, and the reduction of federal government involvement in local governmental affairs. Although the impact of these political aspects has affected organizations differently, some of the impact has been widely experienced. The deregulation of the airline, financial, and telecommunication industries is a case in point. With deregulation, the airline industry has seen a fantastic growth of new carriers (and a number of failures of both new and old carriers), price cutting, mergers and acquisitions, and cutthroat competition. Many organizations were unprepared for such changes in the airline industry. A similar situation has existed in the telecommunications industry ever since the forced divestiture of AT&T's operating companies.

Each of these macro environment considerations should have received thoughtful attention during the mission-formulation phase. Although the degree to which an organization needs to consider each factor will vary, every organization should identify which aspects will impact its future plans and the degree to which those plans are sensitive to changes in the marketplace.

Some General Trends.   According to Naisbitt (1982), the following new directions will transform our lives—especially our organizational lives:

1. The change from an industrial society to an informational society;
2. The development of a high-tech/high-touch requirement;
3. A shift from a national to a world economy;
4. A movement from short-term to long-term thinking, managing, and planning;
5. A change from centralization to decentralization;
6. The reemergence of self-help to replace institutional help;
7. A change from representative democracy to participatory democracy;
8. A shift from hierarchical forms of management to net working;

9. The development of the South as a center of energy and organizational life; and

10. A shift to a search for multiple options rather than an either/or solution.

Although one might argue with Naisbitt's predictions, serious consideration should be given to how those trends and directions may affect the future development of an organization. This would be a worthwhile exercise in the strategic planning process.

To be helpful, the trends in the macro environment must be current. There are numerous sources of up-to-date information on future changes. For example, the Naisbitt Group[1] publishes a yearly forecast (*The Year Ahead: 10 New Trends That Will Shape the Way You Live, Work, and Make Money*) and two monthly newsletters; the World Futures Society[2] holds an annual conference and provides a variety of publications on future trends; the Club of 1000 publishes forecasts irregularly on a variety of trends of concern to business organizations; many banks publish monthly or quarterly letters that focus on local or regional financial trends; business schools of many universities provide published summaries of their research findings on local business trends; and, of course, the national business magazines, such as *Fortune, Forbes, Business Week, Venture,* and *Inc.* provide extensive information on the macro environment. Organizations need to successfully weave the skills of a futurist into the planning process, thereby expanding the resources of the planning group.

The Industry Environment

Clearly, an organization needs to track what is occurring in the environment of its particular industry. By "industry" we mean a group of organizations producing products or services that are close substitutes for one another (Porter, 1980). Understanding industry trends allows an organization to understand what is happening elsewhere in that industry that may affect its continued vitality and

---

[1]Further information is available from the Naisbitt Group, P. O. Box 25536, Washington, DC 20007.

[2]Further information is available from the World Futures Society, 4916 St. Elmo Avenue, Bethesda, MD 20814.

success. For example, a telecommunications company needs to know what is going on in the communications industry; a school system, what is occurring in the education industry; and a restaurant chain, what is happening in the food-service industry. As organizations offer goods or services that can substitute for one another in the same market or to the same potential clients and customers, other organizations become competitors.

The factors that can be considered in tracking the industry environment include potential modifications in the industry structure, changes in the industry technology, changes in the presence of the government in the industry, the introduction of new products or services, the development of new applications for existing products or services, the opening of new markets, changes in the methods of industry financing, changes in the availability of raw material or parts, and the possible unionization or deunionization of industries.

To understand how a few of these factors could impact an organization, consider how the structure of an industry would change if franchising became a strong factor in that industry, as it has in the lodging industry and the fast-food-service industry. One such change in the offing is the repeal of the Glass-Steagle Act, which prohibits interstate banking. With that repeal, the large metropolitan banks in the commercial markets of America—Citicorp, Chase Manhattan, Harris Bank, Security-Pacific—will endeavor to purchase or otherwise take over the smaller banks throughout the country, following the direction set by First Interstate. With this spreading of risk, more central control, national marketing, and a change in marketplace, banking as we know it today will change dramatically and it is difficult to predict what will emerge. Also consider how mass utilization of bank debit cards could affect both the financial-service industry and most retail trades.

If, for example, Internal Revenue codes did not permit personal income-tax deductions for interest payments except for primary dwellings, consider the impact on the vacation-home market and real estate in general. Consider how the rising price of oil has affected the automobile industry, the petroleum industry, the price of products that have to be transported long distances to the retailers, and the general pattern of consumer behavior.

Galbraith and Nathanson (1978) offer an interesting example of how changes in the industry environment affected the aerospace industry. Through the 1960s, technical performance was the criteria upon which defense contracts were awarded, and the price was typically on an actual-cost plus fixed-fee basis. By the middle '60s, however, the environment began to change. Strong pressures to reduce defense costs began to develop, and the Secretary of Defense insisted that technical performance could be maintained at a reduced cost. Cost effectiveness then became a primary criterion, and contracts were granted on the basis of fixed costs with various incentives for cost reduction. Over the next few years the entire pattern of management in the aerospace industry changed; and project managers who were charged with cost control gained power in the organization over the traditional engineering managers who focused on technical requirements.

Because the aspects that need to be monitored in the industry environment are so industry specific, we do not attempt to list specific guidelines for tracking particular industry environments. The planning team must realize nonetheless that the industry environment must be monitored both as part of the strategic planning process and as part of management's general responsibilities.

In each industry a variety of journals, magazines, and newsletters provide useful information about what is happening in that industry. Trade shows and conventions are another useful source, particularly to catch trends early and to pick up rumors, guesses, and hypotheses that rarely find their way into industry publications. Federal bureaus (for example, Census, Economic Analysis, and Domestic and International Business Administration, all under the Department of Commerce; and Labor Statistics, under the Department of Labor) issue many reports containing useful industry data. A variety of private research groups, such as the Conference Board, publish occasional papers on various industries. Since there is no shortage of information about the industry environment, the important issue is to develop the organizational commitment to monitor such data in a systematic fashion.

The Competitive Environment

As we will see in Chapter 11 ("The Performance Audit"), monitoring the competitive environment is of special importance to the success of the organization. Monitoring this environment means keeping track of those organizations that provide or could provide substitute goods and services to the same marketplace.

Various electronic data bases (such as Economic Information Systems, a subsidiary of Control Data Corporation, and *Investex*, published by Business Research Corporation of Brighton, Massachusetts) provide information on competitors' dollar revenues, market shares, number of employees, industrial facilities, and so on. These services charge fees but are perfectly legal sources of information. Another source is the Profit Impact of Marketing Strategy (PIMS) program, developed by the Strategic Planning Institute of Cambridge, Massachusetts, which compares an organization's strategic indices with those from their two-thousand-company data base, thus providing comparative data on strategic strengths and weaknesses. Also, some industries, such as theme parks, regularly share data of importance.

The Customer Environment

A critical area to examine constantly is the customer environment. By staying alert to customer feedback in the form of returned items, complaints or compliments, and patterns of buying, a great deal of information can be gleaned regarding the current and future health of the business. Being aware of trends in customer loyalty (that is, the tendency for customers to move from supplier to supplier or to settle down to sustained buying patterns) can be most helpful in the planning process.

One of the most useful methods of staying alert to customer interests and concerns is to *listen* to the customer. Too many organizations fail to listen because they believe that they—the suppliers, sellers, or professionals — know more than the customers. Other organizations have succeeded, even flourished, primarily by listening carefully to and acting upon what customers were saying. Not only can customer input help identify market trends, but it quite often results in new products or services designed to meet specific, identified customer needs.

The Internal Environment

During the integrating-functional-plans phase, the focus should shift substantially from external scanning to internal scanning, that is, from monitoring how well the competition is doing to monitoring how well the organization itself is doing in terms of profit, revenues, expenses, marketing, and so on. We often strongly recommend that all managers who have responsibility for budget lines — either income, cost of goods, or expenses — need to meet monthly to review, line-by-line, budget versus actual figures for both the preceding month and for the fiscal year to date. Effective applied strategic planning needs to be monitored frequently to assure that the implementation of the plan is synchronized with the specific goals manifested in the strategic business profile (quantified business objectives) as well as the strategic-business-modeling decisions regarding *how* those goals are being met. This monthly monitoring of the operating statement (profit and loss) should also be carefully checked against any triggering levels established in the contingency-planning process (see Chapter 13). Generally, the monthly accounting function should be done within ten working days of the end of the month. If it takes longer than this recommended time, managers are faced with an exasperating delay in being able to make necessary decisions to stay on the course established by the strategic business model.

Another recommendation that we sometime make to organizations, particularly when moderate-to-high levels of growth are targeted, is the establishment of a rolling quarterly budgeting process. This process typically calls for (1) a revision, if necessary, of the next three quarters' budget and (2) a new budget for a fourth quarter that is a year ahead of the quarter just completed. Assuming events covered by contingency planning will require immediate functional realignment. It is the CEO's absolute responsibility to ensure moderately good budgeting skills and a business that is not unreasonably complex, we recommend that this process be done within a month of the close of the quarter, that is, immediately after the actual-to-budget monitoring meeting for the end of each quarter. Additionally, we routinely recommend quarterly balance-sheet meetings in which all assets and liability accounts are fully reconciled.

In the absence of an unusually complex process that can be designed to monitor both original and updated budgets, the trade-off that develops is imbedded in understanding which of the following is more important to the organization: (1) to know how accurate the managers are with respect to the annual budgeting cycle, or (2) to know what is the most accurate picture that can be developed with respect to where the organization will be eight to eleven months hence. We strongly believe that the latter view is more important. While most organizations use an inflexible, yearly budgeting process that is typically out of date six months into the year, the quarterly rebudgeting cycle that we ourselves have used is a much better device to exercise corporate discipline.

We have found that managers who are fully involved in monthly operating-statement monitoring and rolling quarterly budgets see the pragmatic value of the process as opposed to that of the annual budget ritual, which is more typical. Because these monitoring/budgeting skills are kept focused, the quarterly budgeting process only takes about 50 percent more time than the traditional once-a-year, I-cannot-remember-how-we-did-this-last-time method.

When, on occasion, changes in external conditions force adjustments in functional plans or budgets, all managers responsible for major functions must meet to realign their positions with respect to the shifting external conditions and the corresponding responses from others with functional responsibilities. For example, in a large trade association where all revenues are received within sixty days after the annual billing cycle, the short-term interest yield from investing these funds is a significant portion of the total revenue. When short-term interest fell from 10 to 6 percent, it required an extensive rebudgeting to allow for the shortfall in income. Additionally, predetermined response patterns occasioned by the triggering of that adjustments by functional managers are synchronized with the organization's strategic goals.

Typically, near-term functional goals should be planned with a minimum three-year horizon and should be updated annually. Budgeting should be done on a one-year basis; and, as previously mentioned, we recommend rolling quarterly updates. Organizations should adopt time frames that are consistent with their businesses. Functional plans must be fastidiously synchronized with one another and absolutely integrated into the strategic plans.

Near-term functional plans, often referred to as tactical (or operational) plans, should, at a minimum, be translated into *pro forma* profit-and-loss statements, and these should be checked against the business model. Additionally, translation into *pro forma* balance sheets may provide an additional check against the templates of the strategic plan.

Dimensions that may be included are products, pricing, sales programs, manufacturing methods, warehousing and distribution facilities, equipment, location and space requirements, organization and personnel, finance and control procedures, data processing, record keeping, and purchasing. New-product development, marketing, acquisitions, and required capital expenditures may also need to be included.

Depending on the nature of the business, an individual function will often drive others; for example, marketing often drives (or dictates) production and personnel needs, and production may drive purchasing and capital expenditures. In capital-intensive companies, facilities (or capacity) may be the central point from which other functional plans are developed. Because of the intensely complex nature of the interaction among the various functional plans, it is desirable for the CEO to approve the overall, master plan that is built in consultation with the functional heads.

Aside from the obvious limits on financial resources faced by most companies, it is our belief that the major constraint to planned growth is inadequate human resource planning (see Chapter 14).

Environmental Scanning During the Gap Analysis

Environmental scanning is especially important during the gap-analysis phase (see Chapter 12). It could mean the difference between bridging the gap or sitting in the pan and becoming a boiled frog.

Markets are constantly changing. Although this sometimes means growth and opportunity, at other times it may mean decline in size of market and potential sales. It is as critical to properly identify a market that is losing its potential and to respond as it is to spot a new market and leap into it.

Shrinking markets call for tactics of planned withdrawal or reduction of effort to maintain profitability and to free resources for investment in more promising markets. Tactics may be gradual, such as phase-out or phase-down. These both are a series of moves to reduce overhead in line with decreasing sales in order to maintain profitability in the market as long as possible. When phase-out of a product line occurs simultaneously with an overall growth strategy, a unique opportunity is presented. The human, physical, and fiscal resources committed to the LOB (line of business) that is being phased out may be carefully transferred to a growing LOB, thus reducing losses, layoffs, and disruption. In phasing out its retail outlets, a major minicomputer manufacturer offered positions in the marketing groups to all employees who were interested, because these employees were seen as a critically important resource for future growth.

Divesting lines of business by selling them off is more dramatic. Although such a move can cause much internal disruption, it may mean a sale while there still are resources to sell. This may be a very astute tactic if barriers to exit (such as those that are due to capital invested or labor contracts) are very high, making phase-out a potential disaster. Divestment also quickly frees up critical management time and other resources for commitment to markets with higher potential. The sale of the retail division of the computer company is one example of such divestment.

Several potential gaps tend to be related to the leadership style and culture of the organization. If a gap is identified in risk orientation, the planning team must examine the feasibility of reaching the desired future. Risk orientation may be restricted by lack of resources or difficult market conditions, which may be subject to change.

When risk orientation is more clearly related to the style of the key manager, the question becomes "Can this person change or must a new leader or leaders be brought in?" Regardless of desired direction of change (from conservative to risk-oriented or vice versa), these styles are often not easy to change.

IMPLEMENTATION CONSIDERATIONS

There are two sets of concerns regarding implementation of the strategic plan. One set consists of concerns and issues that need to be reviewed *during* the strategic planning process. We will refer to such issues as "implementation considerations" and discuss them primarily in this chapter. The other type of implementation concerns refer to the "final implementation" that is conducted in accordance with the strategic plan *after* the planning process is complete. (See Chapter 15.)

Even though implementation of the strategic plan is the final phase of the model, implementation must continually take place throughout the strategic planning process. If, indeed, a fire-breathing dragon seems to be emerging, steps must be taken immediately to keep a watchful eye on it. Actions must not be delayed until the dragon has devoured the organization. In fact, there are clear implementation aspects of the planning-to-plan process. If the values audit identifies incongruous values in segments of the organization, these need to be addressed *as soon* as they are identified, *not held until the final implementation phase.* The mission statement needs to be distributed for comments and suggestions before it is formally adopted, and no further planning should be done until there is consensus on the statement. Each step of the strategic planning process has its own implementation considerations, and each of these considerations should be addressed during that stage, not postponed until the final implementation phase.

Beginning with the planning-to-plan phase, planning-team members need to understand that the most important test of implementation is the degree to which organizational members, especially managers, use the strategic plan in their everyday management decisions. A strategic plan is being implemented if the initial response of a manager confronted by a problem is to consider whether an answer is found in the organization's strategic plan. Although guidelines for every decision will not be provided in the planning process, consideration of the plan as a first step is the best evidence of the plan's implementation.

Applied strategic planning requires organizations to regard implementation as episodic rather than as just the final stage of the planning process. The Applied Strategic Planning Model requires that the planning team pause after completing each phase of the planning process and consider the implementation issues that can be identified. If, for instance, it is determined that there is low commitment to doing strategic planning in one segment of the organization in the planning-to-plan phase, then working on this commitment must be addressed at that time, not postponed until the final implementation phase. At a major computer organization, strategic planning was regarded as "Mickey Mouse" by the R&D group, and their contributions tended to be humorous rather than serious. Only after several confrontations between the CEO and the director of R&D was serious effort devoted to the R&D planning process.

Similarly, if the values audit brings to the surface serious differences in values that might block the development of a strategic plan or hinder its implementation, then these differences must be addressed and reduced before the next phase is tackled. If the values audit identifies values in one segment of the organization that are incongruous with those in another segment, they need to be addressed immediately. Values need to be clearly articulated, and important value differences need to be resolved for a successful strategic planning process to occur. The envisioning of an organization's future state is a values-based exercise. How an organization considers such ordinary marketplace decisions as market share, dealing with the competition, innovation in products and services, customer or client service, and so on, is a natural outgrowth of the fundamental values that the organization holds — values that need to be examined, or reexamined as part of the strategic planning process. When a planning team arrives at a resolution about the values of the organization, this information needs to be disseminated to the rest of the organization.

Both the mission statement and the organization's statement of philosophy are the tried and true methods for disseminating such information throughout the organization. However, the first time such products are produced, they need to be tested out for feedback before they are widely disseminated.

If the review of the organization's environmental surveillance system identifies gaps in the organization's knowledge base, such as inadequate competitor analysis or market research, then this gap needs to be immediately filled, not held in abeyance until the implementation phase. If the performance audit identifies some internal organizational limitations, such as inadequate capital or manufacturing capacity or quality standards, then these must be immediately addressed, not postponed for the implementation phase. At each phase of our applied strategic planning process there are issues that require an *immediate* organizational response — one that must be made at that time and not delayed.

Implementation efforts following each step in the planning process help members of the organization to feel they are a part of the planning process. These efforts will also increase the members' identification with and support of the final plan.

If the planning process helps the organization face and resolve the concerns of each phase of the strategic planning process as it is encountered, then the implementation of the strategic plan has an excellent chance of being successful. It can be assumed that with each successive iteration of the planning process, fewer and fewer concerns will be encountered and it will be easier and easier to move directly to the implementation phase.

SUMMARY

Throughout their existence, organizations need to be aware of what is happening in their environments that might affect them. This is especially true during the course of the planning process. Five separate but overlapping environments, in particular, need to be monitored: the macro environment, the industry environment, the competitive environment, the customer environment, and the organization's internal environment. Information about each of these environments must be available during the planning process for drafting the mission statement, formulating the strategic business model, identifying the competition, and so on. The environmental scanning process should be continual, so that the appropriate information about what is happening or about to happen in the various environments is always available. Strategic planning provides an opportune time for a major use of this data.

Although implementation is the final step of the model, throughout the planning process there is a continual need to consider implementation concerns. Also throughout the planning process, there needs to be clear awareness of resources available, the existing culture, and what the competition is up to if planning is not to become an academic exercise. Each phase of applied strategic planning has implementation considerations that should be addressed immediately and not postponed until the final implementation phase.

The only reason for strategic planning is the successful implementation of an action plan. This fact must be perceived by the team members as the critical purpose of the entire process, so that as they work they are constantly aware of moving steadily toward this desired outcome.

REFERENCES

Aaker, D. A. (1983). Using a strategic information scanning system. *California Management Review, 25,* 80–81.

Galbraith, J. R., & Nathanson, D. A. (1978). *Strategy implementation: The role of structure and process.* St. Paul, MN: West.

The greying of the U.S. population. (1983, August 12). *New York Times.*

Naisbitt, J. (1982). *Megatrends: Ten new directions transforming our lives.* New York: Warner Books.

Porter, M. E. (1980). *Competitive strategy: Techniques for analyzing industries and competitors.* New York: Free Press.

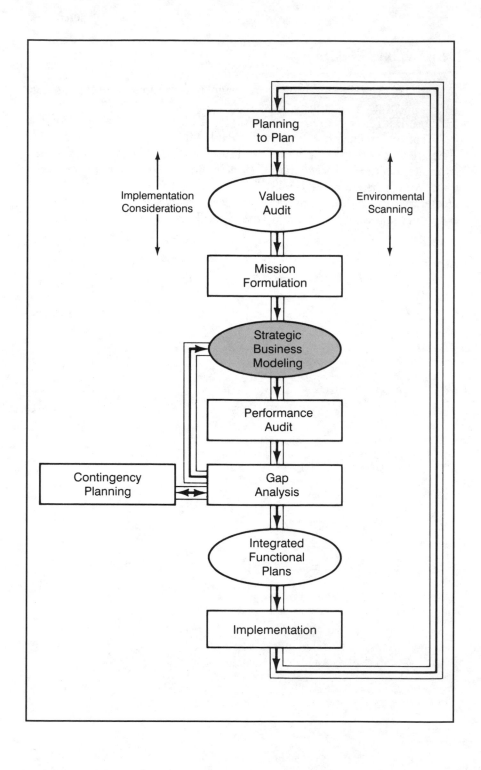

10 STRATEGIC BUSINESS MODELING

Strategic business modeling is the process by which the organization defines success in the context of what business or businesses it wants to be in, how that success will be measured, and what specifically will be done to achieve the success. Strategic business modeling is the most creative aspect of applied strategic planning. Previous steps in the planning process are designed to enable group members to approach strategic business modeling well prepared and free to be creative.

The strategic-business-modeling phase of the Applied Strategic Planning Model provides another point of escape for the frog — or new territories for the bees. Here the planning team is asked to forget about constraints and focus on possibilities. Would it like to jump out of the pan? Take new avenues? And if anyone really believes that a dragon — or any other creature of the imagination — is needed, this is the place to speak up.

The strategic-business-modeling process follows the completion of the mission statement. In this step, time should initially be devoted to defining the organization's desired future, including specific business targets. The future vision of the organization and specific targets that are identified should be congruent with both the values and the major directions defined in the earlier phases of the planning process, especially those spelled out in the mission statement.

The British Airways mission statement is short and sweet, "to make BA the world's favorite airline," but it connotes a great deal. To be the world's favorite anything requires a strong consumer preference. This is especially difficult in air transport, where aircraft, pricing structure, and staffing patterns are almost identical. To achieve this goal requires that priority be given to customer service — from the reservation clerk, through the check-in agent, the ramp agents, the cabin crew, and the luggage handlers. It can be accomplished only through continual training, consistent rewards, and strong management support, all of which become required by the mission statement. British Airways' statement also establishes BA as being in the airline business, not the transportation business — in contrast to Levitt's suggestion to the contrary. No hotels, cruise ships, or the like will display the BA logo in the near future. Instead BA will concentrate on what it knows best, selling airline seats to a cache of continually satisfied customers.

By engaging in strategic business modeling before the performance audit, the planning team will enhance its ability to be creative, since it will not be as unduly influenced by the limitations of the current scope of operations.

The new ideas developed during the strategic-business-modeling phase will be tested later in the gap-analysis phase of our Applied Strategic Planning Model. It is possible, therefore, that many of the ideas generated in this step will never become part of the final strategic plan. Hence, the planning team should be cautioned *not* to communicate tentative ideas, possibilities, and plans prematurely to the rest of the organization. Any discussion of these items should be labeled as "tentative."

Applied strategic planning is distinctly different from long-range planning, and the strategic-business-modeling phase is the point at which these differences are most clear. Long-range planning tends to be merely an extrapolation of what an organization is currently doing. For example, in long-range planning, a furniture manufacturer would plan to sell more units of furniture to consumers through its existing (or expanded) network of retailers, or a service agency would determine that it should open a series of new offices to serve more clients. These plans essentially call for doing more of what is currently being done; the only differences would be variations in or expansions of the type of product or service offered to current or new customers. In contrast, strategic business modeling goes much further. Strategic business modeling actually encourages the frog to jump out of the pan.

In strategic business modeling, key organizational members are asked to conceptualize a series of specific future scenarios. Then they are asked to identify the steps necessary for achieving those scenarios. The advantages of this approach over long-range planning are significant. For example, long-range planning is often myopic and unduly constraining. It is based on an assumption of continuity that is inconsistent with the "discontinuous futures" facing most organizations. The management of discontinuous companies is like playing tennis in the wind; the ball just doesn't go where you aim it (Gallwey, 1979). In addition, working primarily from the perspective of the existing organization often confines future scenarios to the organization's existing customers and marketplace. The result, again, is the boiled frog.

Long-range planning would have dictated a continuation of current marketing activities for British Airways during the summer of 1986, when a series of hijackings and other terrorist activities severely reduced travel by North Americans to Europe. However, the strategic plan of "the world's favorite airline" dictated something rather different. The BA "Get Up, America" campaign, costing several million dollars, involved a raffle giving away, on a Saturday in June, every seat on all BA flights between North America and Great Britain. When BA jumped out of the pan and engineered this highly successful campaign, the result was both an overall increase in trans-Atlantic flights in the next several months and, more importantly, an increased market share for BA.

The challenge of strategic business modeling to *conceptualize* future scenarios is also helpful as a check on decisions to date. Raising questions about what lines of business (LOBs) the organization wants to be in — rather than assuming that the current LOBs are the future LOBs — will enable the planning team to question and discuss the organization's current market practices. IBM's move into the personal-computer business is a case in point. This market required both new capital investments and new marketing and distribution systems, each of which had to be carefully developed in order for this new LOB to become the success it has become for IBM.

KEY CONSIDERATIONS IN STRATEGIC BUSINESS MODELING

Several considerations are critical to the success of the strategic-business-modeling process. The first is the relationship between strategic business modeling and the preceding steps in our Applied Strategic Planning Model. To be effective, the strategic business model must be congruent with and build on the expressed values and the stated mission of the organization. To conceptualize a future that is at odds with the underlying values of key individuals or that is not congruent with the mission statement is to invite failure. To help maintain consistency, the planning team should post the mission statement prominently during strategic business modeling; and business concepts should be regularly tested against the values and mission statements. For example, if the planning-team members propose to enter the consumer electronics industry, as Black and Decker recently did, this proposal would first be tested against the mission statement. Also, as we noted earlier, the BA mission statement keeps it in the airline business and has precluded entry into a variety of related activities. (The subsequent sale of United Airlines' hotel business confirms the risk of straying from the core business.) If the mission statement did notpreclude such a move, this general direction would be further explored. On the other hand, if the mission statement would not permit such a move, the idea would be immediately dropped. Seldom — if ever — should a well-written mission statement be overlooked or rewritten to accommodate potential business ventures.

The second consideration is that strategic business modeling should be done within the context of proactive futuring. Although no one can fully predict the future, significant aspects of the future can be anticipated, a desired end state can be conceptualized, and the organization can work proactively to make this desired future occur. In proactive futuring, the organization takes responsibility for its *own* future. Rather than guessing what the future will bring, through proactive futuring an organization can balance the skills of anticipating the future and managing the organization to attain the desirable goals. Proactive futuring focuses responsibility for the future on leaders and other members of the organization rather than on unseen external forces. The development of disposable diapers, Pampers, by the Procter & Gamble Corporation is an example of proactive futuring. The market for disposable diapers, now a several billion dollar per year industry, simply did not exist prior to the P&G marketing program. But the latent need for such a product had been identified consistently over time by the P&G new-markets group and only required imagination and the courage to develop and bring

Proactive Futuring Comes in Many Guises

the product to market. Procter & Gamble created a different future by its actions. Marketing-driven companies are the most frequently successful organizations in accomplishing such proactive futuring.

A third consideration of effective strategic business modeling is that it should have a creative emphasis. Time should be provided for generating free-flowing ideas that are rich in diversity and that stretch normal limits. Multiple possibilities should be explored, but it is neither realistic nor productive to attempt to explore *all* possibilities. Success in this process is most likely to be found in organizations that maximize creative output *within selected venues*. For example, it is much more productive for a manufacturer of steel fasteners to generate ideas that relate to at least the general areas of manufacturing and the production of comparable products than to generate ideas that emphasize retailing or delivery of services—areas in which the organization has little experience or competence. Since applied strategic planning is such a time-constrained process, such unfocused creativity would be an inappropriate use of time and energy.

However, this is the time to explore conceptually numerous opportunities. Some planning groups have difficulty with being creative about their own futures. Consultant assistance and reaching outside the planning group for creative ideas may be very helpful.

We encourage a "focused-creativity" process at this point. This term refers to the expression of a variety of creative ideas *within the focus* of the key components of the mission statement. If this method is followed, many ideas can be generated; but they need to be congruent with the organizational directions as stated in the mission statement. Focused creativity also serves as a check on the mission statement: If the mission statement fails to provide structure for the process of generating ideas about what business the organization should be in, the mission statement may also lack adequate direction for other areas.

To employ the mission statement as an aid in focusing creativity, the planning team should pull out key words and phrases that are descriptive of the direction that has been set for the organization. These words and phrases will mark the limits of free-flowing creativity so that ideas too far afield will be discarded. For example, if members of a social-service organization generated ideas about the manufacture and distribution of lawn products—

regardless of the attractiveness of such a business—they would simply be wasting time, and the process would be perceived as a useless exercise. What should develop, then, is a variety of ways for the organization to meet its desired goals. Many groups, with proper consultant support, generate lists of more than a hundred business ideas. It is clear—in both research and practice—that the greater the number of ideas, the higher the quality. Once the planning team has developed a variety of ideas, it should select those with the greatest potential for success.

To enhance creativity at this point, the planning-team members can work in brainstorming groups as well as individually. A wide variety of techniques can be employed to develop richer options. For example, in addition to designing the ideal organization, team members may be asked what it would feel like to live in their ideal organization. This softer side can generate insights that will cause the vision of the future to feel real. To further enrich their options, the planning-team members may reach beyond their own membership to other creative people in or outside the organization.

Before the end of this process, the planning team should have identified the proposed ways in which the organization might achieve its quantified business objectives, that is, how the planning elements impact the organization's profitability. These tentative approaches should be developed into a written statement that carries a consensus commitment from the members of the planning team. If this statement is converted to specific percentages of the overall business, then the components of the proposed business model can be expressed visually on a pie chart.

DEFINING THE STRATEGIC PROFILE

An organization's strategic profile is the way in which the organization plans to position itself in its selected marketplace. Components of the strategic profile include orientation toward risk, the approach to competition, and an expression of the critical success indicators.

Orientation Toward Risk

Orientation toward risk results from a mixture of forces. The marketplace may dictate high or low amounts of risk for current inhabitants and potential entrants. High-risk markets tend to be those dominated by two or more leaders that are likely to engage in severe competition with one another. The high costs of entering and/or exiting a market also present a high-risk situation (for example, car rental and airline businesses). If an organization owns facilities that it cannot readily sell, contracts that it must honor, or facilities on which other facets of the organization depend, exiting from a business is more costly than it would be if these encumbrances did not exist. Figure 10-1 illustrates the types of returns that can be expected from businesses with high or low entry or exit barriers. When an organization is contemplating entering a market with these kinds of risks, the decision makers must determine the amount of risk, the payoff for success, and whether the organization could withstand failure in the market. It is clear, for example, that People's Express never adequately assessed the risk involved in the acquisition of Frontier Airlines in 1985. While it did open new

Figure 10-1
Barriers and Profitability

Exit Barriers

		Low	High
Entry Barriers	Low	Low, stable returns	Low, risky returns
	High	High, stable returns	High, risky returns

markets for People's, it exposed the company to a level of debt that it was not able to meet.

Markets dominated by two or more leaders that are engaged in, or that are likely to engage in, severe competition tend to be high-risk areas for all involved. For the leaders, such competition is likely to cut heavily into profitability; price cutting, expensive advertising, and a struggle to maintain or expand carefully guarded market shares increase the risk of failure. For those not in leadership positions in their markets, the future can be treacherous; not only are economies of scale working against organizations with small portions of their markets, but these differences in market portions are magnified by the competition of the market leaders. A good example is the soft-drink market, which has long been dominated by Coke® and Pepsi®. This marketplace sees extensive advertising by the two leaders and constant price cutting by those with smaller market shares. Other entrants into this market — even Seven-Up® — tend to capture only small or unprofitable amounts of the market share or fail entirely. As the leaders compete with each other, the others are left even farther behind with their smaller advertising budgets and more expensive costs of operation.

Orientation toward risk is further defined by forces inside the organization. Internal cash and other reserves facilitate risk taking; so does a strong, diversified organizational market mix. To follow up a prior example, the strong cash position of United Airlines allowed them to purchase, at bargain-basement prices, the "pieces" (the gates, landing slots, and equipment) of the then bankrupt Frontier.

Management must decide its own orientation toward risk. It should ask whether the interests of stakeholders are better served through a more risky (and often potentially more profitable) approach to the marketplace or through a more conservative approach. The risks inherent in a desired marketplace must be carefully assessed. An assessment must also be made of the resources available to support the organization in the risky environment. The desires of key players — and the interests of those they represent — must be honestly evaluated. From this information base, decisions can be made regarding both the selection of a market and also the proposed posture within that market.

Approach to Competition

Another important aspect of strategic business modeling is defining the organization's approach to competition in the markets in which it has decided to compete. Porter's (1980) work in the area of competitive strategy has become the standard in the field. He describes three generic strategies: differentiation, cost leadership, and focus.

- Differentiation — creating something that is perceived in the marketplace as being unique
- Cost leadership — achieving overall cost leadership in an industry through a set of functional policies aimed at delivering products or services at a cost lower than all others in the marketplace
- Focus — focusing on a particular buyer group, segment of the product line, or geographic market

Competition by differentiation requires the development of a unique product or service in the marketplace. Competition on a cost basis is the attempt to consistently offer products or services to customers at costs that are lower than those of the competition. The focus strategy is practiced by carving out a distinct piece of the marketplace — a niche that is readily defensible — and carefully serving that market segment better than the competition does. Focus strategy was exemplified by IBM when it moved into the personal-computer market with its reputation of quality and service.

A strategy of differentiation would require a commitment to marketing, a high degree of creativity, strong research and development skills, and a positive product or service image. Control would be less evident. There would be a drive to encourage product or service innovation that would foster the goal of differentiating the organization from the competition. Mercedes-Benz is a dramatic example of differentiation strategy. Clearly its reputation as both a high-prestige and highly reliable automobile enables MB to price its products at a premium price, one much higher than a simple value-added price would be.

To achieve a competitive advantage within Porter's framework, an organization must make a series of congruent decisions. To achieve a cost advantage, an organization would typically institute tight cost controls, aggressively pursue innovative ways to deliver services or manufacture products at low cost, pursue low-cost distribution systems, and achieve ongoing economies of scale. Tight control, in general, would be typical.

To implement a strategy of focus, careful selection of a market segment is critical. K-Mart has been outstandingly successful as a low-price competitor, saturating the countryside with its outlets. The general upscaling of the consumer marketplace, however, has left K-Mart at a competitive disadvantage. K-Mart has responded with a new, more up-scale image, offering nationally branded merchandise in refurbished stores at a discount price. The potential success of this new strategy is still in question. Having made this selection, the organization would need to develop the appropriate mix of cost and differentiation tactics to achieve leadership.

Alfred Dunhill's philosophy spells out the strategy behind the success of the Dunhill watch. In the words of Dunhill's ads: "It must be useful. It must work dependably. It must be beautiful. It must last. It must be the best of its kind."

Porter believes that it is dangerous to select and concentrate on more than one of these three strategies at the same time. An attempt to be both a cost leader and a differentiated competitor often leaves an organization caught in the middle. Porter gives numerous examples of financial loss or failure that were due to this attempt to combine strategies. One way of understanding the problems of the People's Express acquisition of Frontier is in terms of conflicting market strategies. People's attempted to remake Frontier into its image as the low-cost competitor, lowering its basic fare but charging for meals, beverages, and baggage handling, which resulted in driving off Frontier's repeat, business-person travelers. Discovering that the new strategy resulted in load loss, People's attempted to reverse its strategy, but the business travelers did not return.

In fact, succeeding with one competitive strategy often obviates another strategy. For example, the controls necessary to become an overall cost leader would most likely eliminate the creativity in a differentiation strategy. On the other hand, the expense of marketing and maintaining a well-differentiated product or service often means that the company cannot deliver it to the marketplace in a low-cost manner, thereby negating any hope of cost leadership. Also, the selection of one segment of a market means nonselection of other segments. This aspect of focus strategy will often dictate the related moves regarding cost or differentiation.

In strategic business modeling, an organization must determine how to position itself in reference to competition. As leaders in an organization conceptualize a future, the choice of a competitive strategy is a key aspect of the process. Once the decision is made, this choice further helps to focus the creative process and to identify steps for achieving the desired end state. If, for example, an

Focusing On A Select Segment

organization determines that it wants to be a market leader in the greeting-card business (the desired end state), it must determine whether to position itself as the low-cost seller in greeting cards, differentiate its product line (for instance, by using a particular comic strip character on all its cards), or focus on a select segment of the greeting-card market (such as young adults). It must also determine its capability and willingness to risk organizational resources in achieving the desired leadership in the greeting-card industry.

Establishing *Critical Success Indicators*

As an organization conceptualizes its future, it must identify specific means of measuring both success or failure in reaching that future and the progress toward established goals. These measures, which we call "critical success indicators," are often a mixture of hard financial ratios and soft indicators of attitudes of stakeholders inside and outside the company (see Figures 10-2 and 10-3).

Figure 10-2
Critical Success Indicators — Company A

Critical Success Indicators	1989–1992 Target
1. Profitability	>20%
2. Liquidity	Current on all payables; line of credit equal to 2% of revenue.
3. Compensation-to-Revenue Ratio	1984 rate + 10%
4. Size/Growth	>15% but <20%
5. NPD Reserve	No decrease.
6. Employee Satisfaction	At least as good as 1984 audit.
7. Customer Satisfaction	Develop system for monitoring.
8. Inventory Turnover	No worse than for last 3 years.
9. Marketing-Revenue Ratio	Budget on basis of 1983–85.
10. Income-Tax Rate	<50% of effective tax rate.

Figure 10-3
Critical Success Indicators – Company B

Critical Success Indicators	Annual Target in Five Years
1. Sales Growth	$100 million.
2. Sales per Employee	$100 thousand.
3. Pretax Income	5% of sales.
4. Cash	Equal to pretax income.
5. R & D Expenditures	Not more than 6% of sales.
6. General & Administrative Costs	14% of direct labor rate.
7. Overhead Rate	200% of direct labor rate.
8. Inventory Turnover	3 times a year.
9. Manufacturing Parts	Critical parts: manufacture in house. Others: base on cost.

Dozens of measures (such as new-product introduction, increased market share, revenue, and profits) can be selected to track progress toward goals. Measures selected during strategic business modeling should be relevant to the organization's mission, to the business the organization will engage in, and to those who are responsible for achieving the defined goals. A limit on the number of measures will facilitate tracking. When all the indicators are selected, they should then be listed in the order of their importance. They will also be used to describe the desired targeted levels of success at the end of the strategic planning cycle (three, four, or five years in the future). Critical success indicators, like gauges on the dashboard of an automobile, need to monitor truly important functions. Too few gauges or poorly calibrated gauges result in missing key indicators. By contrast, too many gauges or calibrations that are too complex can cause available data to be lost.

Critical success indicators need to be prioritized to assure that the most important indicators will be used and closely monitored when decisions are made. For example, if profitability is a key feature of the mission statement, then it should show up as a high-priority critical success indicator. For some companies the effective tax rate may be of great importance. According to the *Wall Street Journal* (1985, p. 28), "128 of 250 large, profitable corporations studied paid no taxes in at least one of the last three years, and 53 percent of the companies had an average tax rate over the three-year period of less than 12 percent." For example, the president of Sara Lee, who describes himself as "unintimidated by taxes" is "taking advantage of so-called safe-harbor leasing programs that allowed profitable companies to shelter profits by buying tax benefits from companies with no use for them . . . he reduced Sara Lee's tax rate to about 6 percent, among the lowest of GMA's food processor members" (*Fortune*, 1985, p. 136). Prioritization of success indicators should be achieved through consensus of all of the planning-team members, so that later support and careful goal setting are ensured.

Figure 10-4 provides common financial ratios that may be applied across most organizations. These ratios are divided into four orientations: liquidity, profitability, activity, and leverage. It is desirable to select a number of success indicators that will reflect each of these dimensions.

Output measures that are not reflected in these financial ratios include industry-specific indicators such as promotion-return analysis (for direct-mail companies), warranty work (for manufacturers), test scores (for educational institutions), and recidivism rates (for correctional facilities). Relevant indicators are best selected after careful study of the business in question. The measures selected should supplement financial ratios in an effort to describe the selected future and in regular and periodic monitoring of progress toward that future. The list of indicators is idiosyncratic to each organization and should be tailored carefully.

Soft indicators are also important. These include the image in the marketplace, attitudes of employees, and satisfaction of stakeholders. Although such measures are frequently hard to gather with a high degree of accuracy, they often represent a major variable in the success or failure of an organization. The image of IBM as a service-oriented company, sincerely dedicated to its customers, has been an important factor in its continual success, as is Hewlett-Packard's image as a strong technology leader with a committed, happy work force.

Figure 10-4   Financial Ratios

RATIO	FORMULA	HOW EXPRESSED
1. Liquidity Ratios		
Current ratio	$\dfrac{\text{Current assets}}{\text{Current liabilities}}$	Decimal
Quick (acid test) ratio	$\dfrac{\text{Current assets} - \text{Inventory}}{\text{Current liabilities}}$	Decimal
2. Profitability Ratios		
Net profit margin	$\dfrac{\text{Net profit before taxes}}{\text{Net sales}}$	Percentage
Gross margin	$\dfrac{\text{Sales} - \text{Cost of sales}}{\text{Net sales}}$	Percentage
Return on investment (ROI)	$\dfrac{\text{Net profit before taxes}}{\text{Total assets}}$	Percentage
Return on equity (ROE)	$\dfrac{\text{Net profit after taxes}}{\text{Average Equity}}$	Percentage
Earnings per Share (EPS)	$\dfrac{\text{Net profit after taxes} - \text{Preferred burdens}}{\text{Average number of common shares}}$	Dollar per share
Productivity of Assets	$\dfrac{\text{Gross Income} - \text{Taxes}}{\text{Equity}}$	Percentage
3. Activity Ratios		
Inventory turnover	$\dfrac{\text{Net Sales}}{\text{Inventory}}$	Decimal
Net working capital turnover	$\dfrac{\text{Net sales}}{\text{Net working capital}}$	Decimal
Asset turnover	$\dfrac{\text{Sales}}{\text{Total assets}}$	Decimal
Average collection period	$\dfrac{\text{Accounts receivable}}{\text{Sales for year} \div 365}$	Days
Accounts payable period	$\dfrac{\text{Accounts Payable}}{\text{Purchases for year} \div 365}$	Days
Cash turnover	$\dfrac{\text{Cash}}{\text{Net sales for year} \div 365}$	Days
Days of inventory	$\dfrac{\text{Inventory}}{\text{Cost of goods sold} \div 365}$	Days
Price earning ratio	$\dfrac{\text{Market price per share}}{\text{Earnings per share}}$	Ratio
4. Leverage ratios		
Debt ratio	$\dfrac{\text{Total debt}}{\text{Total assets}}$	Percentage
Times interest earned	$\dfrac{\text{Profit before taxes} + \text{Interest charges}}{\text{Interest charges}}$	Decimal
Coverage of fixed charges	$\dfrac{\text{Profit before taxes} + \text{Interest charges} + \text{Lease charges}}{\text{Interest charges} + \text{Lease obligations}}$	Decimal
Current liabilities to equity	$\dfrac{\text{Current liabilities}}{\text{Equity}}$	Percentage

From Wheelan & Hunger, *Strategic Management & Business Policy*, © 1983, Addison-Wesley, Reading, Massachusetts. Pp. 28–29, Table 2.1. Reprinted with permission.

At the end of the strategic-business-modeling phase, the planning team should have developed a strategic business model that consists of the following:

- A strategic profile, including a risk orientation and an approach to the competition
- A clear, prioritized list of indicators of success with defined end-of-planning-period targets
- A set of statements and a graphic representation to identify the proposed lines of business

All of these pieces should be developed through consensus and should be clearly stated in writing. This information will be valuable in the next two phases (performance audit and gap analysis) of our Applied Strategic Planning Model.

SUMMARY

Strategic business modeling is the process by which the organization more specifically defines success in the context of the business(es) it wants to be in, how that success will be measured, and what will be done to achieve it, while remaining consistent with the mission statement. The strategic-business-modeling phase is the point at which differences between applied strategic planning and long-range planning are most clear. Strategic business modeling requires a conceptualization of specific futures and ways to achieve those futures.

An organization's strategic profile is the way in which the organization plans to position itself in its selected marketplace. Components of the strategic profile include orientation toward risk, the approach to competition, and an expression of the critical success indicators. Strategic business modeling is a point at which the frog has an opportunity to jump out of the pan, and this process clearly encourages it to do so.

REFERENCES

Cheers for tax reform. (1985, September 16). *Fortune*, pp. 135–36.
Corporate income-tax mystery. (1985, April 2). *Wall Street Journal*, p. 28.
Gallwey, W. T. (1979). *The inner game of tennis*. New York: Bantam.
Porter, M. E. (1980). *Competitive strategy: Techniques for analyzing industries and competitors*. New York: Free Press.

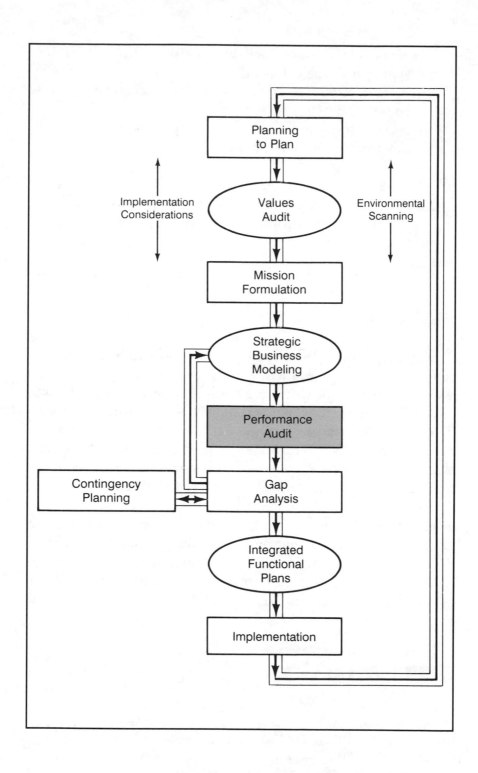

11 THE PERFORMANCE AUDIT

Having envisioned the future the strategic planning team wants to achieve, the team must now establish a clear view of the organization's current performance in a process called the performance audit. This concerted effort involves a simultaneous study of internal strengths and weaknesses of the organization and an effort to identify significant factors outside the organization that may positively or negatively impact the organization's ability to achieve its desired future. The acronym SWOT refers to *strengths* and *weaknesses* (internal factors) and *opportunities* and *threats* (external factors) that must be considered in an effective performance audit.

The performance audit is of critical importance in the applied strategic planning process. The "jumping out of the pan" and the "focused creativity" encouraged in strategic business modeling has likely resulted in some potentially exciting goals. The purpose of the performance audit is to establish the benchmark of capability against which these goals can be tested. Failure to do an adequate performance audit could result in a false sense of security—a belief that the organization is more capable of reaching its goals than it really is. This could lead to serious errors in the process of establishing final strategic goals — and possibly failure to achieve these goals. It is difficult to find a more apt example of a failure to do an adequate performance audit than the previously cited acquisition of Frontier Airlines by People's Express. People's Express simply did not assess the risks involved or their capacity for coping with these risks, which led to a resounding failure of the strategic plan, the bankruptcy of Frontier, and a "forced" merger of People's Express with Texas Air.

THE INTERNAL VIEW

The internal performance audit is an assessment of current organizational strengths and weaknesses. It is accomplished by gathering and studying a wide variety of performance indicators. The audit includes an analysis of current resources — financial and human resources, products or services offered, production capacity, and so on. It also includes a management audit, with a look at current human resources in the organization and an examination of how decisions are made and by whom. The internal performance audit encourages an examination of how the organization *does* business, not just how business is doing. The case of a medium-sized electronics jobber illustrates such issues. Owned by two partners, the organization had grown to $20 million in annual revenues. The partner who had been responsible for managing the internal operations of the company lost interest in the business following a heart attack, abdicating his management role without arranging to have it filled. The performance audit revealed the decay of internal controls and management, all of which required a reconstituting of the corporation.

A comprehensive internal performance audit is very time consuming. In organizations that already maintain numerous outcome measures, the audit will take less time. Complex organizations and organizations that do not routinely track such information will need more time for the performance audit. Time will also vary according to the planning-team members' ability to agree on what the data mean. Discussions of the data are prone to be stretched out, depending on individual defensiveness, the ability of key players to give and receive feedback, and the willingness to grapple with "unhappy truths."

The internal performance audit needs to cover at least four key areas:

1. The critical success indicators identified in the strategic-business-modeling phase of planning
2. An internal resource analysis
3. An analysis of the current way of doing business
4. An external analysis of the business

Critical Success Indicators

Where is the organization in relation to strategic-business-modeling indicators? The first step in the internal performance audit is to analyze each existing LOB (line of business) in the context of both the total organization and also the SBUs (strategic business units). The electronics jobber cited in the prior example actually had three lines of business, each of which could be managed as an individual business unit: lab-designed services for customers, constructing and equipping the customers' labs, and ongoing servicing of customers' labs, including maintenance and providing supplies. The LOBs should also be analyzed in relation to the critical success indicators (CSIs) established during the strategic-business-modeling phase of the planning process. Much of this analysis and data gathering will be done outside the meeting setting. A checklist should be created to identify what data must be collected, who is responsible, and the dates on which this information is needed. Failure to be specific with assignments can lead to frustration, haphazard collection or arrangement of data, lost time, and less solid decision making.

Sufficient time must be allotted to data gathering to allow this considerable amount of work to be accomplished. Data *must* be ready when the planning team meets, and members must be held responsible for completing their homework. They must not use valuable group time to explain noncompletion of assigned tasks.

The planning team should develop an analysis sheet for each LOB to obtain a quick, clear view of the current state of the LOB.

(This information will be used again during the gap-analysis phase.) For each LOB the critical success indicators should be listed; and after sufficient data are collected, the current state of each CSI should be determined and recorded. Table 11-1 illustrates the way a work sheet can be used to analyze critical success indicators. (For examples of other indicators, see Figures 10-2 and 10-3.)

After all the work sheets are completed, the planning team should concentrate on one CSI at a time and share their comments. When a consensus is reached for the targeted level, the work sheet should be altered to reflect the consensus opinion.

Internal Resource Analysis

The internal resource analysis is the process of examining the organization's strengths and weaknesses, the first two elements of SWOT. The purpose of this effort is to identify the weaknesses that need to be managed or avoided as the plan is formulated and also the strengths that can be capitalized on in accomplishing the desired future. It is a good idea at this point to examine the frog's situation and determine some of its options.

Table 11-1
An Example of a Work Sheet for Analyzing Critical Success Indicators

Indicator	Current Level	Time Period Reflected	Comments/ Clarification	Targeted Level
Pre-tax Profitability	9%	8/1/87– 7/31/88	Reflects upsurge in market due to recovery from inflation; 9% is an increase over 7% the previous year with little effort on the organization's part.	12%

Many organizations experience some problems in analyzing their internal resources. These problems may be due to the inability to identify weaknesses honestly and to manage the defenses that may surround them. Often a general myopia occurs when members of an internal strategic planning team identify strengths and weaknesses. This lack of perspective comes from being too close to the items being discussed. Situations that have been in place for years may be overlooked or underestimated in regard to their positive or negative impact. Perhaps the fire-breathing dragon has always been considered a strength when it should have been considered a weakness. In fact, entire areas of weakness or strength may be overlooked. This is a point at which an external consultant or facilitator could become a valuable asset to the members of the planning team, pushing them to deal with areas that might otherwise be neglected.

Few people are excited by focusing on weaknesses, which are often associated with falling short or failure to meet goals. Naturally,

**Some Companies Have Problems
Identifying Weaknesses**

these weaknesses are not prized in most organizations. A particular weakness may be *associated* with a particular person — or may *be* that person, a factor that makes it difficult to clearly identify weaknesses or to plan the organization's future in light of them. Often a planning team will understate weaknesses or even avoid identifying them, thereby creating a serious flaw in the planning process. In the case of the electronics jobber, the most important, and difficult, part of the performance audit was that of surfacing the problem of the "reluctant" partner. This was initially raised in a meeting with the two partners and the strategic planning consultant. Although initially both partners resisted the data, once it was clearly highlighted both were relieved to have matters clarified and a course of resolution identified.

The review of strengths can also be problematic if they are understated or overstated by planning-team members who do not have a clear perception of them.

Rather than merely identifying strengths and weaknesses as a means of establishing a current picture for the strategic planning process, the applied strategic planning team begins immediately to use this information. While the planning process continues, the organization is encouraged not to accept weak elements, but to begin to shore them up immediately. For example, if the internal fiscal reporting system is considered weak because of slowness in getting monthly MIS reports in the hands of management, immediate efforts must be made to speed up the accurate processing and distribution of these critical data. Historically, planners accepted such problems as planning realities and took no action. Today, most organizations cannot afford the luxury of allowing this exposure to continue without action for months or longer as planning progresses.

A solution to the potential problem of not adequately discussing weaknesses and strengths is to reach outside the planning team, for example, by asking a sample of management and nonmanagement employees what they see as the strengths and weaknesses of the organization. In the case of the reluctant partner, it was the internal staff who identified the underlying problem to the consultant, hesitantly at first and then with a real sense of relief. Individual interviews may be appropriate if the sample is a small group of people, whereas larger groups may require the use of a short, written survey. In addition to the likely discovery of previously unidentified strengths or weaknesses, a fringe benefit of these data from employees is the identification of patterns of belief regarding the internal resources. These patterns may point to areas of relatively greater strengths and weaknesses. Additionally, in the case of a written survey, if the survey is properly introduced and results are reported to employees, the employees will more closely identify with the strategic planning process.

Internal Business Analysis

Several concepts and tools have been developed in the past two decades that can help the planning team understand the current state of the organization and how business is being done. We will discuss several that are most useful in the performance-audit phase of applied strategic planning.

Life Cycle Data   Lines of products or given services progress through a series of stages identified as a life cycle. Basically, the stages are introduction, growth, maturity, and decline. These stages are represented graphically and descriptively in Figure 11-1. The concept of life cycle is useful in several aspects of the internal-business-analysis portion of the applied strategic planning process, including identifying what stage of the cycle each LOB is in and what stage key products or services are in. For example, the life-cycle data developed by a medium-sized publisher revealed that over 80 percent of its "back list" (titles in print) were more than four years old and there were only two potentially successful titles currently in press. Since the life cycle of its products was typically less than five years, it became clear that this company did not have enough product either currently available or in development to reach its business growth objectives. This analysis led to the

Figure 11-1
Stages and Implications of Product Life Cycle

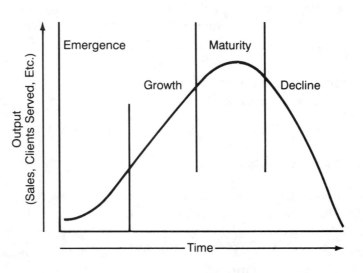

Descriptions	Stage			
	Emergence	**Growth**	**Maturity**	**Decline**
Growth Rate	Accelerating	Faster than GNP	Equal to or slower than GNP	Declining
Number of Competitors	Increasing Rapidly	Increasing; then Shakeout	Stable	Declining
Market Shares	Volatile	Movement Among Top Players	Fixed	Fixed (except for exits)
Customer Behavior	Naive Trial	Trial based on Product Attributes	Price-conscious; Knowledge-able	Price-conscious; Knowledge-able
Profitability	Low	High	High	Usually Low
Cash Flow	–	–	+	Varies

decision to acquire a small publisher with a strong emphasis on acquisitions in order to achieve the growth desired.

Essentially, the relevant output data (sales, clients served, and so on) are examined to determine historical patterns. Members of the planning team should answer the questions independently and then work toward a consensus as to where in the life cycle each product or LOB finds itself. There may well be variance among LOBs. It may be helpful to seek assistance from an outside consultant if significant disagreement results from team discussion. Often an outsider can help identify patterns that insiders find difficult to see.

Who/What/How   Simple models are often among the most potent. The "who, what, how" model discussed in Chapters 5, 8, and 12 (also shown in Figure 11-2) is a prime example. The model requires one to examine key lines of business to determine *who* is

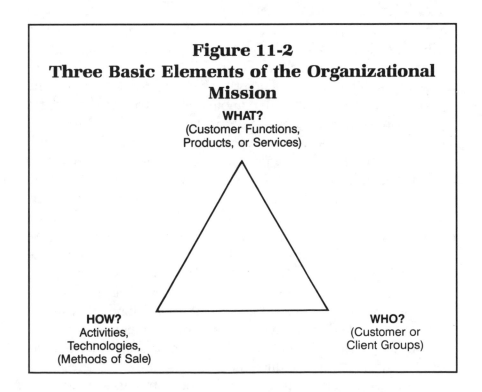

Figure 11-2
Three Basic Elements of the Organizational Mission

WHAT?
(Customer Functions, Products, or Services)

HOW?
Activities, Technologies, (Methods of Sale)

WHO?
(Customer or Client Groups)

served (or who buys the product or service). It next asks *what* is sold or delivered: "What is the product or service?" Finally it asks, "*How* is the product or service delivered?" As shown in the next chapter ("Gap Analysis"), it is extremely risky to change more than one point of this model at any one time. For example, when the Benihana restaurant chain introduced a line of frozen oriental dinners to extend its market, it considered developing a line of plastic chopsticks to package with the products, but because it had no experience in manufacturing or selling such items the company decided not to pursue the idea. Changing the what and the how simultaneously could have severely limited Benihana's chance of success.

The who/what/how analysis should be performed independently by each member of the planning team; then planning-team decisions should be developed for each key LOB. This information will become valuable during the gap analysis.

Portfolio Analysis   Several tools have been developed to enable an organization to analyze its various lines of business. The earliest, simplest, and now classic model is the one developed by the Boston Consulting Group (see Figure 11-3). This model examines LOBs on two dimensions, market growth and market share. The market-share axis indicates the amount of the market share, from low to high, commanded by the particular product being analyzed. The market-growth axis indicates the potential for product growth in terms of future sales. A product that is low in both existing market share and potential for market growth is called a "dog," and what one does with an old, ailing dog is put it out of its misery. Products that are low in market growth but high in market share are called "cash cows"; obviously, one milks these. Products that are low in market share but that have growth potential need to be developed; these are the "problem children" or question marks. If they can be developed efficiently, so that they have high market share and high market growth, they become "stars." If not, they should be dropped. Marketing energy is best put into shining the stars.

Although the analogy is weak in places, the model permits clear identification of the differences among lines of business and has been used effectively to develop business strategies appropriate

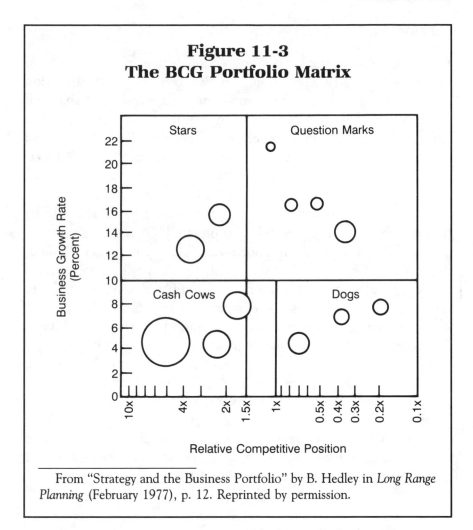

Figure 11-3
The BCG Portfolio Matrix

From "Strategy and the Business Portfolio" by B. Hedley in *Long Range Planning* (February 1977), p. 12. Reprinted by permission.

to each line. The electronics jobber had virtually 100 percent market share in its design and installation business, because there were very few other organizations with its unique combination of services. There was little opportunity for increased market share. Growth depended on a general growth in the electronics industry, not too likely at that time. On the other hand, its service and maintenance business (high balance and lower profit) could easily increase its market share through aggressive marketing and pric-ing—a decision that paid off in both increased revenues and profits.

Distinctive Competency

Almost all organizations function in competitive environments. To succeed — especially when compared to others — an organization should develop a distinctive competency (an advantage) that will enable it to differentiate itself from others in its field. It should then exploit that distinctive competency. The electronics jobber had distinctive competence as a complete "cradle-to-the-grave" designer-installer-servicer of electronic test laboratories. On the other hand, K-Mart is distinctively competent in low-cost distribution.

Ideally, the distinctive competency should be determined by the time the mission statement is formulated. Even so, it should be reviewed during the performance audit. This competency is sometimes obvious, but in other cases — although it may be very much in existence — identifying it will require careful analysis of examples of the organization's success in competitive situations. If a pattern keeps emerging in one success after another, this would be a distinctive competency. The success of Procter & Gamble as a marketing organization with an in-depth understanding of the consumer market and its needs is an example of a distinctive competency. Unfortunately, many organizations lack any clearly distinctive competency. If no distinctive competency can readily be identified, the planning team may need to consider how to develop one. The lack of a distinctive competency limits the organization's ability to differentiate itself in the marketplace.

THE EXTERNAL VIEW

The second major aspect of the performance audit is an examination of the world outside the organization. No organization functions in a vacuum; no organization can succeed without customers, clients, or consumers of its efforts. No organization functions without some impact from other organizations in the form of competition, collaboration, or regulation. Here, again, is a chance to look at the frog's options.

The external view is concerned with the last two categories of SWOT: opportunities and threats. As the planning-team members study competitors, customers, economic trends, and governmental regulation, they must keep in mind that they are trying to identify both threats to the organization and opportunities on which the organization might capitalize. Many planning teams find it difficult to identify opportunity. They typically seem to be much more adept at identifying threats in the environment than opportunities. The planning team may thus find itself most in need of assistance from a consultant at this point. It is often very helpful to reach outside the planning group to others within or outside the organization to enrich the identification of opportunities.

Normally, changes in the market have required internally focused organizations to become *market driven*. In recent years seemingly impervious organizations such as utilities, hospitals, universities, and automobile manufacturers are finding their whole futures dictated by forces outside their own structures. The changes in British Airways have been driven by changes in the airline industry, which has moved from a bureaucratic, controlled industry to a market-driven industry. These changes were intensified in the case of British Airways as it also moved from governmental ownership to a publicly owned corporation in 1987.

The strategic planning team members must devote significant energy to the examination of pertinent forces in the external environment. No plans should be developed without careful study of such external forces as deregulation, demographic shifts, changing markets, and so on. Few plans will work if they do not address both the threats and opportunities that exist in the environment within which the organization must function.

Within the applied strategic planning process, the organization must look outside itself, especially during the performance audit and also during the ongoing environmental scanning process. The data developed in that scanning process, plus other in-depth studies, need to be analyzed during the performance audit. Particular emphasis should be placed on long-term and/or down-board thinking. It is not sufficient to understand what is happening *today*. The planning team needs to be trying to anticipate what will happen one, three, or four years from now. British Airways not only has had to consider the immediate market situation, especially on its North Atlantic routes, but it has had to consider the future as well. What new entrants will test the market? Where are emerging markets? What will present competitors be doing to meet the new marketing initiatives and how will these moves be countered? Clearly, just thinking about the present is not adequate for true strategic planning.

Performing the Analysis of External Forces

In the applied strategic planning process, the look at external forces should be a part of the work of the planning team. As was the case with the internal view, the team may need help. Unlike the internal process, in which the planning team could actively involve the organization employees in gathering data, it is less clear whom to involve in gathering data on the external environment. Organizations usually have less data, and less of a grasp, on the external environment than on the internal environment. Like internal data, external data may well be fraught with bias; but external data are also usually much less complete.

Some organizations put a great deal of energy into tracking external environmental issues such as customer needs, market trends, and relevant legislative activity. Such data can offer an excellent starting point for the external view. The individuals tasked with data gathering will become real assets in the planning process; they may be rich sources of data in areas beyond those with which they normally deal. Similarly, organizations with significant customer contact may have a rich source of data with which to work on developing an applied strategic plan based on customer need.

An effective marketing group within the organization may be most helpful to the external study of the performance audit. This group may already be tracking competitor activity, identifying client desires, and accumulating data on products or services that sell well for the organization. Unfortunately, in many organizations, marketing people are not involved in the strategic planning process. Although we are not advocating that marketing do strategic planning, we definitely are advocating the use of all the expertise available to maximize the quality of decision making. Overlooking potentially pertinent data is not prudent!

Organizations that lack current resources to gather useful data from external sources will need to build, borrow, or buy this talent as soon as possible. Our strong preference is to have internal people maintain control of the process, understand it, and interpret the results of data gathering. The skills in monitoring the environment should also become a regular part of organization development.

Looking at the Competition

Of special importance to organizational viability and success is monitoring the competitive environment, that is, keeping track of those organizations that do provide or could provide substitute goods and services to the same marketplace. Without systematically and thoroughly monitoring this competitive environment, organizations are at direct risk. Competitors typically attempt to increase

Use Skill In Developing Countermoves

their shares of the market by taking customers away from other organizations. Without an early-warning system to detect such competitive strategies and without skills to develop adequate countermoves, an organization may lose significant market shares and resources, thus threatening its continued health or even survival.

Michael Porter (1980), America's foremost analyst of competitive strategy, has argued that there are five basic forces that determine the intensity of competition in any industry:

1. Intensity of rivalry among existing competitors
2. Threat of new entrants
3. Bargaining power of buyers
4. Bargaining power of suppliers
5. Pressure from substitute products or service

Although all five forces should be considered in monitoring the competitive environment, they may be prioritized in terms of potential impact and importance for each organization. Because an understanding of these forces is essential to a successful monitoring of the competitive environment, each will be briefly examined here.

1. Existing Competitors   Competition among existing organizations, the most easily recognized and understood of the five forces, typically takes the familiar form of price wars ("Special this week only: new lower prices!"), competitive advertising campaigns ("Where's the beef?"), new product introductions ("Macintosh, the computer you already know how to use"), and increased customer service or warranties (such as those by U.S. automobile manufacturers).

Rivalry increases because one organization feels pressure to improve its position or sees an opportunity to do so. In most cases, a competitive move by one organization precipitates a countermove by the other(s) most threatened by this action. This sets off an escalating pattern of moves and countermoves that often leaves all the organizations in the industry worse off than had initially been the case.

The negative effect of increased rivalry is especially true when the principal competitive strategy is pricing. Price cuts are typically matched by the competitors (consider the price wars in such deregulated industries as long-distance telephone service). Another example of price wars has occurred in the airline industry. When Continental West announced that it would start flying to the West Coast, it offered the lowest bargain fares in the market in more than three years. Many other airlines responded with lower fares as well (Castro, 1985).

Advertising wars and other competitive strategies, however, often produce increased customer demand and benefit the entire industry.

2. Potential Entrants　The second competitive force is that posed by potential entrants into the industry. New entrants bring new vigor, new resources, and a strong desire to gain a market share. Sometimes these entrants are new organizations; more often they are large organizations that are seeking new opportunities for growth in a related business (such as Procter & Gamble's entrance into the frozen-citrus-juice industry with its new brand, Citrus Hill) or in an unrelated business (such as Mobil Oil's acquisition of Montgomery Ward). Since a competitor may enter the scene from some unexpected quarter, the planning team needs to consider potential sources of new entrants into the industry.

In considering such potential entrants, the planning team needs to recognize that there are barriers to entry that may make the industry resistant to incursions by outsiders. These include economies of scale, capital requirements, product differentiation, switching costs, access to distribution channels, cost disadvantages, and governmental policy (see Figure 11-4). In general, economies of scale for manufacturing, operation, and so on are possible only during the mature phase of the product's life cycle. Thus, getting started is expensive and unprofitable; in addition to capital requirements, the business will have to stick with the entry process for some length of time. Product differentiation is opposed by established brands and consumer brand loyalty that may be difficult to change. Other barriers to entry are the additional costs that potential buyers would incur if they switched to an entrant's products or services. For example, consider the time and psychological costs in

Figure 11-4
Barriers and Profitability

Exit Barriers

		Low	High
	Low	Low, stable returns	Low, risky returns
Entry Barriers	High	High, stable returns	High, risky returns

switching one's personal physician, dentist, or accountant. On a corporate level, consider the difficulties of the Bell system's oper-ating companies, which had been accustomed to simply marketing products manufactured by Western Electric, its captive manufac-turer. The companies had to learn what was available in the competitive market place — from Rohm and Haas, from Northern Telecom, from Ericsonn, and others — not simply negotiate con-tracts to serve their customers' needs.

Still another barrier to entry is access to distribution channels. Nowhere is this more apparent than in retail businesses, where prime shelf space is the continual object of fierce competition. The entrant faces cost disadvantages other than economies of scale. The most important of these is the learning or experience curve in operating a particular kind of organization in a particular kind of industry. Costs decline only as workers and managers gradually become more efficient. Another entry barrier may be governmental policy, especially in those businesses that are regulated to some degree by government agencies or regulations. For example, the federal government limits the number of media outlets (TV, radio, and newspapers) that an individual or organization can own, totally and in combination, to prevent a single organization or person from monopolizing a given market. In the same way, grants from federal and state governments are frequently specifically limited to particular groups (for example, not-for-profit organizations or current grantees).

In addition to entry barriers, there are exit barriers — obstacles that keep organizations in competition even when they would prefer to leave the industry. These exit barriers include specialized assets, such as factories or equipment that have low liquidation value; fixed costs of exit, such as long-term labor contracts or long-term magazine subscriptions that must be fulfilled; strategic interrelationships between the business unit and other units in the company that provide parts or raw materials, image, financing, and so on; emotional barriers, which include pride or loyalty; and governmental or social restrictions to closing down.

The planning team should also look at its own organization with regard to the ease or difficulty of exiting its particular markets. This will provide important information for the performance audit. Pertinent questions would include the following: Is the organization in markets that would be difficult to exit? How deeply entrenched in current markets is the organization? If the organization exited a given market, what might the consequences be on the image of the organization — its perceived reliability, stability, competence, and so on? Would exiting one market positively or negatively affect the organization's products or services in its other markets?

Although entry and exit barriers may be independent, their combined levels affect the level of threat from potential entrants. Where both entry and exit barriers are low, there will always be a high number of potential entrants (for example, Mexican restaurants). With low entry barriers and high exit barriers, there will be fewer potential entrants but not as few as with high entry and low exit barriers. The risk of potential entrants is highest and, of course, the number of entrants lowest when both entry and exit barriers are high.

3. Bargaining Power of Buyers   As Porter (1980) points out, buyers shape the desirability of a marketplace by attempting to drive down prices, by demanding concessions, by insisting on higher quality or additional services, and by playing suppliers off against one another. All of these activities impact the profitability of the industry. This form of competition is typically not recognized by organizations, yet it becomes very important when there is a large-scale buyer or group of buyers representing a significant portion of the organization's revenues.

The federal government is attempting to increase its bargaining power as the largest purchaser of health care through Medicare. Sears is noted for its strong control over those manufacturers who produce merchandise for Sears's private label. Porter's analysis strongly suggests that the environmental scanning process needs to monitor the organization's customers, especially changes in customer patterns, in a fairly careful fashion as part of the competitive environment.

4. Bargaining Power of Suppliers   Not only do buyers compete with an industry, but so do suppliers. Suppliers can impact an industry by raising or threatening to raise prices or by reducing the quality or availability of goods or services. Such moves, of course, dramatically impact profitability, especially when the industry cannot raise prices enough to cover the increased cost. The potential impact of suppliers on an industry increases when the supply is dominated by a few vendors, when there are few substitutes for what is provided, when the industry is not a major customer of the supplier group, and so on. The impact of the OPEC cartel on those businesses producing petroleum-based products, such as plastics, is an example of the important role suppliers play as part of the competitive environment. The behavior of suppliers thus requires routine surveillance as part of the ongoing environmental scanning.

5. Substitute Products or Services   All organizations compete with organizations offering substitute products or services. The degree to which there are clear alternatives to the offered products or services puts a ceiling on the prices that an organization can set for those goods or services. The increase in sales of poultry and fish when the price of beef becomes "too high" is a case in point. The determination of what are reasonable substitutes from the consumers' point of view and the relative availability and price of those substitutes should be considered in monitoring the competitive environment. The manufacturers of Cross ballpoint pens, for example, discovered that a "reasonable substitute" for their pens was not a less expensive pen, as one might expect, but other slightly less expensive gifts, such as leather wallets. They discovered that their major market was people or organizations who were buying gifts — not people who were interested in buying writing instruments.

Sources of information about the competitive environment include published materials such as the competitors' annual reports, trade and industry publications, government reports, patent records, speeches made by executives and managers of competitors, and so on. There are a variety of human sources as well. The customers, vendors, and distributors of one's competitors are often excellent sources of information about competitors' current and future strategies, as are their advertising agencies. Another prime source of information is ex-employees. Some organizations actively recruit new employees from their major competitors primarily as an information source about the competitors' future plans. One major competitor of IBM is proud of its reputation as a home for IBM "retreads" and is always actively recruiting new transfers from "Big Blue."

"Shopping" the competition is another useful, informal source of information; this may include purchasing goods from a competitor and engaging in reverse engineering to learn more about the competitor's material and methods of production. For example, U.S. military forces have purchased captured Russian military equipment from Israel in order to conduct reverse engineering studies and field trials with the Russian equipment. Obviously, many companies are unlikely to cooperate with sharing strategic information with their competitors, and many may actively attempt to prevent their competitors from learning about their present and future strategies. Nevertheless, as we have pointed out, there are ways to obtain a good deal of useful and pertinent information without resorting to unethical or illegal practices.

Scanning the competitive environment is a complex task, and there are aspects of the competitive surroundings in which an organization works that are frequently overlooked. Down-board thinking (described in Chapter 5 as analogous to the way world-class chess players think) is extremely important in planning competitive strategies. The planning team not only must decide on its immediate move, but it must plan ahead for a number of possible moves down board in anticipation of countermoves from the competition. (What it must *not* do is plan to make no move — and become a boiled frog!) Comprehensive, in-depth monitoring of the competitive environment should be high on the management's list of tasks, both for planning and for everyday management.

Figure 11-5 illustrates some key components of the five-pronged competitor analysis framework developed by Porter. The questions it poses can form the basis for an analysis that can be tailored to a particular organization's competitive universe.

The General Environment

Organizations function in an environment that can be readily divided into two parts: (1) the general economic, social, and political environment; and (2) the organization-specific environment. Both are critical to understanding external forces impacting the organization.

Although it is important to be aware of national economic and political trends, it is also valuable to focus on regional economic and sociocultural trends. For example, an organization can find itself functioning simultaneously in a *national* economy in which interest rates are moderate, business good, and the outlook optimistic and in a *region* where — because of its agricultural or industrial focus — the economy is down, unemployment is high, and loans are hard to obtain. For example, sales for national retail chains such as Sears and J.C. Penny's were depressed in the early 1980s in those states with an agriculture-based economy, although sales were generally strong elsewhere.

In the performance audit, the examination of the general environment helps planners understand which important forces

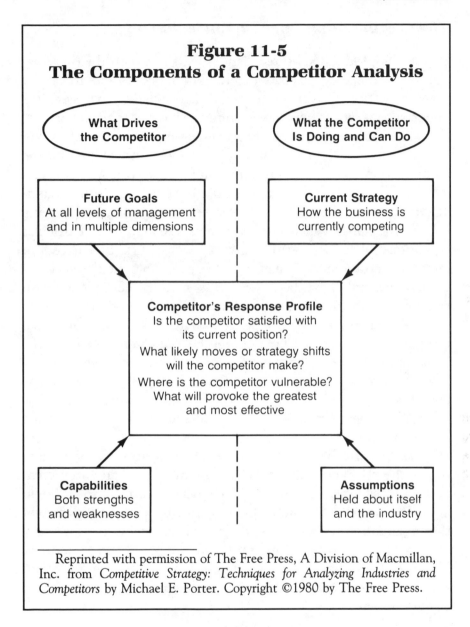

Figure 11-5
The Components of a Competitor Analysis

What Drives
the Competitor

What the Competitor
Is Doing and Can Do

Future Goals
At all levels of management
and in multiple dimensions

Current Strategy
How the business is
currently competing

Competitor's Response Profile
Is the competitor satisfied with
its current position?
What likely moves or strategy shifts
will the competitor make?
Where is the competitor vulnerable?
What will provoke the greatest
and most effective

Capabilities
Both strengths
and weaknesses

Assumptions
Held about itself
and the industry

Reprinted with permission of The Free Press, A Division of Macmillan, Inc. from *Competitive Strategy: Techniques for Analyzing Industries and Competitors* by Michael E. Porter. Copyright ©1980 by The Free Press.

impact the organization today and which may significantly impact it in the future. The strategic planning team should identify and analyze these forces and use them effectively in the planning process.

The Organization-Specific Environment

Porter (1980) identified three distinct ways in which the organization can compete: through differentiation, cost, and focus (or segmenting the market). As the performance audit progresses, it is important to identify how the organization has met the competition.

Understanding the competitive environment is critical to success in applied strategic planning. It provides the basis for the identification of both opportunities and threats (the last two elements of SWOT). It also provides the basis on which the organization's plan can be built, and it represents a constantly changing backdrop against which the plan must be adjusted. Particular conditions in the competitive environment dictate the success or failure of certain tactical maneuvers. For example, numerous community hospitals have been forced to institute new tactics with respect to both their delivery systems and service offerings due to significant changes in the competitive environment. As commercial emergency-room service firms established emergency centers, the community hospitals have in many cases responded with stand-alone emergency centers of their own. Further, as responses to the changing competitive environment, community hospitals are now offering wellness services, opening nursing homes, and offering briefer surgeries.

Using Porter's model to determine where to look for competition, the planning team can identify current and potential competitors. Once these competitors have been identified, they should be sorted into high, medium, and low threats. This sorting enables the organization to put more energy and resources into the study and tracking of the most important of all the potential competitors. However, those classified as medium or low may also be tracked to keep data current and to catch changes that may cause a competitor to grow in importance.

Noncompetitive Aspects

Although it is critical to constantly track competitors and new entrants into the marketplace, analysis must go much further when dealing with the industry-specific environment. Among the aspects that should be studied as part of strategic planning are the customer, the availability of key raw materials, the current marketing mix, the industry life cycle, and the life cycle of major products or services.

SUMMARY

The performance audit is a concerted effort to identify the organization's current position. The four factors of SWOT (strengths, weaknesses, opportunities, and threats) must be considered in an effective and accurate performance audit.

The internal resource analysis is the process of examining the organization's strengths and weaknesses. To succeed in a competitive environment, an organization should develop a distinctive competency that will enable it to differentiate itself from others in its field.

An analysis of external forces considers the organization's opportunities and threats. The competitive environment needs to be monitored, and help may be found both within and outside the organization. As the performance audit progresses, it is important to identify how the organization has met the competition through differentiation, cost, and/or focus.

Looking at the organization's ease or difficulty of exiting its particular markets will also provide information on the likelihood of competition, the desirability of the marketplace, and the risk associated with strategies being proposed.

REFERENCES

Castro, L. L. (1985, October 6). Upstart battling PSA, AirCal, United on West Coast. *San Diego Union*, p. I-1.

Porter, M. E. (1980). *Competitive strategy: Techniques for analyzing industries and competitors.* New York: Free Press.

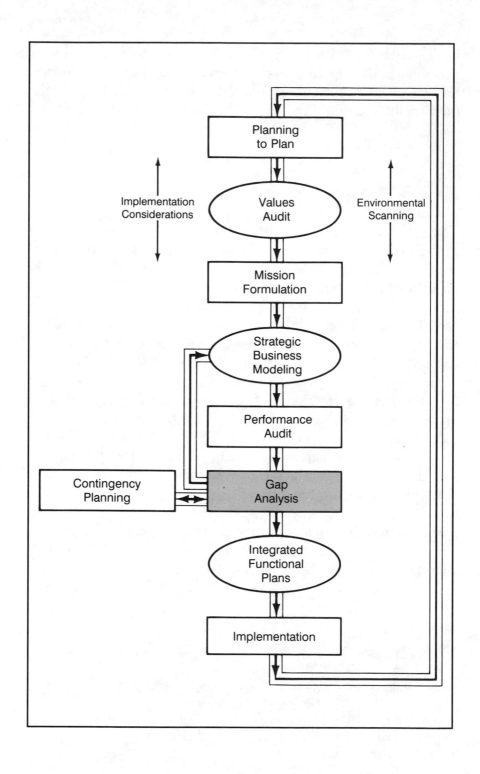

GAP ANALYSIS

12

Gap analysis is a critical step in the applied strategic planning process. It is the time at which the desired future scenario developed during the strategic-business-modeling phase is compared with the current state of the organization. Gap analysis examines how large a leap the frog must take from the pan (the current state) to the desired state. In other words, gap analysis is the process of determining how big the gap is.

Royal Silk, a direct-mail marketing company specializing in women's silk clothing, reached a limitation in its growth. The direct-mail market was saturated and many women asked if there were retail outlets where the clothing could be seen and tried on. The emerging strategic plan proposed the development of a chain of stores in key metropolitan centers. However, the development of such stores — concept, real estate, and personnel — constituted a gap that had to be closed.

During the gap analysis the planning team must determine whether the skills and resources at hand are sufficient to close the gap, that is, to achieve the desired future within the proposed period. Again, an organization's strengths, weaknesses, opportunities, and threats must be considered. If, for example, a dragon is in

Can the Gap Be Closed?

the plan, the planning team must try to determine if it can be used to raise money and close the financial gap or if, instead, it would probably consume the organization.

Gap analysis is also an important *period* in the applied strategic planning process. It is a time for careful decision making. If the gap between the current state and desired state seems too large to bridge, then one of two actions is necessary: (1) Creative solutions for closing the gap must be developed, or (2) the desired future must be redefined, with a focus on those aspects of the strategic business model that are more likely to be accomplished and that will also have the most significant impact. This cycle is graphically illustrated in our Applied Strategic Planning Model with an arrow that leads from gap analysis back to strategic business modeling.

The desired outcome of gap analysis is a strategic plan that has a high probability of success while still reflecting appropriate stretch. The purpose of this step of the process is to bring the test of today's reality to the dreams for the future. Priorities must be based on the normal limits of available resources. In any organization, the equipment, people, dollars, and other resources are finite.

The gap analysis enables planners to properly commit these resources to the pattern of activity that has been determined to have the highest payoff for the organization.

DEFINING THE GAP

Gap analysis is the examination of the distance between an organization's current state, as defined in the performance audit, and the desired state reflected in the strategic business model. Gaps may be observed in numerous areas. During the strategic-business-modeling phase, the planning team might have described the desired state in measurable economic terms. For example, the following is a strategic business model for the hypothetical Delta Company:

> In four years we will have annual sales of $30 million spread across four product lines (three of which will be new). We will have a pretax profit of 15 percent with an annual growth in sales of 30 percent. We intend to display a strong orientation to risk to accomplish these goals, which is necessary as we shift from the development of scientific equipment to more consumer-oriented electronic product lines, an area just beginning to grow. We intend to succeed by becoming a low-cost leader. To accomplish this, we will reduce costs of manufacturing and institute tight controls to assure our goals of cost competitiveness. Our priorities are as follows: (1) growth (increased market share), (2) ultra-effective internal-control systems, and (3) profitability.

As Delta Company completes its performance audit, it must examine its current position on each of the key dimensions of the plan. Assume, for example, that the quick (and incomplete) study of the "current state" of this firm indicated the following:

- Current annual sales, $13.9 million
- Pretax profitability, 4.6 percent
- Current growth rate, 25 percent
- Family-owned firm with conservative history of manufacturing select professional scientific equipment

- Current product sales, based on excellent quality, to a select group of labs
- Strong R&D group fairly free to explore/develop new products
- Current product lines in mature and declining stages of their life cycles
- Strong loyalty among current customers, who trust the company and its products
- Company's main products entering the mature stage with the rate of growth declining
- Company weakness: products taking longer to produce and costing more than first planned

Strategic planners working with this hypothetical firm would need to identify and study a *series* of gaps. They would consider the following factors:

- Time available for changes: four years
- Overall goal: to move company from specialty R&D/manufacture of quality scientific equipment to competitive manufacture of consumer-oriented science-related products
- Increase in sales: from $13.9 million to $30 million
- Improvement in pretax profitability: from 4.6 percent to 15 percent
- Improvement in growth rate: from 25 percent annually (unadjusted for inflation) to 30 percent annually
- Other moves: from conservative to high-risk style of operation; from competitive stance typified by "differentiation" to a stance of "low-cost leader"

Although the above example does not constitute all the dimensions of the strategic business plan nor all the aspects of the performance audit, the flavor is there. The strategic planners would proceed to check the reasonableness of each gap, trying to identify whether it could be closed with the time and resources allotted. If a gap could be bridged, the planning team would carry it into the strategic plan as stated in the strategic business model. If it appeared that a particular goal was too far away to achieve, then the planning process would, by necessity, move back to the strategic-business-modeling stage for a readjustment of the original goal. For example, rather than moving into the retail business to achieve growth, Royal Silk could have reduced its growth and concentrated on increased profitability by cost containment.

Several key considerations exist at this point. When a gap is being examined, a realistic approach must be taken to the question of whether it can be closed. The question is really "Can this gap be closed, given all the other things we are seeking to do?" It is possible that insights gained during the gap analysis will cause the planning team to recycle all the way back to the mission statement. In addition, a gap in one area may lead to the identification of gaps in other areas.

There is also a question of the cumulative impact of trying to close several gaps concurrently. Although a number of individual gaps might be closed by a concerted effort, it may be unrealistic to give the extra effort to several gaps. The fact that a frog could leap in any one of several directions does not mean that it could—or would want to—leap in all directions during a given time period.

ADDITIONAL ASPECTS OF GAP ANALYSIS

As the feasibility of goals set during strategic business modeling are examined, several conceptual tools can be applied. Though simple in concept, they are useful in estimating the amount of risk in a particular move—a critical aspect of gap analysis. Following are four representative growth-feasibility models that can be used for closing gaps:
(1) the "Y" version of the who/what/how model discussed in Chapter 5, (2) increasing-risk ("Z") model, (3) entry/exit barriers, and (4) growth strategies.

Who/What/How ("Y") Model

The simple who/what/how model (see Figure 12-1) was discussed in the chapters on mission formulation and performance audit. During the performance audit, planners were asked to use this model to

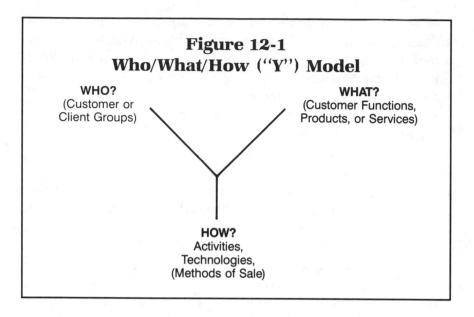

Figure 12-1
Who/What/How ("Y") Model

WHO?
(Customer or
Client Groups)

WHAT?
(Customer Functions,
Products, or Services)

HOW?
Activities,
Technologies,
(Methods of Sale)

describe current lines of business. During gap analysis, the planning team should develop a who/what/how diagram for each major line of business in the strategic business model.

Having created who/what/how models for each proposed area of growth in the business plan, the team would compare them to those prepared as a part of the performance audit. Comparing the proposed line of business to the most similar line of business in the current mix, the team would try to determine how many differences were present or, specifically, how many of the three dimensions would need to change. Experience with the model indicates that it can be used as a quick risk-of-failure gauge. Changing only one axis (with whom business is done, what is sold, or how business is done) carries with it the least risk. Changing two dimensions at once is more risky and in most cases is imprudent; and a three-dimensional switch generally turns out to be almost foolhardy even if the organization has massive resources at hand to simultaneously learn about new customers, new products, *and* a new delivery system. In the Royal Silk example, only *how* the business was conducted was changed. The same merchandise—silk clothing for women—was sold to the same customers. Learning a new distribution system is difficult enough without developing new products and/or new markets at the same time.

The application of the who/what/how model is designed to be a quick test for identifying a potential gap. It should be used to identify potential problems, to give the planning team direction regarding areas requiring further investigation, and to help the team plan a reduction of a potential gap. (This application will be discussed later in the chapter as we explore ways to close the gap.) The planning team should be cautioned to use this tool carefully, however, because there clearly are situations in which changing only one dimension could be a disaster, whereas there are other very selected cases in which changing all three dimensions has succeeded. For example, if an organization has been selling an expensive piece of machinery through a dealer network, converting to direct mail could be a disaster if the item did not lend itself to direct-mail marketing; and the dealer network would also be alienated. Careful thought on the part of team members could catch such an error prior to implementation.

There are also instances in which the product is of such high quality, the market so ready, and the new delivery system so well suited, that it is possible to change all three dimensions at once and still find success. The entry of IBM into the minicomputer market with the introduction of the IBM PC is an outstanding example of such a success. A new product (a personal computer) was successfully marketed to a new market (individuals rather than organizations) through new outlets (retail stores). Again, an alert planning team may be able to spot such an opportunity regardless of warnings by the model. Such situations are *very* rare—*far* more rare than most excited champions of new products would admit. Planners should carefully examine any such dramatic move for flaws, determine whether the payoff is commensurate with the risk, and decide whether the organization is able to assume the risk required. In our example, IBM was clearly able to assume the risk it undertook. Many others will be less able.

Increasing-Risk ("Z") Model

Another model that has a great deal of usefulness is the "Z" model
(see Figure 12-2). Essentially, the model classifies customers and
products according to the same two dimensions—current and new.

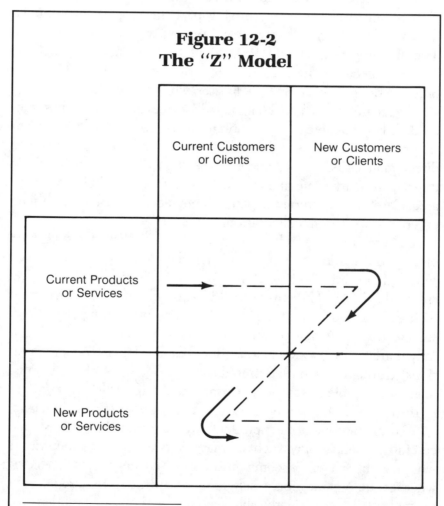

**Figure 12-2
The "Z" Model**

The "Z" model of increased risk was developed by John M. Simonds of
Martin-Simonds Associates, Seattle, Washington.

According to this model, there is least risk in concentrating organizational efforts in the upper left quadrant, that is, in selling more current products or services to current customers. The next in magnitude of risk is the upper right quadrant (selling current products or services to new customers), and the next most risky is the lower left quadrant (selling new products or services to current customers). The most risky is the lower right quadrant: selling new products or services to new customers. The "Z" comes from drawing a line through each of the quadrants according to the degree of risk. The farther an organization travels down the Z, the higher the risk—almost in a geometric progression.

Experience has shown that a strategy of delivering new products or services to new customers can be very risky and is one of the contributing reasons for failure of new businesses—which, by definition, are providing new goods or services for new customers. On the other hand, a new product line that appeals to a new customer base could present such an attractive market niche that pursuing the high risk course would be desirable, as was the case of the IBM PC. The model enables members of the planning group to sort risk factors and gives them a chance to compare the risk of the desired subcomponents of the strategic business plan with the organization's risk orientation. To enter into a strategy of higher risk, the organization should have both a style of willingness to take risks and the availability of resources to support this style.

Entry/Exit Barriers

Different businesses and industries have different degrees of difficulty in starting and liquidating a business. These are commonly known as entry and exit barriers (see Figure 11-4). Attention needs to be given to both entry and exit barriers to prevent a company from being overly attracted to opportunities that may be difficult to abandon if they do not meet expectations. For example, when People's Express hastily bought Frontier Airlines, the "opportunity" became a "threat" and caused extensive financial problems for the parent company. Industries with low entry and low exit barriers (for example, insurance sales and family counseling) tend to have low but stable financial returns because it is easy to get into and out of the business. Those with low entry and high exit barriers (such as insurance underwriting) have low and risky financial returns. Those with high entry and low exit barriers (for example, software) tend to have high, stable financial returns. Those with high entry and high exit barriers (the airline or steel industries) tend to have high but risky financial returns.

Growth Strategies

In the strategic planning of almost all organizations, the long-term survival of the organization is either an explicit goal or a given one. One of the seminal thinkers on strategic planning, Alfred D. Chandler (1962), identified four key growth strategies that typically are sequentially used to ensure the survival of the organization (see Figure 12-3).

Chandler demonstrated that each of these strategies posed different administrative problems and, therefore, tended to lead to different organizational structures. Chandler was the first to both argue and prove that there needs to be a fit between an organization's strategy and an organization's structure if that strategy is to succeed. For example, Procter & Gamble, with its strong marketing emphasis, has a brand-manager structure with each brand manager responsible for a decentralized marketing function. Therefore, one

---

Figure 12-3
Key Growth Strategies

1. Expansion of volume
2. Geographic dispersion
3. Vertical integration
4. Product or service diversification

of the important ways of implementing a strategic plan would be to design the organization to fit the plan, that is, to make certain that structure followed strategy.

Consider each of Chandler's key growth strategies in the light of what organizational design issues emerge for each. The first strategy is expansion of volume or increasing sales, either to a single new market or in existing markets. In most cases an organization starts as a single unit—a plant, a hospital, a store, a warehouse, or a school. As growth occurs, the single unit is required to develop an administrative arm to handle those functions that are not directly involved in the major organizational processes. As a factory produces more and more widgets, as a hospital treats more and more patients, and so on, there is more and more need for record keeping, financial management, supply ordering, and the like. Thus, volume expansion creates the need to develop separate administrative services. When an organization's strategic planning process leads to a principal focus on volume, adequate attention must be paid to having the necessary administrative structure in place to support the increased volume. Otherwise, the plan will fail. One of the major problems confronting the health-care industry is the surplus of hospital beds, or excessive volume. The failure of most hospitals to have the proper administrative controls to monitor the cost of developing and supporting the additional beds is a critical aspect of the problem.

The second growth strategy, geographic expansion, creates multiple field units in the same function or industry but in different geographic locations. For many years, Thomas's English muffins were available only through East Coast markets, causing many transplanted Easterners to ask friendly travelers to bring back a few packages from trips to the East. In the late 1970s, Thomas's successfully expanded geographically and became a national brand. The distribution of Coors beer happened much the same way. Such expansion can provide closer contact with the organization's customers or client base, enhance the delivery of goods or services, increase production volume and market penetration without committing the organization to a limited resource or customer pool, and so on. But problems of interunit coordination, specialization, and standardization arise and need to be solved, typically by the development of functional departments, such as manufacturing, marketing, and sales. These problems often come as a surprise to those involved because only the "economies of scale" are anticipated, not the inversely more costly coordinating problems of scale. Inadequate planning causes the organization to lack the understanding or the resources to develop the functional departments to solve such problems. The development of these functional departments adds to the overhead expense of the organization, often in unforeseen ways. The costs of secretarial support, additional office space, and equipment are all too often overlooked. Failure to solve these problems of coordination, however, would prevent the successful implementation of a strategic plan based on geographic expansion.

The third growth strategy is vertical integration; that is, the organization stays in the same business but develops or acquires related functions. For example, a manufacturer may develop the capacity to produce the component parts or even control the raw materials required for its primary products; paper mills may buy forests, and manufacturers may develop their own distribution centers or their own sales forces. The problems that emerge in the vertical-integration strategy concern balancing the sequential movement of goods, services, and people through the various interdependent functions of the organization. For example, an organization may need to deal with a subassembly manufacturing unit that produces more than the main plant needs in the immediate future. The management of such a problem is typically accomplished through the development of accurate forecasting procedures, scheduling, and capacity-balancing techniques. Any organization contemplating a vertical-integration strategy needs to think through how these coordinating mechanisms will be developed.

The fourth, and final, growth strategy identified by Chandler is that of product diversification. In this strategy, organizations move into new businesses to utilize their existing resources, including physical, human, and capital resources, as their primary markets mature or decline. The movement of community hospitals into residential drug- and alcohol-abuse programs is an example of such diversification—one that also attempts to deal with the problem of overcapacity. The problems that emerge in this strategy are those of appraising and evaluating new-product divisions, each of which must be treated as an investment decision that requires time to make. At the same time, the organization must continue to serve its existing markets. The typical solution to these problems has been the development of the multidivisional structure, wherein each division reports to the organization's headquarters. This structure is based on temporal considerations: The general office is concerned with long-term, strategic decisions, and the product divisions tend to be concerned with short-term, operational decisions. Also typical in this structure are general managers, usually titled group executives, who are expected to tie the strategic direction set by the general office to the internal management of the product divisions.

Another desirable dimension to be examined at this point is the degree of interrelatedness between LOBs (lines of business) and the types of business they do. Experience has demonstrated that there is often value in a strategy of developing LOBs that have a common theme. For example, IBM maintained its focus on information processing with the introduction of the PC. It did not move into a line of business with a dissimilar theme. This common theme can enhance profitability by providing opportunities for economy of scale through procurement of goods or services across LOBs. Additionally, current organizational experience indicates that top management tends to be more successful when operating an organization with related—if not interrelated—parts. Finally, organizations with LOBs that fit a common theme have an enhanced possibility of achieving synergy across LOBs.

MEANS OF CLOSING THE GAP

There are multiple ways to close the gap between the current state and the desired state. Generally the options will fall into either a growth or a retrenchment category, depending on the relationship

When Gaps Cannot Be Closed . . .

of the current organization and its desired future. If growth is necessary to achieve the goals of the strategic business model, options are internal expansion, a new business start-up, an acquisition, or a merger. If the strategic business model calls for retrenchment, options are divestment, phase-out, phase-down, or turnaround.

Internal expansion is often typified by reasonable risk and steady growth. Significant growth from within requires a good deal of financial and other resources. These may be internally identified and committed or may come from outside the organization, often at significant costs. Internal expansion is a reasonable way to close the gap if products or services are strong, if market share seems to be subject to expansion, and if resources are at hand. Products or services offered should be desirable in their marketplace and—if possible—technologically superior to those now available. Planners must keep in mind that current competitors will not view expansion of market share as favorable and will tend to respond aggressively. This competitive factor must be a key consideration in selecting expansion as a strategy. While outstandingly successful with its various models of PC for the first five years, the rise of low-cost competition severely eroded IBM's market share—a development not well anticipated by IBM.

A new business start-up is a growth strategy with a relatively high risk attached to it. On the "Z" model, as we noted earlier, new business means selling new products or services to new customers. If the new business is completely separate from current lines of business, risk is highest. If it is "in tune" with current business, risk may be reduced, because current products or services may help pre-sell the new business. For example, Sears, Roebuck & Company (traditionally a retail store) added a giant new business, the Sears Financial Network Center—covering insurance, real estate, and banking. Knowledge of the interests or needs of customers or clients may also help lessen the risk. Planners should show care in selecting this growth strategy. If selected, creative effort should be placed into the means of reducing the risk. The new business should be run by an individual who understands start-ups and who has the freedom to make decisions necessary for success. There should be a carefully designed supportive relationship with the parent organization.

Acquisitions or mergers are techniques that often accelerate growth goals. Used properly, these approaches can quickly close a gap. Concern must be shown, however, in examining the value of these modes of growth. It is possible to close one or two gaps through an acquisition but to fail in other areas of identified gaps. For example, it is possible for a business to grow in total sales while failing to achieve profitability goals defined in the strategic business model. Care and creativity typify the fully successful acquisition or merger. This move should be made with a specific view to the high priority goals of the strategic business model. The acquisition of Frontier Airlines by People's Express, discussed in an earlier chapter, exemplifies what occurs when the strategic priorities are not kept in mind.

All movements to expand must be done with down-board thinking—examining the impact on the market and on competitors who share or might share the marketplace. Since it takes time to accomplish a change in market share, many things can happen during the process, not the least of which might be the emergence of a competitor that is planning to expand its own market share. Down-board thinking enables the planning team not only to identify the current state, but to anticipate the condition of the market as it will exist in the future. Airline fares have been quite unstable since deregulation. American Airlines frequently precipitates rate wars by reducing its Super Saver fares. They know full well that their price reductions will be met by their competitors but they expect to have significantly increased their market share before the competition can respond and to hold that gain by providing superior service.

Porter (1980, 1985) stresses the need to plan strategy around competitive realities. He encourages planners to anticipate the important factors of tomorrow and stresses that retaliation should be expected. He also coaches his readers in the tactics necessary to meet each of the varied potential challenges.

If the gap dictates retrenchment as part of the strategy, an entirely new set of tactics comes to bear. Such tactics are frequently seen in a more negative light, because often they are tied to failure. This mind-set could lead to serious delays in acting on necessary information. The divestiture of Fireman's Fund Insurance Company by American Express is an example of such a retrenchment, one that did not occur quickly enough to prevent significant deviations from the strategic plan in terms of profit.

WHEN THE GAPS CANNOT BE CLOSED

Gap analysis is a time for candor and honesty. Collusion on the part of the planning-team members to overlook reality at this stage can be most costly. The planning-team members must examine each gap individually. They must reexamine the overall gap between the current state of the business and the desired state. Even when it is possible to close each gap *if treated individually*, it may be impossible to close all gaps simultaneously. An organization that lacks resources is likely to be in that position.

If it appears unlikely that an individual gap can be closed, the planning team must recycle to the strategic business model and reexamine the goal set in this area. This review *may* result in identifying a creative way to close the gap—as did Royal Silk by adding retail outlets to its marketing thrust. If not, the goal in this area must be reworked to a level at which the gap can be closed. Profitability or growth goals may have to be more conservative—a relatively easy readjustment. For example, a goal of 25 percent growth may have to be reduced to 20 percent, the rate that appears to be achievable. Other unachievable goals, such as changing risk orientation, may not only need to be rewritten, but may significantly impact several or all of the remaining dimensions of the strategic business model.

If it appears that each gap can be closed individually but that realistically all gaps cannot be closed simultaneously, additional choices must be made. In the case of Royal Silk, the monies that had to be invested in developing the retail outlets meant that profitability would have to be postponed in order to achieve growth. The two could not be simultaneously achieved. Such choices should be relatively easy, given the early work to prioritize the various aspects of the strategic business model. Care should be taken to maintain congruence both with the mission statement and with the strategic business model.

In the hypothetical Delta Company we mentioned earlier in this chapter, growth was given top priority. Therefore, if tactics to achieve profitability would reduce the company's growth, efforts would have to be made to maintain the growth goal. This could mean looking for more profitable ways to achieve growth goals or reducing the profit target. One of our clients was forced to develop a shape-up-or-divest strategy with one of its manufacturing divisions because of low levels of profitability. Since this division's contributions did not meet the parent conglomerate's financial targets, an 18-month plan to arrive at an acceptable profit level was activated. Because of its low profitability, no emphasis on growth in the future was given to this division in the five-year plan.

Recycling between gap analysis and reworking the strategic business model should continue until a strategic business model emerges that is feasible and realistic. When this happens, two things need to occur. Contingency plans need to be developed to prepare the organization to adjust to significant changes in the internal or external environment (see Chapter 13), and functional plans must be developed to carry the carefully defined strategic plan to the operational level (see Chapter 14).

At this stage, the plan should be expressed as an agreed-upon set of strategic directions. it is important to include rationale for the directions, examples of actions, final critical success indicators with appropriate targets, and the lines of business along with the targeted size for each line.

SUMMARY

Gap analysis is a critical phase of the applied strategic planning process. During the gap analysis the desired future developed through the strategic-business-modeling phase is compared with the current state of the organization. The sizes of the gaps between the current state and the desired future are identified, and decisions must be made about whether the frog can and/or should leap across any of the gaps.

If the gap between the current state and the desired state seems too large to bridge, then either creative solutions for closing the gap must be developed or the desired future must be redefined. Generally, the options for closing the gaps will fall into either a growth or a retrenchment category.

Applying the who/what/how ("Y") test is a quick way to identify a potential gap; however, this tool should be used with caution because of exceptions to the general rule of changing only one dimension at a time. Another useful tool is the "Z" model.

REFERENCES

Chandler, A. D., Jr. (1962). *Strategy and structure: Chapters in the history of the industrial enterprise.* Cambridge, MA: M.I.T. Press.

Porter, M. E. (1980). *Competitive strategy: Techniques for analyzing industries and competitors.* New York: Free Press.

Porter, M. E. (1985). *Competitive advantage: Creating and sustaining superior performance.* New York: Free Press.

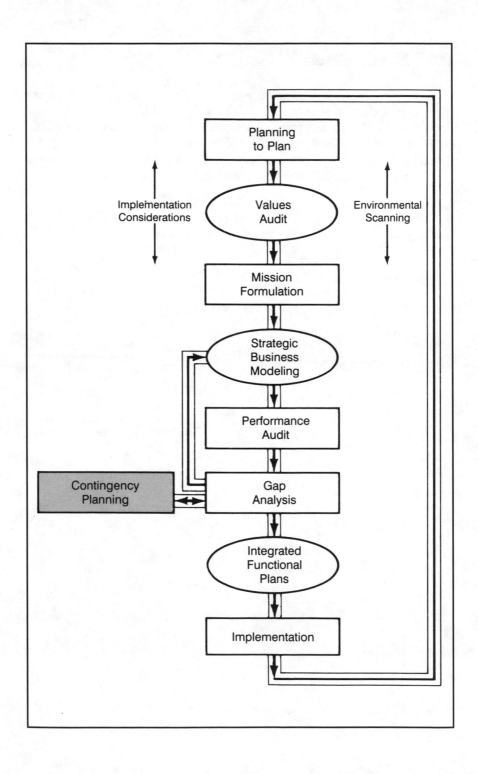

13

CONTINGENCY PLANNING

"Contingency plans are preparations to take specific action(s) when an event not planned for in the formal planning process actually does take place" (Steiner, 1979). Such events include the withdrawal of a competitor from the market, a sudden, unexpected rise in the cost of raw materials, civil unrest, labor problems, changes in the cost of money, and so on. Contingency planning is an integral part of the effective applied strategic planning process.

In discussing contingency planning, we will focus on five key concepts:

1. *The contingency-planning matrix*, which will help an organization to recognize organizational vulnerabilities and opportunities from both internal and external perspectives
2. *The operational-status taxonomy*, which allows an organization to determine a single indicator that is most descriptive of the fiscal viability of the organization
3. *The macroeconomic indices* that are available from the environment and that are determined to be most significant to the organization or, where applicable, to the composite lines of business (LOBs)

4. *Expanded-business indices*, which are to be monitored by the various LOBs and departments

5. *Composite budget-variation indicators*, which provide a single-figure indicator as to the cumulative accuracy of the current year's budget, with a weighted variance indicator that can be keyed to both opportunity and vulnerability triggers for plans identified in the contingency-planning index

Appropriate contingency planning significantly enhances the continued viability and growth of every organization. It is the spare tire, jack, and lug wrench of applied strategic planning. The frog that makes contingency plans recognizes that at some point the heat could increase, so it maps out its escape route.

Contingency planning puts managers in a better position to deal with the unexpected by forcing them to explore scenarios other than the most probable. Contingency planning can dramatically reduce the response time for rectifying threats, such as the loss of productive capacity through a fire or other natural disaster, and/or taking advantage of brief windows of opportunity, such as the opportunity to acquire a competitor due to the death of one of the competitor's principals. In this way, potential problems can become opportunities.

Inasmuch as contingency planning equals preparation for alternative futures, the more turbulent the economic or industrial environment in which a business operates, the more attention needs to be given to contingencies. For example, the fast pace of change in the microelectronics and fashion industries requires a greater degree of attention to contingency planning than do the more staid and traditional markets of the furniture or automotive-parts industries.

THE CONTINGENCY-PLANNING MATRIX

Contingency planning can be divided into two major categories: *internal* vulnerabilities/opportunities, and *external* vulnerabilities/opportunities. Most organizations are more attuned to planning for internal contingencies than for external contingencies, because

Always Have A Contingency Plan

they often have plans for succession, fires, and other disasters. Few organizations, however, have plans for external changes in technologies, drastic shifts in interest rates, and similar factors.

When managers do consider business contingencies, they commonly overemphasize vulnerabilities and underemphasize potential opportunities the organization will face. Our experience as strategic planning consultants has taught us that managers, if undirected, will spend three-quarters of their time developing negative scenarios (destruction of productive capacity through fires and floods, loss of key personnel in airplane crashes, or entry of new, powerful competitors into the market) and one-quarter of their time or less in contemplating scenarios of opportunity (new sources of supply, opportunities for acquisition, lower cost of money, and so on).

Figure 13-1 depicts both the foci and emphases to be considered in contingency planning. If all four cells are *evenly* addressed during the contingency-planning phase, the planning team can be assured that most blind spots will be avoided.

Figure 13-1
Contingency-Planning Matrix

Focus

	Internal	External
Vulnerability	Quadrant 1	Quadrant 2
Emphasis		
Opportunity	Quadrant 3	Quadrant 4

Nowhere in strategic planning literature and practice is "the conventional wisdom" more lacking than in respect to contingency planning. A series of interviews with fifty-eight executives (O'Connor, 1978) indicates that the typical organization plans for a half-dozen critical events or contingencies. Steiner (1979) suggests planning for an equal (or lesser) number of positive contingencies in order not to "generate excessive pessimism on the part of the planning team." We believe that this activity should be much more comprehensive.

Our experience indicates that typical contingencies examined by a planning team include mundane possibilities such as:

1. The computer "eats" all the data.
2. The warehouse/facilities burn down.
3. Key employees leave to work for competitors.
4. A key manager is hospitalized for an extended period.

One can easily see that such contingencies are vulnerabilities, and—with reference to Figure 13-1—we might even place all of them in Quadrant 1. However, as we will detail later, there is much more to contingency planning than simply identifying Quadrant-1 concerns.

The applied strategic planning base plan creates an organizational model built on a series of the highest probability outcomes. Therefore, if the world behaves as we think it most probably will, our planning is optimal. However, contingency planning goes further; it accounts for times when the world behaves other than as expected in the base strategic plan. A "trigger point" is a condition that indicates the base plan is not proceeding as anticipated and that the contingency plan should supersede the base plan. Trigger points need to be carefully *predefined* to determine when assumptions of the base plan would no longer be valid and when new assumptions would be operable. Contingency plans (and trigger points) should be established for key scenarios from each quadrant of Figure 13-1. If a frog would predefine a trigger point for water temperature, it could recognize that it was time to leap into its contingency plan. Otherwise, it would sit there and wonder how on earth it became a boiled frog.

Quadrant I contingencies should include developing back-up strategies for the loss of key personnel, reduction of productive

**Contingency Plans Should Include
Trigger Points**

capacity, and similar problems. Quadrant II should include alternative plans for securing critical resources, the development of unanticipated competitors, and the like. Quadrant III involves consideration of a new application of an existing product, the unexpected development of a new product, the development of new and strikingly significant cost-reduction processes, and so on. Quadrant IV should involve consideration of potential acquisitions, the sudden availability of raw materials, and the like.

Once a contingency variable has been identified, it is essential that timely data are generated and specific trigger points are established. One of the traps of managing in good times is that relatively high profits can mask eroding levels of productivity. If, for example, a CEO monitoring the ratio between revenue and total employee compensation discovers that total employee compensation equals $2,000,000 on annual sales of $10,000,000, then the trigger points for the .20 ratio might be set at two levels: An erosion to .21 (+5 percent) may indicate an alert status (that is, all managers should emphasize their monitoring of productivity concerns), but at .22 (+10 percent) specific action plans should be implemented (for example, a hiring freeze). At .23 or .24 (+15 percent or +20 percent) an emergency exists, and the action plan should call for more drastic actions, such as layoffs.

Similar trigger points can be established around other key indices, such as the revenue/marketing ratio or revenue/scrap-costs (rate) ratios. The key indices generated in the strategic-business-modeling phase should all be bounded by specific contingency actions related to specific, preset trigger points. Again, most managers tend to focus primarily on Quadrant 1 (internal vulnerabilities). It is equally important for them to give comparable emphasis to the other quadrants in the contingency planning matrix (Figure 13-1). For example, if sales of a new product or service exceed projections by 15 percent, the contingency plan may call for accelerated marketing, introduction into new geographic areas, or a crash introduction of spin-off products or services. It is as important to have specific plans for *external opportunities* as it is for *internal vulnerabilities*.

We recommend that the number of key indices to be monitored be somewhere between twelve and twenty and that indices from all four quadrants be included (three to five from each quadrant). It is the CEO's function to see that accurate and timely data are generated so that he or she can *personally* monitor all indices. Although it is acceptable to delegate preplanned actions to managers, in our opinion it is *not* acceptable to delegate the monitoring of the critical organizational indices. This information is so vital that the CEO should have direct and routine access to the data.

IDENTIFYING THE OPERATIONAL STATUS OF THE ORGANIZATION

It is an important aspect of contingency planning to be able to define the operational status of the organization at any point in time. To this end we have found it helpful to establish a definition for an eleven-level operational taxonomy, as is shown in Figure 13-2.

The potency of a single operational-status indicator that is prominently displayed in the offices of managers, meeting rooms, and (one would hope) employees' lounges and/or work areas should not be overlooked. This operational-status indicator can be readily likened to the alert-status indicator of the U.S. Air Force Strategic Air Command. Notwithstanding the thousands of continuous monitorings that the air defense system makes, there is a single, over-riding status indicator that supplies the appropriate context for the ongoing interpretation of all other data collection and monitoring.

As we further explore this notion, we will see that the definition and calibration of the operational-status indicator is the key to establishing trigger points for all quadrants of the contingency planning matrix.

Operational-status indicators need to be distinguished from the budget-variation indicators of Figure 13-4. The operational-status indicator reflects basic organizational health, whereas the budget-variation indicators (which will be reviewed in more detail shortly) reflect the accuracy of the budgeting process. It is conceivable that the accuracy of the budgeting process can be very high while the organization is simultaneously hurtling pell-mell toward failure. It is equally true that profits can be considerably below budgetary expectations while the company is solvent, profitable, and cash rich.

Figure 13-2
Operational-Status Taxonomy (Indicator)

Level Definition

10   Exceptional Performance — outperforming industry, long-term profitable contracts, outstanding commitment from competent/key staff, cash rich.

 9   Exceptional Performance — outstanding performance, optimistic future, significant net worth, good cash flow, or line of credit.

 8   Exceptional Performance — solid performance, reasonable future prospects, moderate net worth with reasonable possibility of access to cash, or line of credit needed for growth.

 7   Transition Down — level eight moving to level five.

 6   Transition Up — level five moving to level eight.

 5   Good Performance — performance equal to industry, balance of strengths and weaknesses, products, services, customer base. Periodic cash shortages and unclear access to cash or line of credit needed for growth.

 4   Transition Down — level five moving to level two.

 3   Transition Up—level two moving to level five.

 2   Survival Mode — insignificant net worth, some prospect, moderate commitment and enthusiasm, cash poor.

 1   Survival Mode — insolvent, operating on guts and credit, waning enthusiasm and commitment.

 0   Survival Mode — insolvent, can operate less than three months without cash infusion, major contract, etc.

It is important that the level of operational-status and budget-variation indices be communicated as broadly as possible throughout the organization. Quarterly in-depth reviews of these indices can help members of the organization become aware of the picture. This is especially true if reviews by top management are followed — in a cascade fashion — by similar reviews on the divisional, departmental, and work-unit levels. This communication activity is the

most important implementation consideration in this phase. We recommend that the status be identified monthly and reported to the organization through departmental meetings, all-personnel meetings, or *thoughtful* memoranda to all managers or employees.

Senior management, under the direction of the CEO, should be able to reach consensus on the operational-status mode of the organization and invoke actions related to trigger points established for each mode. This will help monitor the expansion-contraction behavior necessary to avoid the overexpansion and survival modes as described in Chapter 5 under "Business Cycles."

MACROECONOMIC AND EXPANDED-BUSINESS INDICES

We also suggest that the macroeconomic indices such as changes in the gross national product, the availability of money, and indices of inflation, be defined as relevant indicators for each organization or, where relevant, for each LOB. For example, a general economic downturn may be defined as a decline of two or more percentage points in gross national product for three consecutive quarters. This indicator should serve as a predictor of future buying patterns of an organization's customers, and the organization should adjust accordingly.

Additionally, it is important to monitor inflationary pressures, which may be defined as two or three quarters with annualized consumer-price-index increases of 8 percent or more. This pattern may trigger a move from quarterly (or even annually) to monthly pricing reviews. Perhaps annual reviews were sufficient at one time, and monthly reviews were merely time consuming; but if the pan is now big enough for the whole turkey, there is no reason to keep chopping off the tail.

The indices relevant to any particular organization will, of course, vary widely. For example, construction-related organizations may monitor housing starts; labor-intensive industries may monitor the labor pool through the local unemployment rate; and credit-oriented consumer sales may be monitored through the prime interest rate.

COMPOSITE BUDGET-VARIATION INDICATORS

The budget-variation indicators are intended to be a key triggering point of the contingency-planning matrix. Although Figure 13-3 shows a basic business model for a manufacturing company, it can easily be adapted to any organization.

Figure 13-4 shows sample composite budget-variation indicators for the most recent month and cumulative figures for the fiscal year for this same hypothetical manufacturing company.

By our definition, an organization is outside its strategic base plan when the weighted variation for a three-month period exceeds ± 10 percent. This should be a trigger level for some contingencies in the planning matrix, as shown in Figure 13-5. Weighted variations for a three-month period that exceed the ± 10-percent trigger levels should, at different levels of urgency, be triggers for other planned contingencies in the matrix.

Although these alert levels are expressed in three-month horizons, we do not mean to imply that the process requires only quarterly attention. The CEO *must* assume monitoring of critical

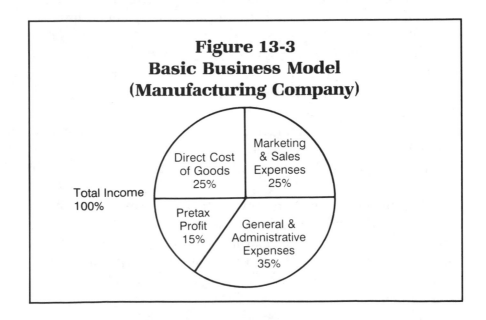

Figure 13-3
Basic Business Model
(Manufacturing Company)

Figure 13-4
Sample Composite Budget-Variation Indicators

	Budget	Most Recent Month (June)	Variation	Last 3 Months (Apr.–June)	Variation	Weighted Average for Fiscal Year to Date (Jan.–June)	Variation
Total Income	100%	96%	–4%	91%	–9%	89%	–11%
Direct Cost of Goods	25%	27%	+8%	26%	+4%	24%	–4%
Marketing & Sales Expenses	25%	30%	+20%	28%	+12%	29%	+16%
General & Administrative Expenses	35%	36%	+2.8%	38%	+8.6%	38%	+8.6%
Pretax Profit	15%	7%	–54%	8%	–47%	9%	–40%

Figure 13-5
Budget-Variation Alert Guidelines

3-Month Cumulative

Altert Level 3 (> ± 10%, < ± 15%)
  Some action required.

Alert Level 2 (> ± 15%, < ± 20%)
  Immediate action required.

Alert Level 1 (> ± 20%)
  Emergency action required.

---

indices on a monthly basis in order to direct tactical/operational interventions that can ameliorate or enhance monthly trends. It is the role of the CEO to monitor these indices regularly and to determine that the necessary interventions are being taken. Our point is that the three-month horizon is a long enough period to remove the issue from the tactical/operational domain; through the contingency-planning matrix, regular monitoring forces the issue into the strategic arena.

SUMMARY

The base strategic plan accounts for predictable changes in an organization's business activities. Contingency plans are preparations for specific actions that can be taken when unusual events occur. Five key concepts should be considered in planning for contingencies: The contingency-planning matrix, the operational-status taxonomy, macroeconomic indices, expanded-business indices, and composite budget-variation indicators. Contingency planning needs to be integrated into the applied strategic plan, primarily by establishing critical "trigger" points that dictate additional actions to be taken.

Contingency planning can be divided into internal vulnerabilities/opportunities and external vulnerabilities/opportunities. Although most companies are more aware of internal contingencies than external contingencies, contingency plans should be established for each quadrant of the contingency-planning matrix. It is also important that the opportunity side of contingency planning be fully developed. The operational status of the organization should be clear to the CEO at any time. The organization's status is best tracked by both operational-status and budget-variation indices. Specific actions need to be planned in advance for various levels of deviation (both positive and negative) of these essential indices.

REFERENCES

O'Connor, R. (1978). *Planning under uncertainty: Multiple scenarios and contingency planning.* New York: Conference Board.

Steiner, G. A. (1979). *Strategic planning: What every manager must know.* New York: Free Press.

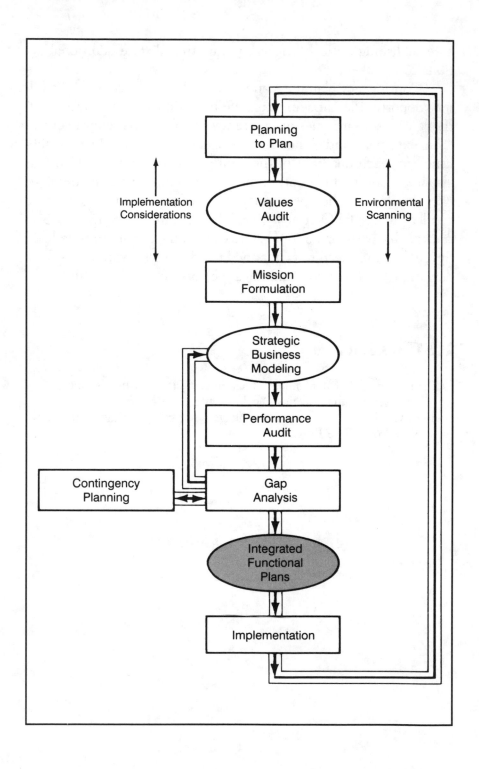

14 INTEGRATING FUNCTIONAL PLANS

After the gap analysis has been completed and the planning team agrees that the remaining gap between the strategic business model and the organization's capacity is a manageable one, detailed planning as to *how* strategic goals can be met is assigned to functional units of the organization, such as engineering, marketing, finance, and human resources (see Figure 14-1). Each functional unit is then required to develop detailed plans that take into consideration any constraint on the human or financial resources of the organization. These largely narrative plans must be integrated by the planning team and specifically approved by the CEOF (chief executive officer function) prior to the initiation of the budgeting process.

Functional plans are then integrated with one another and into the organization through the time-honored practice of resource allocation (budgeting) among the various functional areas. The applied strategic planning process is translated into near-term dimensions by a two-step resource allocation—functional planning and budgeting. The test of the effectiveness of each aspect is the degree to which it supports the strategic planning goals. If the managers who are responsible for the various functional areas

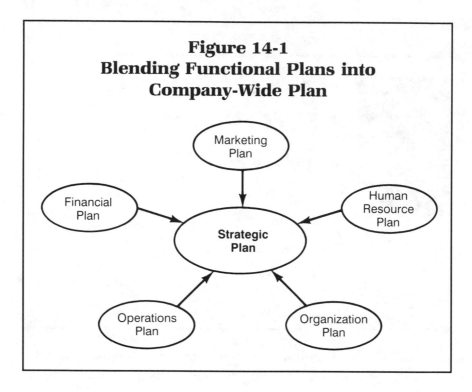

**Figure 14-1
Blending Functional Plans into
Company-Wide Plan**

understand and support the strategic goals, their respective functional plans will demonstrate that understanding and support.

The strategic plan of British Airways to become the world's favorite airline required a strong commitment to marketing and human resource development—marketing to "sell the image" and human resources to ensure that customer-service attitudes were learned and practiced to "make the image real." Prior to the new strategic plan, the human resources function at BA was a traditional personnel function, concern with the bureaucratic control of people. The plan required a new function: supporting managers in a system-wide effort at change that would involve training, performance approval, and the development of a system to compensate employees for meeting customer-service criteria. Each of the resul-tant BA budgets has reflected the increased emphasis on marketing and human resource

**Functional Plans Must Be
Integrated**

development. British Airways thus exemplifies the manner in which the overall strategic plan impacts the detailed functional plan.

Particular attention needs to be given to integrating marketing plans and human resource plans, because these are two areas in which most organizations too quickly reach or exceed their existing capacity. It is absolutely essential that these functional plans be completed and integrated before the fiscal-year budget cycle begins.

Changing the human resources function at BA did not prove to be easy. Old attitudes die slowly and new skills must be painfully acquired through training and practice. Like frogs, we sometimes find it more comfortable to sit in the pan and adapt than to jump into unfamiliar territory. In fact, it was two years before the human resources staff at BA began to initiate the necessary programs and processes to empower themselves to support the strategic plan.

**When Integrating Functional Plans,
It Is Natural For Managers To
Compete For Resources**

CHANGE OF FOCUS

At this point, a shift in the way in which the planning team functions is desirable. As discussed in Chapter 6 and also depicted in Figure 14-2, members of the planning team typically start to shift from an organizational to a functional focus. That is, managers begin to shift from the organizational view they held during earlier planning sessions to constituency-based approaches. This shift is manifested in comments such as "*I can't meet my commitment if I am not allowed the necessary resources.*"

The functional plans are often in conflict with one another or in direct competition for finite organizational resources. In fact, if the strategic business model is even moderately aggressive, competition for the scarcer resources of the organization is inevitable among the various operational functions. Although this competition should be viewed as both natural and healthy, the CEO needs to manage it carefully. It is the CEOF's responsibility to see that all

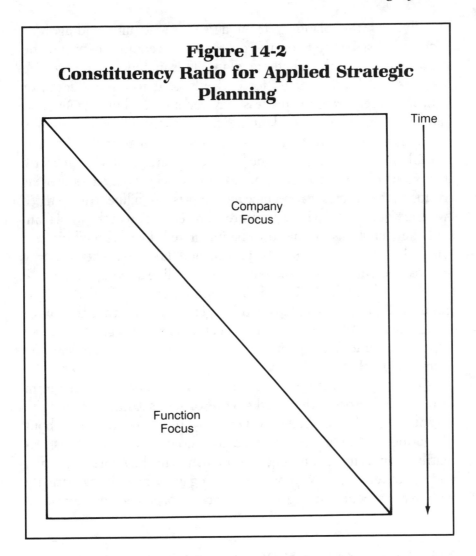

Figure 14-2
Constituency Ratio for Applied Strategic
Planning

conflicts in functional plans or budgets are resolved. This is accomplished by making certain that the overall organization budget does not exceed the predetermined total and that the functional managers agree that they have the necessary resources to do their jobs. The CEO can manage the competition for resources first by surfacing it in regular staff meetings, then by requiring the competing managers to arrive at the "fair" solution, and finally — if no other way can be developed — by dictating a solution.

Even if the planning team agreed to acquire a dragon, a decision must be made on the degree of fit required between the strategic plan and the functional plans. This includes planning time horizons and level of detail for both plans. If too much detail or tightness is required, the process may become too burdensome and may dull the thrust of planning and execution. For example, aligning the marketing and human resources plan at British Airways (see Chapter 9) was done on the basis of specific goals on a quarterly basis with only total budget estimates. Conversely, if the relationship is too loose, the process may become meaningless. A failure to align these two plans at BA would have prevented any realization of the total plan. Only key functions may need to be integrated. Plans should be kept relatively simple, short (a few pages), and limited to high-priority actions, thereby avoiding the pitfalls of mere linear extrapolation.

The role of the CEO and the planning team at this stage is to monitor the functional plans and budgets to ensure that they have a high degree of fidelity with respect to strategic goals. Equally important, functional plans and budgets must be implemented according to that plan.

In most organizations, managers are experienced in some form of budgeting process that works more or less satisfactorily for the organization. There are, however, two recommendations about budgeting that organizations need to follow: One is to focus primarily on monitoring profit goals established in the strategic profile, and the other is to focus more on meeting growth goals, particularly if they are moderately aggressive (that is, 15 percent or more).

HUMAN RESOURCE PLANNING

"Effective human resource planning is a process of continually analyzing an organization's human resource needs under changing conditions and developing the activities necessary to satisfy these needs" (Walker, 1980). Human resource planning is basically a two-part process. The first part consists of analyzing what human resources the organization has and forecasting what resources it is going to need on a year-by-year basis to meet the goals outlined in the strategic plan. As mentioned earlier, British Airways moved into requiring a strong, proactive human resource function; the number of people adequate to fulfill this new function was calculated and projections were developed for a five-year period. The resultant shortfall helped management decide what additional resources needed to be developed internally or acquired externally. The second part of human resource planning, in its most simplistic terms, is to develop a functional plan to close the gap identified in the first step in a timely and cost-efficient manner.

Succession Planning

One of the most difficult aspects of human resource planning, and one that is often neglected or totally avoided, is succession planning at senior levels of the organization. Succession is a topic frequently avoided in many organizations; if it is discussed, it tends to have a more casual, conversational orientation than befits such an important concern.

The inevitable test for promoting someone consists of two questions. The first is "Can the person proposed for the promotion do the job?" The second is "Has the proposed person groomed someone to take his or her job?" Very often the answer to this latter question is so emphatically negative that the potentially successful candidate cannot be promoted. Although succession in case of the unforeseen is typically covered in the contingency-planning phase, it is a rare small-to-medium-sized company that links succession planning to career development of managers.

We contend that a functional human resource plan *must* include specific succession plans for all senior managers. If the succession cannot come from within, as is often the case with chief financial officers and senior data-processing managers, a succession plan can nevertheless be prepared through the establishment of a well-written job description and a clear plan of where to look for the prospective new executive.

The most complex dimension of this compelling problem is the succession for the CEO, particularly in closely held companies in which the CEO is either the entrepreneur/founder or the son or daughter of the entrepreneur/founder. Bennis and Nanus (1985), in a detailed summary of in-depth interviews with ninety top leaders in all aspects of American life, conclude that "the almost-universal common failing of entrepreneur/founders is that they fail to make a successful plan for their succession."

Human Resource Planning: A Model

A model for human resource planning is presented in Figures 14-3 through 14-6. It starts with the Human Resources Forecast (Figure 14-3) in which the human resources necessary for the execution of the various aspects of the strategic plan are carefully identified on a year-by-year basis. Although a five-year planning cycle is common, the actual cycle might be shorter or longer than that. The identified yearly needs must then be corrected by adding to the human resource requirement the replacements necessitated by losses from retirements, turnovers, promotions, and other changes in staffing patterns.

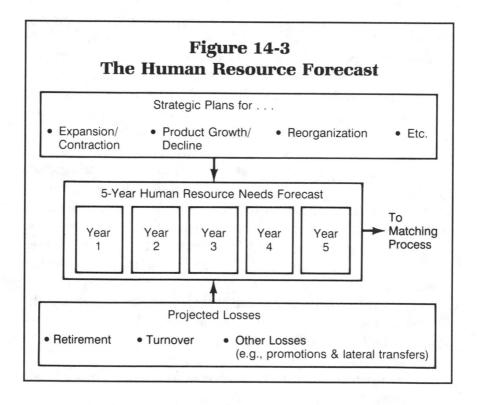

Figure 14-3
The Human Resource Forecast

Strategic Plans for . . .

• Expansion/ Contraction • Product Growth/ Decline • Reorganization • Etc.

5-Year Human Resource Needs Forecast

| Year 1 | Year 2 | Year 3 | Year 4 | Year 5 |

To Matching Process

Projected Losses

• Retirement • Turnover • Other Losses (e.g., promotions & lateral transfers)

The next step (Figure 14-4) is to carefully inventory the current human resources of the organization on an individual-by-individual basis: what each person's career and work interests are, especially as these impact the organization, and how each person's actual performance compares with his or her interests and aspirations. These comparisons should be the focus of regular performance/development discussions between employees and managers, with some involvement by a human resource specialist. These discussions need to focus on what potential opportunities exist for a particular individual, stemming from the strategic planning process, and what the individual *and* the organization need to do in order to have these plans come to fruition. These steps may include training courses, mentoring, cross-training, and so on. All of these processes are intended to facilitate and enhance the assessment of advancement potential, which needs to be stored in the human

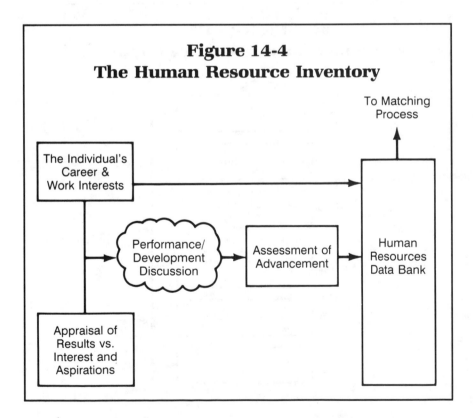

Figure 14-4
The Human Resource Inventory

resource data bank. We predict that the application of computer technology will make this data bank more readily accessible to managers and human resource specialists.

Once the organization identifies its human resource supply and demand for the strategic planning time frame, the supply and demand need to be matched and the imbalances need to be identified (see Figure 14-5). The supply of current human resources may not be adequate to meet the organization's demand, especially in periods of rapid growth, or it may be too large in periods of "down-sizing" or entrenchment. There are circumstances in which both conditions exist at the same time, for example, when old products and services are being phased out, new products or services are being introduced, and the delivery of the new requires new and different skills that are not teachable to the present work force.

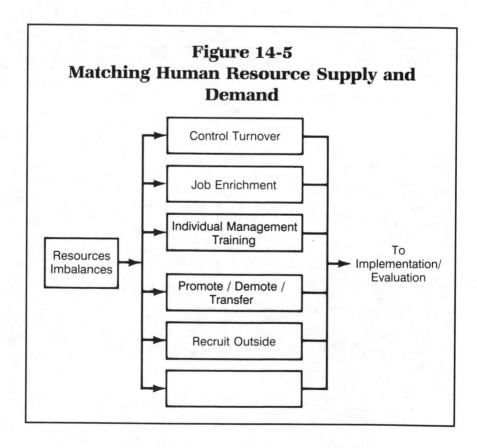

Figure 14-5
Matching Human Resource Supply and Demand

Clearly, the introduction of robotics in manufacturing organizations and computers in service industries are creating this type of condition. The matching process identifies any imbalances that must be addressed and resolved.

Figure 14-6 suggests that alternatives need to be considered when the organization's human resource demands exceed its supply. Plans for alternatives need to be developed for the managerial level as well as for the technical staff and other human resource needs. The potential for filling these needs by several development alternatives needs to be realistically evaluated if the organization's human resource needs are to be met.

Our experience shows that the human resource requirements for executing this element of the strategic plan are too often given short shrift. There is little doubt that the plans will be reevaluated when there is inadequate capital or equipment for execution, but too little attention is paid to the human resource requirements. Such requirements must be carefully thought through.

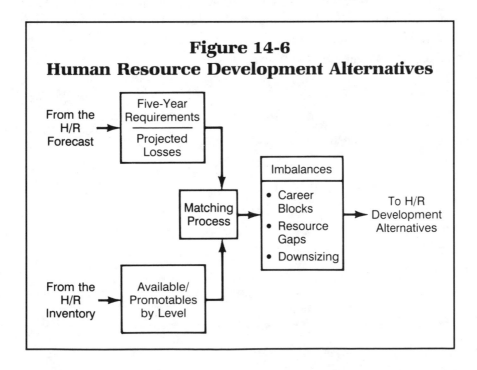

Figure 14-6
Human Resource Development Alternatives

One of our clients, a public utility, completely rebuilt its system at a cost of two billion dollars. The resulting cutting-edge technology required 400 rather than 650 employees—with largely different skills from those previously required. The company's nine-year human resource plan, which was developed congruently with the strategic plan, enabled the organization to offer all employees who desired retraining the opportunity to prepare for a new position. Through orderly retraining and natural attrition, our client was able to downsize without layoffs—all in a heavily political and unionized environment.

SUMMARY

Prior to the planning-team meeting on integrating functional plans, all functional managers should write plans for their respective areas. These plans must be integrated by the planning team and CEO and approved by the CEO prior to the initiation of the budgeting process.

During the phase of integrating functional plans, a shift should be made away from the *organizational* view and toward a *functional* view. Human resource planning, including succession planning, is an important part of this phase.

REFERENCES

Bennis, W. G., & Nanus, B. (1985). *Leaders: The strategies for taking charge*. New York: Harper & Row.

Walker, J. W. (1980). *Human resource planning*. New York: McGraw-Hill.

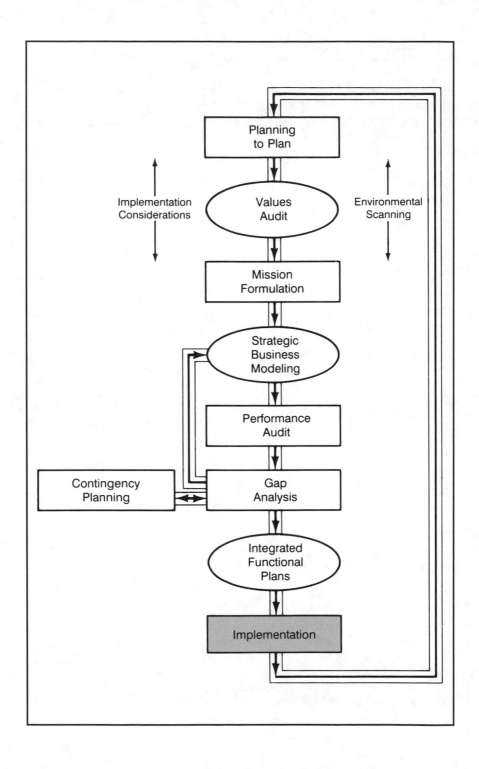

15

IMPLEMENTATION

The payoff of strategic planning is in the implementation of the strategic plan. The implementation phase can be compared to the moment in which the frog actually makes the leap from the pan.

Galbraith and Nathanson (1978) emphasize the implementation aspects when they define strategy as "specific actions deriving from the 'strategy formulation process.'" The aim of strategic planning is to develop a better road map to guide the organization, and the planning process fails unless this road map actually does guide organizational decision making and actions.

All organizations have a strategy, but this strategy is often implicit and has not been thoughtfully examined. We believe that management of an organization according to an *explicit* strategic plan is *strategic management*. Strategic management involves the execution of an explicit strategic plan that is consistent with the values and beliefs of those people who must execute it and that has gained the commitment of those same individuals.

As exemplified in the parable of the dragon, there is a big difference between a vision and its implementation. The acid test for any strategic planning process is the degree to which it impacts the ongoing daily activities and behavior of members of the organization. "Quality" is a key component of the Celanese Corporation's strategic plan. Employees, including top managers, wear CQ (Celanese Quality) pins, posters fill the plant walls, quality statistics are posted everywhere, and employees are evaluated against quality standards as an important aspect of their performance review. The heavy emphasis on process considerations and concrete action steps in our model strongly raises the probability that organizations that follow this model will find obvious behavioral consequences throughout the organization, especially at the managerial level. At Celanese, managers, supervisors, and line workers are all expected to be quality conscious, although how these behaviors are played out differs at each level.

THE STRUCTURAL ASPECTS OF IMPLEMENTATION

Chandler (1962) and others have provided strong empirical support for the concept that the successful execution of an organization's strategy requires that an organization either have the appropriate structure for that strategy in place or quickly develop such a structure. For example, Galbraith (1971) traced the changes over a decade in the structure of the commercial airplane division of the Boeing Company as a function of changes in the division's strategy. At the beginning, the 707 (the civilian version of the military KC-135 transport) provided Boeing with a vehicle to enter the commercial aircraft market.

Boeing "made a market" for commercial jet aircraft where there had previously been only propeller-driven aircraft. Boeing built a prototype, demonstrated it to the airlines, and took the resulting orders from the impressed airline officials. The success of the 707 resulted in the development of competition (DC-8 and Convair 880) for the intercontinental aircraft market. Boeing next "made a market" by introducing the 727 for intermediate-length flights. The strategy was the same as it had been for the 707. Boeing carefully developed and tested a model that resulted in orders before production began. All of this was accomplished with a traditional functional organization.

The commercial aircraft business changed dramatically in the mid-1960s. Rather than developing a competitor to the 727, Douglas developed the DC-9, a short-haul aircraft. This further subdivided the market, and soon there were a host of competitors. Rather than being able to "make a market," Boeing then had to face the fact that the market was changing and that it had to change quickly with it. Boeing's initial strategy (slowly and carefully developing a new model and temporarily monopolizing the market as a consequence of its technological innovation) was no longer functional. It quickly had to develop new models (new versions of the 727, the short-haul 737, and the jumbo 747) and market them in the face of extensive competition. The combination of competition, internal demands for various resources, and a shortened time frame produced serious internal problems of inadequate engineering resources, poor designs, and an inability to meet deadlines. These problems made it clear to Boeing's top management that the earlier functional organization of the company was no longer adequate for solving emerging problems in Boeing's marketplace.

Boeing's response was to reorganize its commercial aircraft division into a multidivisional structure. One division was created for each of its major product lines, together with a central fabricating division. Once this structure was firmly in place, Boeing was able to solve its internal problems and resume its profitable course. The divisional structure thus enabled Boeing to adapt to its new market, its diverse product lines, and the increased competition.

More recently, increased competition and reduced market share has forced Procter & Gamble (one of America's most successful marketing organizations) to speed up its product-development and release cycle. Procter & Gamble (*New York Times*, 1985) has rolled out several of its new products, such as Ivory Shampoo and Liquid Tide, from test market to nationwide distribution in less than four months, rather than the three or four years that the organization previously required. Accomplishing this feat required a realignment of its marketing and product-management structures and staff.

If we examine in greater detail the nature of the mechanisms used by organizations to implement strategic plans, the research of Galbraith (1973) is instructive. Over two decades he compared three industries that differed dramatically in the introduction of new products. The container industry introduced no new products during the period, but new products introduced by the food industry accounted for 15 percent of all its products, and the plastics industry's new products accounted for 35 percent. All three industries used four common integrative/control mechanisms: rules, hierarchical authority to resolve disputes, goal setting, and direct contact among diverse elements for problem solving. The food industry, however, also used cross-functional task forces and product managers who served an integrative product-development function; and the plastics industry used multilevel, cross-functional integrative teams as well as a higher percentage of integrative product managers.

Galbraith concludes that it is these additional mechanisms for coordination (cross-functional task forces and multilevel integrative teams) that enabled the food and plastics industries to be innovative and develop new products. He notes that these product managers serve a general management function that is necessary for coordinating the interfunctional work required to develop new products. This added structural element is required to execute the strategic plans for product innovation that typified the plastics and food industries, but it was not required for the more predictable and less diverse container industry. (This situation is in sharp contrast to the reality of high innovation in the container industry since the Galbraith study.)

It should be clear by now that any applied strategic planning process must involve an in-depth analysis of whether or not the organization's structure "fits" its strategic plan; if it does not fit, either the structure or the plan needs to be revised, depending on the situation. Structure alone, however, is not sufficient to guarantee that the strategic plan will be implemented. A number of functional factors need to be considered as well.

THE FUNCTIONAL ASPECTS OF IMPLEMENTATION

Once a strategic plan is in place, together with an organizational structure that "fits" that plan, the plan needs to become the template against which organizational decisions are made, the scale on which resource allocations are made, the focus of organizational energy, and so on. If these descriptions of the strategic plan are seen simply as clichés, however, the plan will never be implemented. On the other hand, even if the planning team and top management are committed to the plan and its success, how a strategic plan becomes part of the lifeblood of an organization still needs to be resolved.

If the applied strategic planning process that we have outlined has been followed, then the organization is well aware of the planning process. This awareness will be heightened if the planning team makes periodic reports to the employees about planning developments and where it stands in the process. The final announcement and presentation of the plan needs to be accomplished with the pomp and ceremony that signal an important event in the life of the organization. All-personnel meetings, special issues of newsletters, and videotape presentations are several ways to alert and involve the rank-and-file of the organization. The preferred communication vehicle will vary according to the organization's size, facilities, history, and so on. For example, in Silicon Valley, elephants are rented to get employees' attention.

The process by which "buy-in" and commitment to the strategic plan are accomplished does not stop with the introduction of the plan. *A strategic plan is not an event; it is a process*, and for most organizations it must be an ongoing process. For this process to "take," managers, especially top managers, need to be clearly committed to the strategic plan and need to use it in obvious ways. When a decision based on a strategic consideration is made, the basis for that decision needs to be explicitly and fully communicated to those involved. The top management of an American automobile manufacturer discovered that each unit produced resulted in a sizable cost disadvantage when compared with the Japanese competition. This discovery led to a strategic plan to downsize the

Announce the Plan with Pomp and Ceremony

organization. The failure of top management to fully explain the rationale or to develop a strong implementation plan meant that two years after the plan was announced, there still had been no change in the number on staff!

When a decision is requested by subordinates, managers need to discuss how the organization's strategic plan can guide that decision. Even with operational decisions that have no bearing on the execution of the strategic plan, management's commitment to the plan enhances its credibility throughout the organization. For example, in launching a new product that has been in the pipeline for some time, simply taking time out to review the implications of the new product on the future plan helps cement attention on the plan.

The role of the CEO in the implementation of the strategic plan cannot be overemphasized. The CEO must lead the support and must be totally committed to the strategic plan. This commitment goes far beyond annual talks to employees and reports to shareholders or to the board of directors. The implementation of an organization's strategic plan requires the CEO to internalize the plan emotionally. The CEO has to *want* to effect the changes that the strategic plan requires, and his or her actions must indicate a deep, strong belief in what is being done. Once the strategy is internalized by the CEO and by those who report directly to that person, it impacts every key operating decision and becomes the driving force for the organization.

Some supporting functional elements, the most important of which is the budget, help incorporate the strategic plan into the workings of the organization. As noted in Chapter 14, the budgets of the functional units of the organization need to be integrated into a single organizational budget that is the personification of the organization's strategic plan. The process by which the organization's management reviews the variances from budget, positive and negative, is the most obvious and clear-cut way of identifying the degree to which the strategic plan is being executed. In a sense, the budget can be considered as the navigator's tactics for arriving at the ship's destination; and budgetary variances, especially serious ones, suggest that the ship is off course and may be delayed or may not even arrive at the intended port. In fact, serious budgetary variances may be an indication that the frog is boiling.

The use of the budget to operationalize the strategic plan and the use of the budget-review process as a constant measure of the organization's success in executing its strategic plan not only give life to the organization's budgeting processes, but also demand a strong commitment to the use of the budget—and budget controls—on an ongoing basis. When budget forecasts of revenues are not met, when expenditures exceed budgetary limits, and when resources are allocated "off-line," there is clear evidence that the strategic plan is not being executed.

Other indices also need to be included in the evaluation of the degree to which the strategic plan is being implemented. An organization that aims to increase market share as an important aspect of its strategic plan needs to involve some indices of market share in its review process. In a similar fashion, an organization that holds quality as part of its strategic plan needs to include a variety of quality indices, such as scrap rate, in-warranty service calls, and customer complaints. None of these, however, should take the place of the budget as the main measure of the organization's success in executing its strategic plan. The relationship between the strategic plan and the accuracy of the budget is analogous to the relationship between the game of tennis and the scoreboard. You do not win tennis matches by watching the scoreboard, but when the game is over, it's the score that ultimately matters.

Nevertheless, the implementation of the strategic plan requires more than adherence to an adequate budgetary system and the emotional and psychological commitment of management. The strategic plan needs to be embedded in the performance-management and performance-appraisal systems of the organization. The strategic-focused performance-management system is one of the key tools of strategic management. In such a plan, the performance appraisals of all members of the organization should include a test of activities since their previous review that have helped carry out the strategic plan of the organization. For instance, at British Airways, managers and others are measured on commitment to customer service, the key ingredient of trying to make BA the world's favorite airline. Thus the performance of an operator on a production line is not measured simply on the basis of output, but also on the basis of how that output (or quality, or whatever) has helped the organization accomplish its strategic targets. Opryland Showpark in Nashville carefully designed a management-by-objectives system that was tied to bonuses and directly fitted with its strategic plan. Each director was evaluated for his or her contribution to the plan. This accountability was extended downward another layer of management in the second year of the applied strategic planning process.

Another example is NASA, which was enormously successful in capturing the commitment of its employees, down to the janitorial level, in fulfilling its mission to "put a man on the moon by the end of the decade." There was constant internal publicity about NASA's strategic goal, and all employees were regularly informed by their supervisors that their efforts—regardless of their job—were critical and essential to the successful achievement of the goal.

Installing such a performance-management system takes both some imagination and a high degree of commitment to the implementation of the strategic plan.

Each time a significant milestone is reached in implementation, a celebration is needed. Organizations that regularly attend to such accomplishments with verbal praise, recognition pins, company picnics, bonuses, and the like are clearly demonstrating two things to their employees: the organization's commitment to the accomplishment of its strategic plan and the organization's awareness that the accomplishment of the plan requires everyone's involvement and hard work.

The successful implementation of a strategic plan is no small accomplishment. It requires the initial creativity and energy to develop the plan, the courage and commitment to introduce it, and the persistence and thoroughness to fully implement it. But without a strong process for ensuring its implementation, there is little or no reason for developing a strategic plan. An experienced strategic planner expressed it this way: A "B" quality plan executed in an "A" manner is always better than an "A" quality plan executed in a "B" manner.

A "B" Quality Plan Implemented in an "A" Manner Is Better Than an "A" Quality Plan Implemented in a "B" Manner

Finally, it is necessary to point out that strategic planning, even applied strategic planning, does not necessarily lead to success. The Edsel was a monument to the failure of a strategic planning process, as are the more recent attempts of the oil (or energy) industry to develop oil shale as a major fuel source. In some cases of failure the reason is simply that there was no way to know (until after the fact) whether or not the necessary ingredients were present. Proper assumptions that are continually tested, sophisticated environmental surveillance, a high degree of organizational competence, and luck are all necessary ingredients to the success of any strategic planning process.

The real measure of whether strategic planning is able to optimally impact the organization takes place in the second and third years of the process. Many organizations "do a plan." They commit time and energy to a planning effort they hope will set the direction for the next three, five, or some other chosen number of years. They put a plan in place and check some time later to determine whether the plan has worked. This approach is most likely to result in failure.

This approach can be compared to the weapons used in World War II; those weapons were aimed at a target, but the projectiles were uncontrollable after they were launched. The gunner would shoot at the enemy, wait to see whether he hit the target, then shoot again if he missed. In World War II this method was acceptable, but in today's environment it will not work. Now the weaponry must be capable of guiding projectiles after they are launched and compensating for any change in the movement of the target. Today's business environments are likewise more demanding than markets of the past. Whereas well-conceived plans could once be launched and expected to hit the targets with little attention, today's targets change direction too fast. Furthermore, failure can mean disaster in environments of intense international competition.

For example, in the late 1970s, General Motors, using the best data available, designed a highly ambitious, sophisticated strategic plan to restore the automaker to its past preeminence. GM committed forty billion dollars and several years to a plan that would retool every manufacturing facility in high-tech fashion while simultaneously redesigning both the corporation and every vehicle it produced. Greatly sophisticated computer models were developed. By 1987, sixty billion dollars had been spent. GM's quality was uneven, automobile sales were weak, and for the first time since the Model T, Ford was reporting a greater profit than the much larger GM. What had happened? GM had launched an "unguided projectile" of a plan in an environment that demanded a carefully guided missile that could be constantly adjusted for changing market conditions. The GM plan was soundly built on key factors of the late 1970s: fuel shortages and demands by consumers for smaller cars. The GM plan was *not* designed to adjust to changes in the marketplace once fuel was no longer in shortage and buyers returned to buying larger cars.

Planning must take place annually, and the plan must be constantly tested against rapidly changing market conditions. Strategic planning can become a highly potent management tool if it leads to deliberate strategic management with careful implementation and guidance. We believe that strategic planning, when skillfully applied, can make the difference between healthy, leaping frogs and the poor little lifeless boiled frog.

Strategic planning can give organizational leaders the ability to shape the future of their organizations. Applied strategic planning offers the sense of control that is all but absent in many organizations today. Proper assumptions, environmental surveillance, organizational competence, and luck are all necessary ingredients for a successful strategic planning process. But, please, no boiled frogs.

SUMMARY

The payoff of strategic planning is in the implementation of the strategic plan. The acid test for any strategic planning process is the degree to which it impacts the ongoing behavior of the organization.

The strategic plan needs to become the template on which organizational decisions are based. Whereas plans could once be launched and expected to hit the target, today's targets change direction fast; strategic plans must be designed to follow the target period. The final announcement and presentation of the plan needs to be accomplished with the pomp and ceremony that signal an important event in the life of the organization.

Proper assumptions, environmental surveillance, organizational competence, and luck are necessary for a successful strategic planning process.

REFERENCES

Chandler, A. B. (1962). *Strategy and structure.* Cambridge, MA: M.I.T. Press.

Galbraith, J. R. (1971). Matrix organization designs. *Business Horizons,* 14, pp. 29–40.

Galbraith, J. R. (1973). *Designing complex organizations.* Reading, MA: Addison-Wesley.

Galbraith, J. R., & Nathanson, D. A. (1978). *Strategy implementation: The role of structure and process.* St. Paul, MN: West.

A new-found pep at P. & G. (1985, February 3). *New York Times,* Sec. 2, p. 4.

APPENDIX

This appendix is for use during the values audit (see Chapter 7).

THE PERSONAL VALUE STATEMENT (PVS)

John E. Oliver

Instructions: For each of the following groups of three words, place a *3* by the word that is *most* important to you and a *1* by the word that is *least* important to you. Place a *2* by the remaining word.

1.	a.	Power	_____	11.	a.	Conquest	_____
	b.	Style	_____		b.	Art	_____
	c.	People	_____		c.	Sympathy	_____
2.	a.	Thinking	_____	12.	a.	Learning	_____
	b.	Practicality	_____		b.	Production	_____
	c.	Winning	_____		c.	Strength	_____
3.	a.	Taste	_____	13.	a.	Harmony	_____
	b.	Unselfishness	_____		b.	Giving	_____
	c.	Reason	_____		c.	Solutions	_____
4.	a.	Tangibility	_____	14.	a.	Prosperity	_____
	b.	Overcoming	_____		b.	Struggles	_____
	c.	Appearance	_____		c.	Form	_____
5.	a.	Helping	_____	15.	a.	Understanding	_____
	b.	Science	_____		b.	Logic	_____
	c.	Efficiency	_____		c.	Wealth	_____
6.	a.	Control	_____	16.	a.	Influence	_____
	b.	Charm	_____		b.	Elegance	_____
	c.	Kindness	_____		c.	Charity	_____
7.	a.	Knowledge	_____	17.	a.	Explanation	_____
	b.	Utility	_____		b.	Profit	_____
	c.	Position	_____		c.	Authority	_____
8.	a.	Culture	_____	18.	a.	Symmetry	_____
	b.	Warmth	_____		b.	Freedom	_____
	c.	Analysis	_____		c.	Theories	_____
9.	a.	Usefulness	_____	19.	a.	Effectiveness	_____
	b.	Command	_____		b.	Privilege	_____
	c.	Refinement	_____		c.	Beauty	_____
10.	a.	Aid	_____	20.	a.	Assistance	_____
	b.	Information	_____		b.	Research	_____
	c.	Application	_____		c.	Earnings	_____

From "The Personal Value Statement (PVS): An Experiential Learning Instrument" by J. E. Oliver, 1985. In L. D. Goodstein and J. W. Pfeiffer (Eds.), *The 1985 Annual: Developing Human Resources* (pp. 107–116). San Diego, CA: University Associates. Reprinted with permission.

PERSONAL VALUE STATEMENT SCORING SHEET

Instructions: Enter your scores from the PVS form in the spaces below. Then add the scores in each column and enter the total for the column in the space provided.

VALUES				
Political	Aesthetic	Social	Theoretical	Economic
1a _____	1b _____	1c _____	2a _____	2b _____
6a _____	6b _____	6c _____	7a _____	7b _____
11a _____	11b _____	11c _____	12a _____	12b _____
16a _____	16b _____	16c _____	17a _____	17b _____
2c _____	3a _____	3b _____	3c _____	4a _____
7c _____	8a _____	8b _____	8c _____	9a _____
12c _____	13a _____	13b _____	13c _____	14a _____
17c _____	18a _____	18b _____	18c _____	19a _____
4b _____	4c _____	5a _____	5b _____	5c _____
9b _____	9c _____	10a _____	10b _____	10c _____
14b _____	14c _____	15a _____	15b _____	15c _____
19b _____	19c _____	20a _____	20b _____	20c _____
Total _____	Total _____	Total _____	Total _____	Total _____
Rank _____	Rank _____	Rank _____	Rank _____	Rank _____

ORGANIZATIONAL BLASPHEMIES: CLARIFYING VALUES

Tony McNulty

Goals

    I.   To provide an opportunity for the planning-team members to be creatively open about aspects of the organization.

   II.   To identify and compare the organizational values of members of the planning team.

 III.   To provide an opportunity to explore the match between the goals or values of the planning-team members and those of the organization.

Materials

    I.   Three sheets of blank paper and a pencil for each member of the planning team.

   II.   A newsprint flip chart and a felt-tipped marker.

 III.   Masking tape for posting newsprint.

Physical Setting

A room with a chair and a writing surface for each member of the planning team. Each member should be seated so that he or she can see the other members as well as the facilitator and the newsprint flip chart.

Process

    I.   The facilitator introduces the activity by stating that it is useful for the members of an organization to think from time to time about the organization's objectives and whether they, as individuals, are working toward those objectives.

From "Organizational Blasphemies: Clarifying Values" by T. McNulty, 1983. In L. D. Goodstein & J. W. Pfeiffer (Eds.), The 1983 Annual for Facilitators, Trainers, and Consultants (pp. 77–79). San Diego, CA: University Associates. Adapted with permission.

II. The facilitator distributes three sheets of blank paper and a pencil to each member of the planning team and explains that each member is to write an organizational blasphemy[1] — a phrase or slogan so alien to what the group represents that the members will squirm in their seats when they hear it. The facilitator then gives examples of blasphemies for other organizations:

University Associates: "You can't teach an old dog new tricks."

Four-Star Restaurant: "If we run out of veal, use lean pork; no one will notice."

III. The planning-team members are told that they will have five minutes in which to invent blasphemies and are instructed to work independently. Each member is to use one of the sheets of blank paper.

IV. The facilitator calls time, collects the blasphemies, and reads them aloud while a member of the planning team records them on newsprint.

V. The newsprint is posted, and the group discusses the activity thus far. The following topics may be included in this discussion:

1. How did it feel to consider and write down ideas of this nature?
2. Why did members select these particular blasphemies?
3. Is there a common theme running through the blasphemies? What might this mean in terms of the way the members perceive the organization?
4. What blind spots or biases in the organization might these blasphemies indicate?
5. What taboos are there within the team that appear clearly in the list of blasphemies?
6. What does this imply about the goals of the organization? The way in which the organization works?
7. Does any team member's blasphemy differ significantly from the rest? What might be the reason?

---

[1]The idea of an organizational blasphemy was suggested in *The Corporation Man* by Anthony Jay, Penguin Books, Ltd., 1975.

6. What implications do the results of this activity have for the organization? The group? The individual members? The fit among these three?

VI. The facilitator states that blasphemies often highlight beliefs or aspects of behavior that have been "socialized out" of the members by the organization's processes. The members are then invited to contribute their own examples of how this process of socialization has operated.

VII. The facilitator states that groups like the planning team are often cultures within other cultures and that the values of these cultures can differ to a great extent. The facilitator then posts a diagram (see illustration) and explains that the larger the shaded area, the more "comfortable" individuals are likely to feel in the organization or group. If the shaded area is large, the individual is confronted by less value conflict. The facilitator says that tension can be present whenever the individual perceives a clash between the values of one culture and the values of another culture to which it is connected (e.g., personal and work or department and organization) and that these values may conflict more than one often realizes.

VIII. The facilitator asks the members to think of two departments or groups to which they belong. Ideally, these would be groups

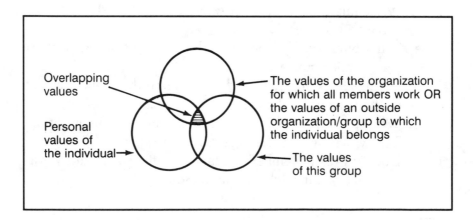

that form part of a larger organization. The members are then directed to think about themselves in relation to these groups and, using the diagram of the three circles as a model, to draw circles (of approximately the same size) to represent their own values in relation to their two chosen groups, departments, or organizations, and to list the values in each circle.

IX. When all members of the planning team have completed this task, the facilitator directs the members to discuss their respective drawings and to explain the rationale behind these drawings.

X. The facilitator leads a discussion on the experience, focusing in particular on the following questions:

1. What does the shaded area on each drawing indicate about the match between the individual and the work area?
2. What values are seen as common (shaded areas)? What values outside the common areas are shaded by individuals in the group?
3. Is there a common theme running through the blasphemies? What might this mean in terms of the way the members perceive the organization?
4. How can the blasphemies be turned around and stated in terms of agreed-on goals?

Variation

If the planning team is large, Step IX may be accomplished in dyads.

ORGANIZATIONAL DIAGNOSIS QUESTIONNAIRE

Robert C. Preziosi

From time to time organizations consider it important to analyze themselves. It is necessary to find out from the people who work in the organization what they think if the analysis is going to be of value. This questionnaire will help the organization that you work for analyze itself.

   Directions: Do not put your name anywhere on this questionnaire. Please answer all thirty-five questions. *Be open and honest.* For each of the thirty-five statements circle only *one* (1) number to indicate your thinking.

1 — Agree Strongly
2 — Agree
3 — Agree Slightly
4 — Neutral
5 — Disagree Slightly
6 — Disagree
7 — Disagree Strongly

	Agree Strongly	Agree	Agree Slightly	Neutral	Disagree slightly	Disagree	Disagree Strongly
1. The goals of this organization are clearly stated.	1	2	3	4	5	6	7
2. The division of labor of this organization is flexible.	1	2	3	4	5	6	7
3. My immediate supervisor is supportive of my efforts.	1	2	3	4	5	6	7
4. My relationship with my supervisor is a harmonious one.	1	2	3	4	5	6	7
5. My job offers me the opportunity to grow as a person.	1	2	3	4	5	6	7
6. My immediate supervisor has ideas that are helpful to me and my work group.	1	2	3	4	5	6	7

   From "Organizational Diagnosis Questionnaire (ODQ)" by R. C. Preziosi, 1980. In J. W. Pfeiffer & J. E. Jones (Eds.), *The 1980 Annual Handbook for Group Facilitators* (pp. 115–120). San Diego, CA: University Associates. Reprinted with permission.

7. This organization is not resistant to change.　　　　　　　　　　1　2　3　4　5　6　7

8. I am personally in agreement with the stated goals of my work unit.　　　1　2　3　4　5　6　7

9. The division of labor of this organization is conducive to reaching its goals.　1　2　3　4　5　6　7

10. The leadership norms of this organization help its progress.　　　　　　1　2　3　4　5　6　7

11. I can always talk with someone at work if I have a work-related problem.　　1　2　3　4　5　6　7

12. The pay scale and benefits of this organization treat each employee equitably.　1　2　3　4　5　6　7

13. I have the information that I need to do a good job.　　　　　　　　　　1　2　3　4　5　6　7

14. This organization introduces enough new policies and procedures.　　　　1　2　3　4　5　6　7

15. I understand the purpose of this organization.　　　　　　　　　　　　1　2　3　4　5　6　7

16. The manner in which work tasks are divided is a logical one.　　　　　　1　2　3　4　5　6　7

17. This organization's leadership efforts result in the organization's fulfillment of its purposes.　　　　　　　　　　　　　1　2　3　4　5　6　7

18. My relationships with members of my work group are friendly as well as professional.　　　　　　　　　　　　1　2　3　4　5　6　7

19. The opportunity for promotion exists in this organization.　　　　　　　1　2　3　4　5　6　7

20. This organization has adequate mechanisms for binding itself together.　　1　2　3　4　5　6　7

21. This organization favors change.　　　1　2　3　4　5　6　7

22. The priorities of this organization are understood by its employees.　　　　1　2　3　4　5　6　7

23. The structure of my work unit is well designed. 1 2 3 4 5 6 7

24. It is clear to me whenever my boss is attempting to guide my work efforts. 1 2 3 4 5 6 7

25. I have established the relationships that I need to do my job properly. 1 2 3 4 5 6 7

26. The salary that I receive is commensurate with the job that I perform. 1 2 3 4 5 6 7

27. Other work units are helpful to my work unit whenever assistance is requested. 1 2 3 4 5 6 7

28. Occasionally I like to change things about my job. 1 2 3 4 5 6 7

29. I have enough input in deciding my work-unit goals. 1 2 3 4 5 6 7

30. The division of labor of this organization helps its efforts to reach its goals. 1 2 3 4 5 6 7

31. I understand my boss's efforts to influence me and the other members of the work unit. 1 2 3 4 5 6 7

32. There is no evidence of unresolved conflict in this organization. 1 2 3 4 5 6 7

33. All tasks to be accomplished are associated with incentives. 1 2 3 4 5 6 7

34. This organization's planning and control efforts are helpful to its growth and development. 1 2 3 4 5 6 7

35. This organization has the ability to change. 1 2 3 4 5 6 7

ODQ SCORING SHEET

Instructions: Transfer the numbers you circled on the questionnaire to the blanks below, add each column, and divide each sum by five. This will give you comparable scores for each of the seven areas.

Purposes	Structure	Leadership	Relationships
1 _____	2 _____	3 _____	4 _____
8 _____	9 _____	10 _____	11 _____
15 _____	16 _____	17 _____	18 _____
22 _____	23 _____	24 _____	25 _____
29 _____	30 _____	31 _____	32 _____
Total _____	Total _____	Total _____	Total _____
Average _____	Average _____	Average _____	Average _____

Rewards	Helpful Mechanisms	Attitude Toward Change
5 _____	6 _____	7 _____
12 _____	13 _____	14 _____
19 _____	20 _____	21 _____
26 _____	27 _____	28 _____
33 _____	34 _____	35 _____
Total _____	Total _____	Total _____
Average _____	Average _____	Average _____

ODQ PROFILE AND INTERPRETATION SHEET

Instructions: Transfer your average scores from the ODQ Scoring Sheet to the appropriate boxes in the figure below.[1] Then study the background information and interpretation suggestions that follow.

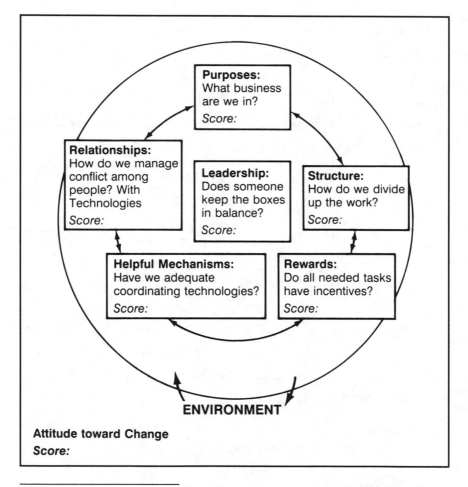

Purposes:
What business are we in?
Score:

Relationships:
How do we manage conflict among people? With Technologies
Score:

Leadership:
Does someone keep the boxes in balance?
Score:

Structure:
How do we divide up the work?
Score:

Helpful Mechanisms:
Have we adequate coordinating technologies?
Score:

Rewards:
Do all needed tasks have incentives?
Score:

ENVIRONMENT

Attitude toward Change
Score:

[1]From "Organizational Diagnosis: Six Places To Look for Trouble with or Without a Theory" by M. R. Weisbord, 1976. In *Group & Organization Studies*, 1 (4), 430–477. Reprinted by permission of Sage Publications, Inc.

Background

The ODQ is a survey-feedback instrument designed to collect data on organizational functioning. It measures the perceptions of persons in an organization or work unit to determine areas of activity that would benefit from an organization development effort. It can be used as the sole data-collection technique or in conjunction with other techniques (interview, observation, etc.).

Weisbord's Six-Box Organizational Model (see figure) is the basis for the questionnaire, which measures seven variables: purposes, structure, relationships, rewards, leadership, helpful mechanisms, and attitude toward change. The first six areas are from Weisbord's model, while the last one was added to provide the consultant/facilitator with input on readiness for change.

The instrument and the model reflect a systematic approach for analyzing relationships among variables that influence how an organization is managed. The ODQ measures the informal aspects of the system. It may be necessary for the consultant/facilitator also to gather information on the formal aspects and to examine the gaps between the two.

Using the ODQ is the first step in determining appropriate interventions for organizational change efforts. Its use as a diagnostic tool can be the first step in improving an organization's or work unit's capability to serve its clientele.

Interpretation and Diagnosis

A crucial consideration is the diagnosis based upon data interpretation. The simplest diagnosis would be to assess the amount of variance for each of the seven variables in relation to a score of 4, which is the neutral point. Scores above 4 would indicate a problem with organizational functioning. The closer the score is to 7 the more severe the problem would be. Scores below 4 indicate the lack of a problem, with a score of 1 indicating optimum functioning.

Another diagnostic approach follows the same guidelines of assessment in relation to the neutral point (score) of 4. The score of each of the thirty-five items on the questionnaire can be reviewed to produce more exacting information on problematic areas. Thus diagnosis would be more precise. For example, let us suppose that the average score on item number 8 is 6.4. This would indicate not only a problem in organizational purpose, but also a more specific problem in that there is a gap between organizational and individual goals. This more precise diagnostic effort is likely to lead to a more appropriate intervention in the organization than the generalized diagnostic approach described in the preceding paragraph.

Appropriate diagnosis must address the relationships between the boxes to determine the interconnectedness of problems. For example, if there is a problem with relationships, could it be that the reward system does not reward relationship behavior? This might be the case if the average score on item 33 was well above 4 (5.5 or higher) and all the items on relationships (4, 11, 18, 25, 32) averaged above 5.5.

ORGANIZATIONAL NORMS OPINIONNAIRE

Mark Alexander

Instructions: This opinionnaire is designed to help you determine the norms that are operating in your organization. The opinionnaire asks you to assess what the reaction of most persons in your organization *would be* if another person said a particular thing or behaved in a particular manner. For example, the first item reads:

> "If an employee in your organization were to criticize the organization and the people in it . . . most other employees would . . ."

To complete the statement, choose one of the following five alternatives.

A. Strongly agree with or encourage it
B. Agree with or encourage it
C. Consider it not important
D. Disagree with or discourage it
E. Strongly disagree with or discourage it

Choose the alternative that you think would be the most common response to the action or behavior stated and place the letter corresponding to that alternative in the blank space following each item. Complete all forty-two statements in the same manner, being as honest as possible.

Most Other Employees Would:

If an employee in your organization were to . . .

1. criticize the organization and the people in it . . . _____
2. try to improve things even though the operation is running smoothly . . . _____
3. listen to others and try to get their opinions . . . _____
4. think of going to a supervisor with a problem . . . _____

From "Organizational Norms Opinionnaire" by M. Alexander, 1978. In J. W. Pfeiffer & J. E. Jones (Eds.), *The 1978 Annual Handbook for Group Facilitators* (pp. 83–88). San Diego, CA: University Associates. Reprinted with permission.

5. look upon himself/herself as being responsible for reducing costs . . . _____

6. take advantage of a fellow employee . . . _____

7. keep a customer or client waiting in order to look after matters of personal convenience . . . _____

8. suggest a new idea or approach for doing things . . . _____

9. actively look for ways to expand his/her knowledge in order to be able to do a better job . . . _____

10. talk freely and openly about the organization and its problems . . . _____

11. show genuine concern for the problems that face the organization and make suggestions about solving them . . . _____

12. suggest that employees should do only enough to get by . . . _____

13. go out of his/her way to help other members of the work group . . . _____

14. look upon the supervisor as a source of help and development . . . _____

15. purposely misuse equipment or privileges . . . _____

16. express concern for the well-being of other members of the organization . . . _____

17. attempt to find new and better ways to serve the customer or client . . . _____

18. attempt to experiment in order to do things better in the work situation . . . _____

19. show enthusiasm for going to an organization-sponsored training and development program . . . _____

20. suggest confronting the boss about a mistake or something in the boss's style that is creating problems . . . _____

21. look upon the job as being merely eight hours and the major reward as the month-end paycheck . . . _____

22. say that there is no point in trying harder, as no one else does . . .   _____

23. work on his/her own rather than work with others to try to get things done . . .   _____

24. look upon the supervisor as someone to talk openly and freely to . . .   _____

25. look upon making a profit as someone else's problem . . .   _____

26. make an effort to get to know the people he/she works with . . .   _____

27. sometimes see the customer or client as a burden or obstruction to getting the job done . . .   _____

28. criticize a fellow employee who is trying to improve things in the work situation . . .   _____

29. mention that he/she was planning to attend a recently announced organization training program . . .   _____

30. talk openly about problems facing the work group, including personalities or interpersonal problems . . .   _____

31. talk about work with satisfaction . . .   _____

32. set very high personal standards of performance . . .   _____

33. try to make the work group operate more like a team when dealing with issues or problems . . .   _____

34. look upon the supervisor as the one who sets the standards of performance or goals for the work group . . .   _____

35. evaluate expenditures in terms of the benefits they will provide for the organization . . .   _____

36. always try to treat the customer or client as well as possible . . .   _____

37. think of going to the boss with an idea or suggestion . . .   _____

38. go to the boss to talk about what training he/she should get in order to do a better job . . .   _____

39. be perfectly honest in answering this questionnaire . . . _____

40. work harder than what is considered the normal pace . . . _____

41. look after himself/herself before the other members of the work group . . . _____

42. do his/her job even when the supervisor is not around . . . _____

ORGANIZATIONAL NORMS OPINIONNAIRE SCORE SHEET

Instructions: On the ten scales below, circle the value that corresponds to the response you gave for that item on the questionnaire. Total your score for each of the ten categories and follow the indicated mathematical formula for each. The result is your final percentage score.

I. Organizational/Personal Pride

Item			Response		
	A	B	C	D	E
1	-2	-1	0	+1	+2
11	+2	+1	0	-1	-2
21	-2	-1	0	+1	+2
31	+2	+1	0	-1	-2

Total
Score _____ ÷ 8 × 100 = ☐ **Final** **% Score**

II. Performance/Excellence

Item			Response		
	A	B	C	D	E
2	+2	+1	0	-1	-2
12	-2	-1	0	+1	+2
22	-2	-1	0	+1	+2
32	+2	+1	0	-1	-2
40	+2	+1	0	-1	-2

Total
Score _____ ÷ 10 × 100 = ☐ **Final** **% Score**

III. Teamwork/Communication

Item			Response		
	A	B	C	D	E
3	+2	+1	0	−1	−2
13	+2	+1	0	−1	−2
23	−2	−1	0	+1	+2
33	+2	+1	0	−1	−2
41	−2	−1	0	+1	+2

Total
Score _____ ÷ 10 × 100 = [ ] **Final % Score**

IV. Leadership/Supervision

Item			Response		
	A	B	C	D	E
4	+2	+1	0	−1	−2
14	+2	+1	0	−1	−2
24	+2	+1	0	−1	−2
34	+2	+1	0	−1	−2
42	+2	+1	0	−1	−2

Total
Score _____ ÷ 10 × 100 = [ ] **Final % Score**

V. Profitability/Cost Effectiveness

Item			Response		
	A	B	C	D	E
5	+2	+1	0	−1	−2
15	−2	−1	0	+1	+2
25	−2	−1	0	+1	+2
35	+2	+1	0	−1	−2

Total
Score _____ ÷ 8 × 100 = [ ] **Final % Score**

VI. Colleague/Associate Relations

Item			Response		
	A	B	C	D	E
6	−2	−1	0	+1	+2
16	+2	+1	0	−1	−2
26	+2	+1	0	−1	−2

Total

Score _____ ÷ 6 × 100 = [＿＿＿] **Final % Score**

VII. Customer/Client Relations

Item			Response		
	A	B	C	D	E
7	−2	−1	0	+1	+2
17	+2	+1	0	−1	−2
27	−2	−1	0	+1	+2
36	+2	+1	0	−1	−2

Total

Score _____ ÷ 8 × 100 = [＿＿＿] **Final % Score**

VIII. Innovativeness/Creativity

Item			Response		
	A	B	C	D	E
8	+2	+1	0	−1	−2
18	+2	+1	0	−1	−2
28	−2	−1	0	+1	+2
37	+2	+1	0	−1	−2

Total

Score _____ ÷ 8 × 100 = [＿＿＿] **Final % Score**

IX. Training/Development

Item			Response		
	A	B	C	D	E
9	+2	+1	0	−1	−2
19	+2	+1	0	−1	−2
29	+2	+1	0	−1	−2
38	+2	+1	0	−1	−2

Total
Score _____ ÷ 8 × 100 = [   ] **Final % Score**

X. Candor/Openness

Item			Response		
	A	B	C	D	E
10	+2	+1	0	−1	−2
20	+2	+1	0	−1	−2
30	+2	+1	0	−1	−2
39	+2	+1	0	−1	−2

Total
Score _____ ÷ 8 × 100 = [   ] **Final % Score**

ORGANIZATIONAL NORMS OPINIONNAIRE PROFILE SHEET

Instructions: For each of the ten scales, enter your final percentage score from the score sheet and then plot that percentage by placing an "X" on the graph at the appropriate point. (Negative percentages are plotted to the left of the center line and positive percentages are plotted to the right.) Next, connect the "X"s you have plotted with straight lines. The result is your Organizational Norms profile.

Scale	Final Score	−100%	−50%	0%	+50%	+100%
I. Organizational/Personal Pride						
II. Performance/Excellence						
III. Teamwork/Communication						
IV. Leadership/Supervision						
V. Profitability/Cost Effectiveness						
VI. Colleague/Associate Relations						
VII. Customer/Client Relations						
VIII. Innovativeness/Creativity						
IX. Training/Development						
X. Candor/Openness						

INDEX

Here's how to receive your free catalog and save money on your next book order from Scott, Foresman and Company.

Simply mail in the response card below to receive your free copy of our latest catalog featuring computer and business books. After you've looked through the catalog and you're ready to place your order, attach the coupon below to receive $1.00 off the catalog price of Scott, Foresman and Company Professional Books Group computer and business books.

✂ _

YES, please send me my *free* catalog of your latest computer and business books!

NAME (please print) _____

COMPANY _____

ADDRESS _____

CITY _____ STATE _____ ZIP _____

Mail response card to: Scott, Foresman and Company
                                Professional Books Group
                                1900 East Lake Avenue
                                Glenview, IL 60025

✂ _

PUBLISHER'S COUPON   NO EXPIRATION DATE

SAVE $1.00

Limit one per order. Good only on Scott, Foresman and Company Professional Books Group publications. Consumer pays any sales tax. Coupon may not be assigned, transferred, or reproduced. Coupon will be redeemed by Scott, Foresman and Company Professional Publishing Group, 1900 East Lake Avenue, Glenview, IL 60025.

Customer's Signature _____